Reading Klein

Reading Klein provides an introduction to the work of one of the twentieth century's greatest psychoanalysts, known in particular for her contribution in developing child analysis and for her vivid depiction of the inner world. This book makes Melanie Klein's works highly accessible, providing both substantial extracts from her writings, and commentaries by the authors exploring their significance.

Each chapter corresponds to a major field of Klein's work, outlining its development over almost 40 years. The first part is concerned with her theoretical and clinical contributions. It shows Klein to be a sensitive clinician deeply concerned for her patients, and with a remarkable capacity to understand their unconscious anxieties and to revise our understanding of the mind. The second part sets out the contribution of her ideas to morality, to aesthetics and to the understanding of society, introducing writing by her associates as well as herself.

The book provides a lucid account of Klein's published writing, presented by two distinguished writers who know her work well and have made creative use of it in their own clinical and extra-clinical writing. Its aim is to show how substantial her contribution to psychoanalytic thinking and clinical practice was, and how indispensable it remains to understanding the field of psychoanalysis.

Reading Klein will be a highly valuable resource for students, trainees in psychoanalysis, psychoanalytic practitioners and all who are interested in Melanie Klein and her legacy.

Margaret Rustin is a child, adolescent and adult psychotherapist and a child analyst at the British Psychoanalytical Society. She trained at the Tavistock Clinic in London and worked there from 1968 to 2009, becoming Head of Child Psychotherapy and Dean of Postgraduate Studies. Since retiring she continues to teach and maintains a private practice.

Michael Rustin is Professor of Sociology at the University of East London, and a Visiting Professor at the Tavistock and Portman NHS Foundation Trust and the University of Essex. He is an associate of the British Psychoanalytical Society and, like Margaret Rustin, is the author and editor of many books and articles.

THE NEW LIBRARY OF PSYCHOANALYSIS TEACHING SERIES

General Editor: Alessandra Lemma

The New Library of Psychoanalysis was launched in 1987 in association with the Institute of Psychoanalysis, London. It took over from the International Psychoanalytical Library which published many of the early translations of the works of Freud and the writings of most of the leading British and Continental psychoanalysts. The purpose of the New Library of Psychoanalysis is to facilitate a greater and more widespread appreciation of psychoanalysis and to provide a forum for increasing mutual understanding between psychoanalysts and those working in other disciplines such as the social sciences, medicine, philosophy, history, linguistics, literature and the arts. It aims to represent different trends both in British psychoanalysis and in psychoanalysis generally. The New Library of Psychoanalysis is well placed to make available to the English-speaking world psychoanalytic writings from other European countries and to increase the interchange of ideas between British and American psychoanalysts.

Through the *Teaching* subseries, the New Library of Psychoanalysis publishes books that provide comprehensive, yet accessible, overviews of selected subject areas aimed at those studying psychoanalysis and related fields such as the social sciences, philosophy, literature and the arts.

For a full list of all the titles in the New Library of Psychoanalysis main series and the New Library of Psychoanalysis 'Beyond the Couch' subseries, please visit the Routledge website.

TITLES IN THE NEW LIBRARY OF PSYCHOANALYSIS TEACHING SERIES

Reading Freud: A Chronological Exploration of Freud's Writings Jean-Michel Quinodoz

Listening to Hanna Segal: Her Contribution to Psychoanalysis Jean-Michel Quinodoz

Reading French Psychoanalysis Edited by Dana Birksted-Breen, Sara Flanders and Alain Gibeault

Reading Winnicott Lesley Caldwell and Angela Joyce

Initiating Psychoanalysis: Perspectives Bernard Reith, Sven Lagerlöf, Penelope Crick, Mette Møller and Elisabeth Skale

Infant Observation Frances Salo

Reading Anna Freud Nick Midgley

Reading Italian Psychoanalysis Edited by Franco Borgogno, Alberto Luchetti and Luisa Marino Coe

Reading Klein Margaret Rustin and Michael Rustin

Reading Klein

Margaret Rustin and Michael Rustin

Routledge
Taylor & Francis Group
LONDON AND NEW YORK

First published 2017
by Routledge
2 Park Square, Milton Park, Abingdon, Oxon OX14 4RN

and by Routledge
711 Third Avenue, New York, NY 10017

Routledge is an imprint of the Taylor & Francis Group, an informa business

British Library Cataloguing in Publication Data
A catalogue record for this book is available from the British Library

Library of Congress Cataloging in Publication Data
Names: Rustin, Margaret, author. | Rustin, Michael, author.
Title: Reading Klein / Margaret Rustin and Michael Rustin.
Description: New York : Routledge, 2017. | Series: New library of psychoanalysis "Teaching" series ; 9 | Includes bibliographical references and index.
Identifiers: LCCN 2016027220| ISBN 9780415452939 (hardback : alk. paper) | ISBN 9780415452946 (pbk. : alk. paper) | ISBN 9781315544618 (e-book)
Subjects: LCSH: Psychoanalysis. | Child analysis. | Child psychology—Research—Methodology. | Klein, Melanie.
Classification: LCC BF173 .R887 2016 | DDC 150.19/5092—dc23
LC record available at https://lccn.loc.gov/2016027220

ISBN: 978-0-415-45293-9 (hbk)
ISBN: 978-0-415-45294-6 (pbk)
ISBN: 978-1-315-54461-8 (ebk)

Typeset in Times New Roman
by Swales & Willis Ltd, Exeter, Devon, UK

Contents

Acknowledgements

We are most grateful to the Trustees of the Melanie Klein Trust for asking us to prepare this book, supporting us in doing so, and bearing with patience the time it has taken to complete. Particular and generous help has also been given by Lisa Miller in reading the whole book, by Sue Sherwin-White in allowing us to make use of her unpublished work on the details of Melanie Klein's life, by Kate Stratton, whose editorial and bibliographical expertise has been invaluable, and by Kate Paul, Suchen Hung and Hsui Nien Wei for help with individual chapters. The whole project has depended on our long-shared involvement in psychoanalysis and in thinking about Klein, one of us as a clinician and one as an academic. We owe a great deal to our analysts and to the psychoanalytic community within which we have been nourished for over 50 years.

The authors and the Melanie Klein Trust are very grateful to Penguin Random House UK for their generous permission to quote extensively from the works of Melanie Klein. Passages from two of Hanna Segal's articles from 1952 and 1957, 'A psycho-analytical approach to aesthetics' and 'Notes on symbol formation', are reprinted by permission of *The International Journal of Psycho-Analysis* and Wiley.

Extracts from 'A case-study in the functioning of social systems as a defence against anxiety: a report on a study of the nursing service of a general hospital' by Isabel Menzies, *Human Relations,* 1960, vol. 13, no. 2, pp. 95–121, are reprinted by permission of Sage Publications.

Chapter 1

Introduction

Melanie Klein had become widely recognised as one of Freud's most original and important psychoanalytic successors. Her initial contribution grew from her early work with children in emotional difficulty, some of them very young and seriously disturbed, and her writings document her gradual discovery of a method of analysing children through providing a setting for the child to express him- or herself in play activities. Working as a child analyst gave her access to the nature of the child's developing mind and led her to revise crucial aspects of psychoanalytic theory. She became convinced that the infant related actively to the maternal figure from birth onwards, though initially perceiving the mother in fragmentary ways rather than as a complete person. These partial experiences of mother were rooted in the many different aspects of early bodily care. This was a challenge to the belief that babies begin life in a state which is prior to relating to the world outside themselves – the psychoanalytic theory of a period of primary narcissism. Klein also found evidence in her work with very young children of a much earlier form of the superego – the judging function of the mind – than that described by Freud and linked by him to the resolution of the Oedipal preoccupations of the child aged around 5. She described vividly the ferocity of this early form of conscience by which a child could be tormented, suffering severe anxiety and guilt. Linked with this was her recognition of early precursors of the classical Oedipus complex. She was profoundly aware of the bodily roots of psychoanalytic theory, including Freud's important discoveries about the sexual nature of young children.

Her openness to learning about the more primitive building blocks of the mind entailed facing the implications of the small child's capacity for hatred as well as seeing the passionate nature of his love. This meant that her ideas shocked many of her contemporaries and, indeed, her picture of the inner world of baby and young child still has a capacity to stun her readers at first sight.

In her later work, she built on her extraordinary achievements as the first analyst of young children to revise the psychoanalytic understanding of mental development. Her focus on anxieties in her clinical practice led her to describe two constellations of anxieties and defences within the mind. The first of these, developmentally, she named the paranoid-schizoid position (choosing the term position to denote the overarching and lasting significance of this structure in mental life) and the later one, the depressive position. While paranoid-schizoid states centre on anxieties about the self, fears for its survival and well-being, in depressive states the individual is also concerned about the fate of the people towards whom his emotions are directed, and particularly about the primary family figures whom he fears are damaged by his hostile feelings. The formation of the personality, Klein believed, depended on the outcome of the continuous interchange between the individual and his primary objects – 'objects' being used in psychoanalytic theory to mean the significant others of the individual's emotional world. This interchange involved ongoing projection – pushing parts of one's own experience into another – and introjection – the taking in of emotional experience from others. Klein's concrete way of understanding projective processes, something she understood very profoundly from her clinical experience with young children, led to her proposing the concept of projective identification which has become important in contemporary psychoanalysis.

Other significant contributions to theory included her work on mourning and depression, on manic states, on the importance of the desire to understand and on envy and gratitude as powerful features of human relationships.

As will be evident in our account of Klein's developing understanding of the mind, she not only made significant analytic discoveries across a lifetime of clinical work, but she also revised some of her earlier formulations in the light of further experience. Perhaps of special importance in this respect is her later strongly held view that love was an essential part of the infant's relation to mother from the start. Readers of her early papers are often taken aback by her detailed description of the ferocity of early infantile phantasy, but when this depiction of hatred and sadism is set clearly alongside the infant's passionate love and longing for mother, the overall picture of the emotional life of the baby reads very differently. *Narrative of a Child Analysis*, her day-by-day account of one child's analysis in the early days of the war, is a moving example of how balanced was her work with her patients. Her capacity for theoretical revision comes out particularly clearly in the early and later papers on the Oedipus complex.

This book aims to present Klein's ideas through extensive selected quotations from her major writings, with commentary and some brief indication of the direction in which her ideas have led other psychoanalytic thinkers. We hope this will encourage readers to explore her remarkable work more fully, and we include some suggestions for further reading at the end, including important scholarly publications which draw on the Klein archive held at the Wellcome Library. Klein's writing has often been described as quite difficult, and it is of course important to keep in mind that much of the English edition is translated from her original German, but our re-reading of her work in preparing this book evoked very great admiration.

We have organised the material in two parts, one looking roughly chronologically at her developing clinical and theoretical perspective, and the other examining the relevance of her ideas for a psychoanalytically informed understanding of ethics, aesthetics, and social and political matters. This second part underlines our belief in the very wide implications of Klein's understanding of the mind, going much beyond the practice of child and adult psychoanalysis in the consulting room.

Brief biographical note

Melanie Klein was born in 1882, the daughter of Moriz Reizes, a doctor from an orthodox Jewish family who chose medicine instead of rabbinical studies, and Libussa Deutsch, a much younger woman from a liberal Jewish family. After their marriage in 1875 they moved to Vienna. Melanie was the youngest of their four children. She was particularly attached to Sidonie, the sister a little older than her, and deeply distressed by Sidonie's early death. Her older brother, Emanuel, also died when she was still a young woman. These painful early losses are likely to have played a part in her profound interest in the nature of mourning and in her awareness of the importance of siblings in psychic life (Sherwin-White, 2014).

Klein loved learning and school and was ambitious for education, and her parents supported this. However, her plan to study medicine at Vienna University had to be set aside when she became engaged and later married Arthur Klein in 1903.

The marriage was not a happy one but Klein and Arthur had two children in quick succession, Melitta and Hans, and a third, Erich, some years later. Klein struggled with serious episodes of depression in these years. In 1910 the family moved to Budapest and Klein found solace in the lively culture of the society there after the years of living in less congenial small towns. She began there an analysis with Sándor Ferenczi, the foremost psychoanalyst in the Hungarian Society, and this provided both personal help to her and an opportunity to begin professional work in analysing children with his encouragement. In 1919 she separated from her husband and two years later she moved to Berlin with the children. In Budapest she had already become a member of the Hungarian Psychoanalytic Society and in Berlin she found a very flourishing psychoanalytic community. She entered an analysis with Karl Abraham in 1925, sadly prematurely terminated at his death after less than a year. During the years in Berlin she involved herself in extensive clinical work with children (Frank, 2009). From this time onwards she wrote many psychoanalytic papers.

In 1926 she moved to London, at the invitation of Ernest Jones and colleagues, following a visit in which her lectures had greatly impressed members of the British Psychoanalytical Society. The early years in London were a time of great intellectual creativity. However, the professional home provided by the British Society changed its character with the arrival of many analysts coming as refugees from Vienna, following the rise of Nazism. The serious disagreements between Klein and Anna Freud, which had already surfaced in the 1920s when their very different approaches to child analysis became a matter of public debate, now threatened to disrupt the world of psychoanalysis in Britain. The Viennese group saw Klein's revision to theory as attacks on Freudian orthodoxy. This was very painful to Klein, who always saw herself as building on Freud's psychoanalytic foundations and extending these in ways that were true to the spirit of psychoanalytic inquiry.

The institutional difficulties in the British Psychoanalytic Society were resolved through a political compromise following the scientific discussions recorded in *The Freud–Klein Controversies 1941–45* (King and Steiner, 1991). The intense intellectual efforts of Klein and her close group of analytic allies at this time proved to be the spur to a fresh period of theoretical creativity. In the post-war years she published several very important papers and her writing continued up to her death in 1960.

Part I

Chapter 2

Klein's early work

Children's upbringing, education and child analysis

Klein's first paper, read to the Hungarian Psycho-analytical Society in 1919, was entitled 'The development of a child'. The theme of development is therefore signalled at the outset of her career as at the heart of her interest and her approach to psychoanalysis. It is obvious that this is profoundly linked to her personal and family circumstances at that time. She had begun an analysis with Ferenczi in the context of unhappiness in her marriage and an as-yet uncharted professional path for herself. She had three children, with whose individual personalities and development she was intensely involved. Living with and thinking about them seems to have been a huge stimulus to detailed observation and reflection on their day-to-day preoccupations, their thoughts and the whole direction and shape of their mental lives. Her analysis no doubt opened her up to all sorts of questions about her own life as a child and the way in which she had arrived at this juncture in her life. Ferenczi's encouragement of her interest in children's minds and the possibilities for psychoanalytic investigation and intervention with young children must have drawn on his awareness of her unusual capacities for combining tender interest and rigorous enquiry in her relationships with children. The wider historical context possibly played a part too: just as the later story of post-1945 child psychoanalysis in Britain was deeply influenced by the post-war hopes of a better world and the particular emphasis on improved education and health for children (the 1944 Education Act and the launch of the National Health Service in 1948), so perhaps the concern with understanding early development, which Ferenczi embraced with enthusiasm, and which Klein found again with Abraham when she moved to Berlin in 1921, had its roots not only in the evolution of psychoanalysis but also in the intellectual response to the horrors of the First World War.

Here is the Introduction to this first paper, which signals a challenge to the conventions of the time with respect to children's upbringing, tackles headlong the idea of childhood innocence and links the necessity for opening up the acknowledgement of children's sexual interests (as Freud had done for Little Hans) with the lifting of childhood anxieties and the freeing of intellectual development:

> The idea of enlightening children in sexual matters is steadily gaining ground. The instruction introduced in many places by the schools aims at protecting children during the age of puberty from the increasing dangers of ignorance, and it is from this point of view that the idea has won most sympathy and support. The knowledge obtained
>
> *(continued)*

(continued)

by psycho-analysis, however, indicates the necessity, if not of 'enlightening', at least of bringing up children from the tenderest years in such a fashion as will render any special enlightenment unnecessary, since it points to the completest, most natural enlightenment compatible with the rate of development of the child. The irrefutable conclusions to be drawn from psycho-analytic experience demand that children shall, whenever possible, be protected from any over-strong repression, and thus from illness or a disadvantageous development of character. Alongside the certainly wise intention of countering actual and visible dangers with information, therefore, analysis aims at avoiding dangers that are equally actual, even if not visible (because not recognized as such), but which are much commoner, deeper, and therefore call much more urgently for observation. The results of psycho-analysis, which always in every individual case leads back to repressions of childish sexuality as the causes of subsequent illness, or of the more or less operative morbific elements or inhibitions present even in every normal mentality, indicate clearly the path to be followed. We can spare the child unnecessary repression by freeing – and first and foremost in ourselves – the whole wide sphere of sexuality from the dense veils of secrecy, falsehood and danger spun by a hypocritical civilization upon an affective and uninformed foundation. We shall let the child acquire as much sexual information as the growth of its desire for knowledge requires, thus depriving sexuality at once of its mystery and of a great part of its danger. This ensures that wishes, thoughts and feelings shall not – as happened to us – be partly repressed and partly, in so far as repression fails, endured under a burden of false shame and nervous suffering. In averting this repression, this burden of superfluous suffering, moreover, we are laying the foundations for health, mental balance and the favourable development of character. This incalculably valuable result, however, is not the only advantage we can expect for the individual and for the evolution of humanity from an upbringing founded upon unqualified frankness. It has another and not less significant consequence – a decisive influence upon the development of the intellectual powers.

('The development of a child', 1921; pp. 1–2)

It is of great interest that Klein's attention to children's intellectual development began in this earliest publication, and is also taken further in the next papers she wrote. This distinctive focus on the capacity for thinking and understanding has remained characteristic of the style of work of many of the analysts who represent later developments of her ideas (e.g. Bion, Money-Kyrle, O'Shaughnessy, Britton). Likierman (2001) suggests that Klein's approach represents a bringing together of Freud's theory of infantile sexuality and sexual curiosity of children with Ferenczi's interest in the transition from omnipotent to reality-based thinking.

The child she wrote about in her first paper she called Fritz, but he is known in fact to be her own son Erich. In the early days of psychoanalysis the practice of analysts analysing their own children was quite widespread, most famously in the case of Freud and his daughter Anna, and in this paper it does of course make it possible for her to draw on an extraordinary mix of observations. We learn of Fritz's overall 'slow' development, and the late onset of his asking the sort of challenging questions young children do pose to their parents: about birth, death, time, God and so on. He comes vividly alive as a child in Klein's descriptions. She focuses on the time when Fritz seems to wake up to a great many things he wants to get to the bottom of: why do grown-ups tell stories to cover up true facts? What is the role of father? What goes on inside mother's body? How are things made and how do things work? What is the difference between boys and girls? She describes the growth of Fritz's reality sense in contrast to the omnipotence of wishes.

Klein's emphasis is on what gets locked up in repression, and the problem of false authority.

Pedagogic and psychological perspectives

> New vistas open before me when I compare my observations of this child's greatly enhanced mental powers under the influence of his newly acquired knowledge with previous observations and experiences in cases of more or less unfavourable development. Honesty towards children, frank answering of all their questions, and the inner freedom which this brings about, influence mental development profoundly and beneficially. This safeguards thought from the tendency to repression which is the chief danger affecting it, i.e. from the withdrawal of instinctual energy with which goes a part of sublimation, and from the accompanying repression of ideational associations connected with the repressed complexes, whereby the sequence of thought is destroyed.
>
> ('The development of a child', 1921; pp. 18–19)

She goes on to discuss the idea of analysing children under the age of six, which would be new territory, as Hug-Hellmuth (1921), the first child analyst, had suggested that analysis was only adapted to children above this age, in other words to children entering the latency period following the intense Oedipal period Freud had described as located between three and five years, going to school, and being able to speak about their thoughts. But first she lays out her view of parental responsibilities in the light of psychoanalytic knowledge:

> I shall now, however, bring forward the question of what we learn from the analyses of adults and children that we could apply in regard to the mind of children under six, since it is well known that analyses of the neuroses reveal traumata and sources of injury in events, impressions or developments that occurred at a very early age, that is, before the sixth year. What does this information yield for prophylaxis? What can we *do* just at the age that analysis has taught us is so exceedingly important, not only for subsequent illnesses but also for the permanent formation of character and of intellectual development?
>
> The first and most natural result of our knowledge will above all be the avoidance of factors which psycho-analysis has taught us to consider as grossly injurious to the child's mind. We shall therefore lay down as an unconditional necessity that the child, from birth, shall not share the parental bedroom; and we shall be more sparing of
>
> *(continued)*

(continued)

compulsory ethical requirements in regard to the tiny developing creature than people were with us. We shall allow him to remain for a longer period uninhibited and natural, less interfered with than has hitherto been the case, to become conscious of his different instinctive impulses and of his pleasure therein without immediately whipping up his cultural tendencies against this ingenuousness. We shall aim at a slower development, that allows room for his instincts to become partially conscious, and, together with this, for their possible sublimation. At the same time we shall not refuse expression to his awakening sexual curiosity and shall satisfy it step by step, even – in my opinion – withholding nothing. We shall know how to give him sufficient affection and yet avoid a harmful superfluity; above all we shall reject physical punishment and threats, and secure the obedience necessary for upbringing by occasionally means of withdrawing affection.

('The development of a child', 1921; pp. 25–26)

Klein describes the torment of meaningless or unanswerable questions many parents are familiar with, and comments that the conscious spoken question conceals the unconscious and unspoken one. She then turns her attention to the 'attitude' of the child from 'the very tenderest years' which limits the impact of the most enlightened upbringing:

It appears, e.g., in spite of all educational measures aiming amongst other things at an unreserved satisfying of sexual curiosity, that this latter need is frequently not freely expressed. This negative attitude [towards knowledge] may take the most varying forms up to an absolute unwillingness to know. At times it appears as a displaced interest in something else which is often marked by a compulsive character. At times this attitude sets in only after partial enlightenment and then, instead of the lively interest hitherto displayed, the child manifests a strong resistance against accepting any further enlightenment and simply does not accept it.

(p. 27)

The story of Fritz is resumed, with many details outlining her understanding of his Oedipal phantasies of competition with father for mother and his splitting of the mother imago. Klein recounts the interpretations of his play and stories which she gave him alongside the answering of questions and summarises her work as 'upbringing with analytic features'. Here is an example of the kind of conversations they had. Klein herself thought this particular one was important:

He is sitting early in the morning on the chamber, and explains that the kakis [poos] are on the balcony already, have run upstairs again and don't want to go into the garden (as he has repeatedly designated the chamber). I ask him, 'These are the children then that grow in the stomach?' As I notice this interests him I continue, 'For the kakis are made

> from the food; real children are not made from food.' He, 'I know that, they are made of milk.' 'Oh no, they are made of something that papa makes and the egg that is inside mamma.' (He is very attentive now and asks me to explain.) When I begin once more about the little egg, he interrupts me, 'I know that.' I continue, 'Papa can make something with his wiwi that really looks rather like milk and is called seed; he makes it like doing wiwi only not so much. Mamma's wiwi is different to papa's' (he interrupts) 'I know that!' I say, 'Mamma's wiwi is like a hole. If papa puts his wiwi into mamma's wiwi and makes the seed there, then the seed runs in deeper into her body and when it meets with one of the little eggs that are inside mamma, then that little egg begins to grow and it becomes a child.' Fritz listened with great interest and said, 'I would so much like to see how a child is made inside like that.' I explain that this is impossible until he is big because it can't be done till then but that then he will do it himself. 'But then I would like to do it to mamma.' 'That can't be, mamma can't be your wife for she is the wife of your papa, and then papa would have no wife.' 'But we could both do it to her.' I say, 'No, that can't be. Every man has only one wife. When you are big your mamma will be old. Then you will marry a beautiful young girl and she will be your wife.' He (nearly in tears and with quivering lips), 'But shan't we live in the same house together with mamma?' I, 'Certainly, and your mamma will always love you but she can't be your wife.' He then enquired about various details, how the child is fed in the maternal body, what the cord is made of, how it comes away, he was full of interest and no further resistance was to be noticed. At the end he said, 'But I would just once like to see how the child gets in and out.'
>
> (pp. 33–34)

A few days later, Fritz told Klein this dream which she interpreted directly:

> 'There was a big motor that looked just like an electric car. It had seats too and there was a little motor that ran along with the big one. Their roofs could be opened up and then shut down when it rained. Then the motors went on and ran into an electric car and knocked it away. Then the big motor went on top of the electric car and drew the little one after it. And then they all got close together, the electric car and the two motors. The electric car had a connecting-rod too. You know what I mean? The big motor had a beautiful big silver iron thing and the little one had something like two little hooks. The little one was between the electric car and the motor. Then they drove up a high mountain and came down quickly again. The motors stayed there in the night too. When electric cars came they knocked them away and if any one did like that' (with an arm) 'they went backwards at once.' (I explain that the big motor is his papa, the electric car his mamma and the little motor himself, and that he has put himself between papa and mamma because he would so much like to put papa away altogether and to remain alone with his mamma and do with her what only papa is allowed to do.)
>
> (p. 35)

Fritz went on to develop the dream story expansively and Klein comments thus:

> Subsequent to this phantasy the pleasure in play was increased and became permanent. He now played alone for hours with the same amount of pleasure as it gave him to relate these phantasies. He would also say straight out, 'Now I shall play what I told you', or 'I won't tell this but just play it.' Thus while unconscious phantasies are usually ventilated in play-activities, in this case it seemed probable, as no doubt in other similar cases, that the inhibition of phantasy was the cause of the play-inhibition, both of which were simultaneously removed. I observed that the games and occupations that had been previously pursued now dropped into the background. I mean especially the endless 'chauffeur, coachman, etc.' game that had generally consisted in his shoving benches, chairs or a box, up against one another and sitting on them. He had also never given up running to the window whenever he heard a vehicle pass and was quite unhappy if he ever missed one. He could put in hours standing at the window or at the front door mainly in order to look at the passing carriages. The vehemence and exclusiveness with which he pursued these occupations led me to consider them as of the nature of compulsions.
>
> (pp. 36–37)

It is important to note here her use of the term 'unconscious phantasies', which was to become such a prominent feature of Kleinian theory, and her interest in the resolution of the inhibitions which she believed were restricting Fritz's development.

Some months later, Fritz began to express anxiety which she linked to his enthusiasm for listening to Grimm's fairy tales (sadly she does not tell us which ones) and a period of illness in herself which was severe enough to deprive him of her day-to-day care. She describes his difficulties in falling asleep, over-zealous efforts to learn to read and his being 'naughtier and less cheerful'. This is such a good example of the close connection between internal and external factors. We could suggest that his mother's illness arouses deep worry in Fritz (perhaps intensified by the intimacy of exchange between them which had preceded this) and his unconsciously determined response is to struggle to be a big boy, to acquire the capacity as reader to be able to solve problems himself and to turn away from the dangerous free play he is now somewhat afraid of. But all this is a great strain and indeed the boundary between phantasy and reality does not feel so solid when a child's basic security is undermined, as happens when a parent is ill. (This is something Klein discusses in *Narrative of a Child Analysis* in relation to Richard's father's serious illness.) This is clear in another sequence Klein reports:

> Here is another dream that was not, however, associated with feelings of fear. Everywhere, behind mirrors, doors, etc., were wolves with long tongues hanging out. He shot them all down so that they died. He was not afraid because he was stronger than them. Subsequent phantasies also dealt with wolves. Once when he was frightened again before falling asleep, he said about it that he had been frightened of the hole in the wall where the light peeped in (an opening in the wall for heating purposes) because on the ceiling it looked like a hole too, and a man might get up from there with a ladder on

> to the roof. He also spoke about whether the devil did not sit in the hole in the stove. He recounted that he saw the following in a picture book. A lady is in his room. Suddenly she sees that the devil is sitting in the hole in the stove and his tail is sticking out. In the course of his associations it is shown that he was afraid that the man with the ladder might step on him, hurt him in the belly and finally he owns up that he was afraid for his wiwi.
>
> (pp. 40–41)

Klein's regular work with Fritz continued for some time, dealing with anal-erotic, homosexual and paranoid features in his phantasies. She concludes her paper with some broad reflections on the place of analysis in bringing up children:

> I am of the opinion that no upbringing should be without analytic help, because analysis affords such valuable and, from the point of view of prophylaxis, as yet incalculable assistance.
>
> (p. 45)

She first suggests 'Psychoanalysis would have to serve education as an assistant – as a completion' but then more boldly asserts:

> how advantageous and necessary it is to intervene with analysis quite early in upbringing in order to prepare a relationship to the child's unconscious as soon as we can get in touch with his conscious. Then probably the inhibitions or neurotic traits could be easily removed as they were beginning to develop. There is no doubt that the normal three-year-old, probably indeed the still younger child, who so often shows such lively interests, is already intellectually capable of grasping the explanations given him as well as anything else. Probably much better than the older child, who is already affectively hampered in such matters by a more strongly fixed resistance, while the little child is far nearer to these natural things so long as upbringing has not extended its injurious influences too far. *This* would be, then, much more than in the case of this already five-year-old boy, an upbringing with the aid of analysis.
>
> (pp. 47–48)

She produces all kinds of arguments to defend the idea of early analysis: it does not make children difficult or uneducable, but rather the opposite. Her hopefulness about the benefits of analysis and her ambition for it to benefit children widely – for example, by analysts being involved in running kindergartens – is impressive.

The next paper Klein wrote explored explicitly what she called 'The role of the school in the libidinal development of the child' (1923). Again, one can sense here the importance of her experience as a mother overseeing her children's education as well as her analytic focus. She writes about the child's experience of school with an eye to the unconscious sexual meaning of aspects of the school as institution, of the nature of the learning process and of the particular significance of different subjects studied at school.

She begins with a reference to fear of examinations and this almost universal and therefore easily recognisable everyday fear sets the scene for a dazzling array of observations about the range and meaning of inhibitions and anxieties aroused in the school setting. Klein notes that the pressure on the child is a consequence of the demand for the sublimation of 'libidinal instinctual energies', and suggests that there is also a shift from the 'passive feminine' attitude of the pre-school child – here she seems to be referring to the idea of a preponderance of the pleasure principle in the early years in the undemanding life of the child free to play – to the requirement to be more active and confront tasks. Her later discoveries about the very early severe anxieties of the infant and young child, the much earlier dating of the superego, and the complexity of projective and introjective processes do, of course, provide a very different picture of the pre-school child, but nonetheless the enormity of the change for the child now expected to begin formal learning is a reality. The small child's 'work' is to play, but the schoolchild's work includes a great deal of adaptation to the demands of being one of a large group and completing tasks set by teachers.

Klein is attentive to the school as an institution, with its imposition and provision of external structures. She suggests that the headmaster and class teacher are often unconsciously experienced as father whereas the school as a whole is felt to be mother. This vision of the whole school space and its widest functions evoking feelings similar to those aroused by the maternal body is a theme taken up by later writers, including the psychoanalytic art historian Adrian Stokes in his writings about architecture (Stokes, 1951, 1958, 1965). In line with her overall emphasis at this time on Freud's theory of infantile sexuality and especially the fear of castration, she describes the school mistress as likely to be experienced as a castrating mother. She offers original insights into the meaning of many particular activities. She shows how speaking and singing can be felt as linked to phantasies about intercourse because the movement of the tongue in the mouth can be imaginatively associated with the movement of father's penis inside mother's body. In similar style (that is, always alert to the potential unconscious sexual significance of what is encountered), Klein discusses how individual letters of the alphabet can be equated with the genitals, or faeces, capital letters given specific potency and so on, and the numbers of arithmetic are also full of potential symbolic reference. The number three evokes the Oedipal trio and five the fingers of the hand, for example. Division sums can arouse anxiety because of the evocation of phantasies of chopping up mother, and learning grammar, in which sentences must be taken apart, can similarly be felt as a disturbing demand to dismember something. One can note here Klein's understanding of pre-symbolic forms of thought, which Bion's later work on the origins and development of thinking capacity will address. History as a subject naturally suggests the questions of personal and family history, including the basic one about one's own conception and origins, and geography, maps in particular, stirs infantile thoughts about the world we first meet after birth, the world of the maternal body. Klein's overall argument is summarised in the following quotations:

> I have endeavoured to show that the fundamental activities exercised at school are channels for the flow of libido and that by this means the component instincts achieve sublimation under the supremacy of the genitals. This libidinal cathexis, however, is carried over from the most elementary studies – reading, writing and arithmetic – to wider

efforts and interests based upon these, so that the foundations of later inhibitions – of vocational inhibition as well – are to be found, above all, in the frequently apparently evanescent ones concerned with the earliest studies. The inhibitions of these earliest studies, however, are built upon play-inhibitions, so that in the end we can see all the later inhibitions, so significant for life and development, evolving from the earliest play-inhibitions . . .

. . . We must refer the establishment of all the inhibitions which affect learning and all further development to the time of the first efflorescence of infantile sexuality which, with the onset of the Oedipus complex, gives its greatest momentum to the castration-fear, that is, to the early period between three and four years of age. It is the consequent repression of the active masculine components – in both boys and girls – that provides the chief basis for inhibitions of learning.

The contribution which the feminine component makes to sublimation will probably always prove to be receptivity and understanding, which are an important part of all activities; the driving executive part, however, which really constitutes the character of any activity, originates in the sublimation of masculine potency. The feminine attitude towards the father, which is connected with admiration and acknowledgement of the paternal penis and its achievements, becomes by sublimation the basis of an understanding for artistic and other achievements in general. I was able repeatedly in analyses of boys and girls to see how important the repression of this feminine attitude through the castration complex might be. As an essential part of every activity, repression of it must contribute largely to the inhibition of any activity. It has also been possible to observe in analysing patients of both sexes how, as a part of the castration complex became conscious and the feminine attitude appeared more freely, there often occurred a powerful onset of artistic and other interests . . .

. . . I will briefly sum up my conception of the teacher's part in the development of the child. The teacher can achieve much by sympathetic understanding, for he is able thereby considerably to reduce that part of the inhibition that attaches to the person of the teacher as 'avenger'. At the same time, the wise and kindly teacher offers the homosexual component in the boy and the masculine component of the girl an object for the exercise of their genital activity in a sublimated form, as which [in], as I suggested, we can recognize the various studies. From these indications, however, the possibilities of injury that can result from a pedagogically wrong or even brutal procedure on the part of the teacher can be deduced.

('The role of the school in the libidinal development of the child', 1923; pp. 73–76)

It is worthy of note that Klein's early interest in the school and in the psychological aspects of education has proved an inspiration to later generations of child analysts and child psychotherapists. The idea, implicit in these early papers, that psychoanalysis has a great deal to contribute to the understanding of the pupil–teacher relationship and the functioning of the school as a whole has been fruitfully developed in a number of ways. These have included involvement in the training of teachers (Susan Isaacs's work at the Institute of Education in London was the start of this), the longstanding provision of courses exploring the emotional aspects of teaching and learning for teachers at the Tavistock Clinic (Salzberger-Wittenberg *et al.*, 1983; Youell, 2006; Rustin, 2012) and direct work in school offering consultancy to staff (Harris, 1987) and clinical work to children and young people.

The creative imagination with which Klein investigated the anxieties and inhibitions in learning which her young patients revealed remains a vital resource for those involved in education as well as for clinical psychoanalysis. There is a delightful footnote in her next paper on 'Early analysis' (1923) which draws on her analysis of Fritz, who was fascinated by railways, stations and roads which featured largely in his play. Klein discusses his profound interest in the 'geography of the mother's body' – he used to explain, aged 4, that his mother was 'a mountain which he was climbing' – and explains clearly her understanding of the importance of the free play of phantasy in development:

> The circular railway which came into his phantasies appeared in all his games as well. He constructed trains which ran in a circle and he drove his big hoop round and round in a circle. His gradually increasing interest in the direction and names of streets had developed into an interest in geography. He pretended that he was going on journeys on the map. All this showed that the advance in his phantasies from his home to his town, his country and the world at large (an advance which manifested itself when once the phantasies were set free) was having its effect on his interests also, for their sphere was widening more and more. Here I should like to draw attention to the very great importance of inhibitions in play from this point of view as well. The inhibition and restriction of interests in play leads to the diminishing of potentialities and interests both in learning and in the whole further development of the mind.
>
> ('Early analysis', 1923; p. 97)

She links this matter of freedom to explore versus inhibition to most profound issues of orientation and the growth of the mind:

> Apart from the interest in geography I discovered that it was one of the determining factors in the capacity for drawing and the interest in natural science and everything to do with the exploration of the earth.
>
> In Fritz I found also a very close connection between his lack of orientation in space and in time. Corresponding to his repressed interest in the place of his intra-uterine existence was the absence of interest in details as to the time when he was there. Thus both the questions 'Where was I before birth?' and 'When was I there?' were repressed.
>
> The unconscious equation of sleep, death and intra-uterine existence was evident in many of his sayings and phantasies, and connected with this was his curiosity as to the duration of these states and their succession in time. It would appear that the change from intra-uterine to extra-uterine existence, as the prototype of all periodicity, is one of the roots of the concept of time and of orientation in time.
>
> (p. 99)

In the paper on 'Early analysis' (1923), Klein is clearly intending to ground her work closely on Freudian instinct theory, fixation points, sublimation and so on. The centrality of the primal scene is summarised in this quotation:

> To sum up what I have said, I have found that artistic and intellectual fixations, as well as those which subsequently lead to neurosis, have as some of their most powerful determining factors the primal scene or phantasies of it. An important point is which of the senses is more strongly excited: whether the interest applies more to what is to be seen or to what is to be heard. This will probably also determine, and on the other hand will also depend upon, whether ideas present themselves to the subject visually or auditorily. No doubt constitutional factors play a great part here.
>
> In Fritz it was the movement of the penis to which he was fixated, in Felix the sounds which he heard, in others the colour-effects. Of course, for the talent or bent to develop, those special factors which I have already discussed in detail must come into play. In fixation to the primal scene (or phantasies) *the degree of activity*, which is so important for sublimation itself, undoubtedly also determines whether the subject develops a talent for creation or reproduction. For the degree of activity certainly influences the mode of identification.
>
> ('Early analysis', 1923; p. 103)

But in this summary, the lines of enquiry which Klein was to take further are also evident: the emphasis on phantasy, on identification and on the importance of early sensory experience. Klein's attention to the differentiation between sound and vision might be taken as a precursor of her later idea of part-objects and her attempt to understand the complex process of integration between part-objects (or aspects of the object) towards the creation of an object perceived as a whole. The great breadth of her deployment of the concept of inhibition is the other notable feature of this as of her other early papers and the consequent ambition for and hopefulness about the development of child analysis.

Her next paper, 'A contribution to the psychogenesis of tics' (1925), is her first published case history, and links directly with her concern about inhibited development. Thirteen-year-old Felix is described as very inhibited in 'intellectual interests and social relations', interested only in games and physical prowess, and lacking in emotionality. Klein became interested also in a tic mentioned to her at the point of referral and this is the explicit focus of the paper. She worked with Felix for over three years, and was impressed by the intensification of his sexual anxieties at the onset of puberty. She gives a very careful early history of significant events, including sharing his parents' bedroom until he was six, two medical interventions, and his father's absence during the war and subsequent return. Some of the details are poignant: Felix had enjoyed singing as a young child, but had then given it up. The picture of extreme physical restlessness, fidgeting at school and an aversion to school work puts one in mind of the contemporary diagnosis of attention deficit hyperactivity disorder (ADHD). Klein understood his overall anxiety state and defensive efforts to be closely linked to sexual preoccupations and strong impulses to masturbate, which he tried to control as his parents demanded. This picture of the power of repression is the background to her complex analysis of his tic. Here is her account of it:

> An increase in the frequency of the tic was to be noticed at this time. It had first appeared a few months prior to the analysis, the precipitating factor being that Felix had clandestinely witnessed sexual intercourse between his parents. Immediately afterwards the symptoms, out of which the tic developed, appeared: a twitching of the face and a throwing back of the head. The tic comprised three phases. At the beginning Felix had a feeling as though the depression in his neck, under the back of his head, were being torn. In consequence of this feeling he felt constrained first to throw his head back and then to rotate it from right to left. The second movement was accompanied by a feeling that something was cracking loudly. The concluding phase consisted of a third movement in which the chin was pressed as deeply as possible downwards. This gave Felix a feeling of drilling into something. For a time he performed these three movements three times over consecutively. One meaning of the 'three' was that in the tic – I shall refer to this later in detail – Felix played three rôles: the passive rôle of his mother, the passive rôle of his own ego, and the active rôle of his father. The passive rôles were represented predominanty by the first two movements; though in the feeling of 'cracking' was contained also the sadistic element representing the active rôle of the father, an element which came to fuller expression in the third movement, that of drilling into something.
>
> ('A contribution to the psychogenesis of tics', 1925; pp. 108–109)

She notes that to 'bring the tic within the scope of the analysis', Felix's free associations were necessary, and this is an instructive example of her careful clinical technique. Klein shows how his concern with his parents' sexual relationship – stimulated by his exposure to the 'primal scene' – underlay the inhibition of his pleasure in sound, particularly his musical sensibility, and his use of his eyes. Instead of the expression of his wish to see in ordinary curiosity there was repression of this desire, manifested in the compulsive rubbing of his eyes and later blinking. The marked degrees of closure in his cultural interests Klein linked to Felix's tendency to close both eyes and ears rather than experience the anxiety which was evoked by opening up his organs of perception. These observations are fascinating precursors of many later analysts' interest in the processes of the splitting up of 'common sense' (Bion, 1970) and the problems in the development a capacity for thought when perceptual capacities are attacked by the self.

In this paper, Klein shows a surprising combination of analytic exploration and rigour with an anxious decision to interfere directly in Felix's life. She became worried that mutual masturbation with another boy was not 'in the interest of the analysis' and 'in view of all the complications . . . I had to put a stop to this relation between the two boys'. Felix seems to have accepted her instruction – echoing in his submission to his analyst the earlier struggles to go along with parental injunctions – and indeed Klein could then analyse his unconscious homosexual attitude to his father. Perhaps the difficulty for child analysts of sustaining loyalty to the child patient in the context of parental expectations and the dependence of the analyst on parental support if the analysis is to be allowed to take its course may have played a part in this sequence of events. The text does not make this clear. Possibly Klein's recognition of the sexual activities of young adolescents disturbed her, though she later wrote in a startlingly open-minded way about sexual expression among children, seeing it as having important creative potential rather than something to be strongly discouraged.

Analysing masturbation phantasies, however, was absolutely central to her analytic work with Felix. The analysis of the tic led her to a deep understanding of the object relationships which were at its core, and to a view that these unconscious object relationships were closely linked to overall character. Noting the similarities between Felix's behaviour and the restlessness of another patient, Werner, led to many reflections on the psychic meaning of motor discharge. Werner was one of those helpful child patients who alert their analyst both to underlying phantasy and to the suffering that their compulsive behaviour occasions. Werner could explain that 'Fidgeting is fun, but it isn't always fun, you can't leave off when you want to – as, for instance, when you ought to do your lessons', and he also referred to his 'fidgeting thoughts', which were the complex phantasies represented in the compulsive actions which Klein realised were based on identification with both male and female bodies in intercourse. Werner told her, touchingly, that he could not 'fidget properly' in the company of other people, thus revealing how close to consciousness was the sexual element in his phantasy life, but of course also illustrating how much Klein's child patients came to trust her.

These observations of behaviour which has sexual phantasy at its heart remain strikingly fresh and provide us with a theory with which to approach some of the familiar diagnoses of modern child psychiatry. Klein's ideas illuminate not only a central aspect of the internal object relations which characterise the hyperactive children given an ADHD diagnosis, but also in her discussion of tics and their genesis, the phenomena of Tourette's syndrome. Klein's work here follows Freud's interest in sexual desires. One can see modern psychiatric approaches to ADHD as repeating the earlier resistant reaction to Freud's hypotheses about infantile sexuality and Klein's about the importance of underlying anxieties.

Klein's own on-going dialogue with her psychoanalytic forebears is also in evidence in this paper, in which she discusses Ferenczi's view of the tic. She is aware of a difference in their points of view, and locates this in her belief that the tic behaviour involves a 'retreat from the object relations already achieved to a secondary narcissism'. She saw the tic, therefore, not only as an 'indication of inhibition and asocial development' but as what contemporary analysts might understand as constituting a pathological defensive organisation, trapping the patient in a narcissistic inner world consequent on confusion of self and object – the self being the child who had dealt with Oedipal difficulties via intrusive identification (Meltzer, 1967) into the object. Klein notes the seriousness of the fact that a symptom can, in this way, subvert development. By contrast, in a wonderful footnote, she points out, 'The connection between auditory impressions and their reproduction in movement is seen as a normal phenomenon in the urge to dance which is aroused by listening to dance music' (p. 125). The contrast suggested here between the development of symbolic activity and the entry into cultural space and the non-symbolic imitative activity of Felix and Werner anticipates the work of Segal and others in differentiating the symbolic realm from the one-person world of symbolic equations. It also reminds us of how in touch Klein was with the range of children's ordinary behaviour, and how grounded her theoretical ideas are in close observation.

In two papers from 1926 and 1927, Klein outlines her technique. The first of these, 'The psychological principles of early analysis', tackles the issue of how to adapt psychoanalytic technique to the task of understanding the mind of the young child and presents an account of her play technique. The second is her contribution to a 'Symposium on child-analysis' held in the British Psychoanalytical Society that year, and confronts the considerable difference between Klein's approach and that of Anna Freud. It is, therefore, a historical document of importance in setting out the background to the two distinct lines of development in child analysis and the underlying differences in the conception of psychoanalysis which became so dominant a matter in the 1930s and 1940s, as described in *The Freud–Klein Controversies 1941–45* (King and Steiner, 1991).

The first paper is characteristic of Klein's method in that it starts with a clinical vignette of a 3¼-year-old patient. This is set within the following theoretical assumptions about early childhood:

- The child seeks pleasure from relations with other people (objects).
- The initial relationship to objects is narcissistic.
- A relationship to reality grows out of these relationships.

In Klein's vignette, she highlights the child's sense of deprivation, that is to say, it is the experience of frustration which inaugurates a relationship to reality. In particular, the sense of deprivation arising from the Oedipus situation has to be tolerated if a child is to have a 'successful adaptation to reality'. Klein's Freudian heart is on her sleeve, but she then goes on to locate Oedipal issues in the second year of life, a major difference with Freud's theory. She also notes, in a footnote, the importance of the early feeding experience and the weaning process, signalling her interest in the earlier deprivation involved in the loss of the breast which was so central to her thinking. She is also keen to emphasise that early analysis of children supports them in becoming able to bear parental and educational expectations. All these comments suggest the importance in Klein's thinking of her experience as a mother. Her everyday intimacy with the lives of very young children enables her to see quite new things, in ways which were less accessible to Freud.

She goes on to discuss the typical features of 'neurosis' in young children. We can understand 'neurosis' here as referring to obvious unhappiness and difficulty in adapting to ordinary parental expectations. Klein describes the importance of anxiety, including night terrors, bodily accidents and fears, extreme sensitivity, inhibition in play, ambivalence to family festivities and behavioural difficulties. She proposes that guilt was a central cause of these varied phenomena, and gives clinical examples to show that small children's aggressive phantasies and wishes leave them vulnerable to enormous feelings of guilt. She shows from her clinical material that the fear of severe punishment is not only experienced in relation to real external figures but also to harsh internal figures. Here she is describing the early cruel superego which her work with young children introduced her to so vividly, and their determined efforts to control their hostile feelings. Of Rita, aged 2¼, she wrote:

> [O]n one occasion an elephant was put beside its [the doll's] bed. This elephant was supposed to prevent the baby-doll from getting up; otherwise it would steal into the parents' bedroom and do them some harm or take something away from them . . . [B]etween the ages of fifteen months and two years, she had wanted to usurp her mother's place with her father, to steal from her mother the child with which she was pregnant, and to injure and castrate the parents.
>
> ('The psychological principles of early analysis', 1926; p. 132)

Thus Klein both announces her theory of the early Oedipal conflict and asserts a historical event in Rita's mind provoked by the awareness of her mother's pregnancy. The enormity of these claims within the psychoanalytic community of the time can hardly be overestimated, and the disturbing picture of the hostile and sadistic phantasies of early childhood was and remains to this day a source of shock and discomfiture, often leading to rejection of her ideas. Klein, however, goes calmly on to discuss the inhibitions which follow deep unconscious guilt, and to assert that these earlier forms of the superego are properly continuous with Freud's depiction of the later superego. She emphasises the link between the early phase of the Oedipal conflict and the origin of this early cruel conscience, thus sustaining the Freudian link between Oedipal development and the establishment of the superego. Her wish is to free her little patients from their infantile neuroses and she describes how open young children can be to this work, since 'in certain strata of the child-mind there is a much easier communication between Cs [the conscious mind] and Ucs [what is unconscious], and therefore it is much simpler to retrace the steps from the one to the other' (p. 134). This observation is indeed borne out by generations of child analysts and psychotherapists who often find themselves taken aback by the speed at which things move in analytic work with young children, in marked contrast with the slow pace of most analysis of latency-aged children, not to mention adults, whose capacity for resistance of all kinds can be difficult to bear.

Klein suggests that children's play symbolically expresses wishes, phantasies and experiences in a way analogous to adult dreaming:

> We can only fully understand it if we approach it by the method Freud has evolved for unravelling dreams. Symbolism is only a part of it; if we want rightly to comprehend children's play in connection with their whole behaviour during the analytic hour, we must take into account not only the symbolism which often appears so clearly in their games, but also all the means of representation and the mechanisms involved in dream-work, and we must bear in mind the necessity of examining the whole nexus of phenomena.
>
> ('The psychological principles of early analysis', 1926; p. 134)

Here is a succinct statement of Klein's understanding of what she later came to call the 'total situation' (Klein, 1952).

She goes on to give proper place to the child's associations and to the observing role of the analyst, and to argue strongly for the depth of child analysis:

> In their play children represent symbolically phantasies, wishes and experiences. Here they are employing the same language, the same archaic, phylogenetically acquired mode of expression as we are familiar with from dreams. . . . If we employ this [Freud's] technique we soon find that children produce no fewer associations to the separate features of their games than do adults to the elements of their dreams. The details of the play point the way for an attentive observer; and, in between, the child tells all sorts of things which must be given their full weight as associations.
>
> Besides this archaic mode of representation children employ another primitive mechanism, that is to say, they substitute actions (which were the original precursors of thoughts) for words: with children, *acting* plays a prominent part.
>
> *(continued)*

(continued)

In 'From the history of an infantile neurosis', Freud (1918) says: 'An analysis which is conducted upon a neurotic child itself must, as a matter of course, appear to be more trustworthy, but it cannot be very rich in material; too many words and thoughts have to be lent to the child, and even so the deepest strata may turn out to be impenetrable to consciousness'.

If we approach children with the technique appropriate to the analysis of adults we shall assuredly not succeed in penetrating to the deepest layers of the child's mental life. But it is precisely these layers which are of moment for the value and success of an analysis. If, however, we take into account the psychological differences between children and adults and bear in mind the fact that in children we find Ucs still in operation side by side with Cs, the most primitive tendencies side by side with those most complicated developments known to us, such as the super-ego – if, that is to say, we rightly understand the child's mode of expression, all these doubtful points and unfavourable factors vanish. For we find that, as regards the depth and scope of the analysis, we may expect as much from children as from adults. And still more, in the analysis of children we can go back to experiences and fixations which in analysing adults we can only *reconstruct*, while in children they are *directly* represented. Take for instance, the case of Ruth who, as an infant, had gone hungry for some time because her mother had little milk to give her. At the age of four years and three months, when playing with the wash-basin, she called the water-tap a milk-tap. She declared that the milk was running into mouths (the holes of the waste-pipe), but that only a very little was flowing. This unsatisfied oral desire made its appearance in countless games and dramatizations and showed itself in her whole attitude. For instance, she asserted that she was poor, that she only had one coat, and that she had very little to eat – none of these statements being in the least in accordance with reality.

Another little patient (who suffered from obsessional neurosis) was the six-year-old Erna, whose neurosis was based on impressions received during the period of training in cleanliness. These impressions she dramatized for me in the minutest detail. Once she placed a little doll on a stone, pretended that it was defæcating and stood other dolls round it which were supposed to be admiring it. After this dramatization Erna brought the same material into a game of acting. She wanted me to be a baby in long clothes which made itself dirty, while she was the mother. The baby was a spoilt child and an object of admiration. This was followed by a reaction of rage in Erna, and she played the part of a cruel teacher who knocked the child about. In this way Erna enacted before me one of the first traumata in her experience: the heavy blow her narcissism received when she imagined that the measures taken to train her meant the loss of the excessive affection bestowed on her in her infancy.

In general, in the analysis of children we cannot over-estimate the importance of phantasy and of translation into action at the bidding of the compulsion to repetition. Naturally, *little* children use the vehicle of action to a far greater extent, but even older ones constantly have recourse to this primitive mechanism, especially when analysis has removed some of their repressions. It is indispensable for carrying on the analysis that children should have the pleasure that is bound up with this mechanism, but the pleasure must always remain only a means to the end. It is just here that we see the

> predominance of the pleasure-principle over the reality-principle. We cannot appeal to the sense of reality in little patients as we can in older ones.
>
> Just as children's means of expression differ from those of adults, so the analytic situation in the analysis of children appears to be entirely different. It is, however, in both cases *essentially* the same. Consistent interpretations, gradual solving of resistances and persistent tracing of the transference to earlier situations – these constitute in children as in adults the correct analytic situation.
>
> ('The psychological principles of early analysis', 1926; pp. 134–137)

'Consistent interpretations, gradual solving of resistances and persistent tracing of the transference to earlier situations – these constitute in children as in adults the correct analytic situation.' There could hardly be a stronger statement of the viability of child analysis and its essential theoretical and clinical link to the psychoanalysis of adults.

In the 'Symposium' paper (1927), the confident tone of the paper just presented is there, but so is a sense of pressure to defend herself from attack, and a determination to locate herself at the heart of psychoanalysis. One can readily imagine the visceral emotional impact on Klein of Anna Freud's fierce assault on her work and similarly the outrage of Anna Freud to hear Klein claim to be the inheritor of Freud's legacy. These two remarkable women were battling over what was to be seen as the proper way forward in child analysis and for both of them it was a matter of deep principle but also of intense personal importance. The roots of the institutional conflict in the British Psychoanalytical Society and the debates of the Controversial Discussions are starkly present. Klein's postscript of 1947 notes changes in Anna Freud's position since the Symposium which bring their views closer together but her underlying anger about being misrepresented remains. The sense of being in opposing camps that characterised the experience of people trained within these two traditions in the years from the late 1940s to the 1980s seems an inevitable and unsurprising outcome of the conjunction of such irreconcilable mutual hurt with profound differences of analytic theory and technique. The role of Klein's two analysts, Ferenczi and Abraham, in enabling her to follow an independent psychoanalytic direction must have been important (Likierman, 2001). Perhaps the Anna Freud–Melanie Klein conflict can be seen as enacting some repetition of the fierce issues of loyalty between Freud and the first generation of psychoanalysts.

Klein's statement of position starts with Freud and Little Hans. She quotes Freud's reflections on the beneficial effects of the analysis of the Oedipus complex on the relationship between Little Hans and his father to set the scene for her own conviction about the value of child analysis, and the importance of keeping analysis separate from educational or more limited approaches to the child which were characteristic of Hug-Hellmuth's and later Anna Freud's technique. What Klein liked about Little Hans and about Freud's approach was the thorough-going pursuit of Hans' phantasies, wherever they led. She writes:

> [I]t is the attitude [of the analyst], the inner conviction which finds the necessary technique. I must reiterate what I have said: if one approaches child-analysis with an open mind one will discover ways and means of probing to the deepest depths.
>
> ('Symposium on child-analysis', 1927; p. 142)

She follows this manifesto about what is to be regarded as truly analytic with a substantial discussion of Anna Freud's views at this time. These included the belief that a child's current relationship to parents was an impediment to the evolution of a transference relationship to the analyst, that educational elements had to be combined with analytic technique to introduce a child to analytic work and persuade her to co-operate, that the child's conscious anxiety and guilt were important foundations for the analysis, and that the encouragement of a positive transference is beneficial. Klein argues, by contrast, that analysis deals with the internalized earlier aspects of the child's relationship to parents (the infantile elements) and that it is vital to interpret both positive and negative transferences, which will both regularly transmute into their opposites, and that the aim is to *resolve* anxiety and guilt. Of the analytic task she writes uncompromisingly: 'Analysis is not in itself a gentle method: it cannot spare the patient *any suffering*, and this applies equally to children' (p. 144).

In defending her play technique from Anna Freud's accusations of wild symbolic interpretation, she gives a rather striking account of her technique:

> Supposing that a child gives expression to the same psychic material in various repetitions – often actually through various media, i.e. toys, water, by cutting-out, drawing, etc. – and supposing that, besides, I can observe that these particular activities are mostly accompanied at the time by a sense of guilt, manifesting itself either as anxiety or in representations which imply over-compensation, which are the expression of reaction-formations – supposing, then, that I have arrived at an insight into certain connections: then I interpret these phenomena and link them up with the Ucs and the analytic situation. The practical and theoretical conditions for the interpretation are precisely the same as in the analysis of adults.
>
> The little toys I use are only one means I provide; paper, pencils, scissors, string, balls, bricks and, above all, water are others. They are at the child's disposal to use if he likes and the purpose of them all is simply to gain access to and to liberate his phantasy. There are some children who for a long time will not touch a toy or perhaps for weeks on end will only cut things out. In the case of children altogether inhibited in play the toys may possibly simply be a means of studying more closely the reasons for their inhibition. Some children, often the very little ones, as soon as the playthings have given them the opportunity of dramatizing some of the phantasies or experiences by which they are dominated, often put the toys aside altogether and pass on to every imaginable kind of game in which they themselves, various objects in my room and I have to take part.
>
> ('Symposium on child-analysis', 1927; pp. 147–148)

These paragraphs convey what a wealth of experience Klein has already amassed of work with children. A whole range of children at play pass before one's eyes in reading this description: the inhibited child, the young child busy with water, the more organised latency child using paper, pens, scissors and glue, free play with small toys, and pretend play involving both child and analyst in different roles.

Klein's delight in the natural symbolism of play is evident. 'Let us follow them along this path, that is to say, let us come into contact with their Ucs, making use of its language through our interpretation' (p. 148). She goes on to state her belief in the importance of reaching verbal expression which:

> bridges the gulf to reality . . . On this account I would not regard any child-analysis, not even that of a quite little child, as terminated unless I could finally succeed in its being expressed in speech, to the degree to which the child is capable of this, and so of linking it up with reality.
>
> (p. 150)

Following this discussion of technique, Klein pursues the theoretical underpinning of her understanding of the structure and development of the superego in young children. Its early development and its great severity she links to the Oedipal elements of the child's experience at weaning, the awareness of loss of the intimate relationship to mother's body being influenced by the child's passionate rage and possessiveness. Here she is urging the revision of Freud's dating of superego development in the light of her discoveries in analysing very young children:

> What Anna Freud says in this connection gives me the impression that she believes the development of the super-ego, with reaction-formations and screen-memories, to take place to a large extent during the period of latency. My analytic knowledge of little children forces me to differ from her quite definitely on this point. My observations have taught me that all these mechanisms are set going when the Oedipus complex arises and are activated by that complex. With its passing they have accomplished their fundamental work; the subsequent developments and reactions are rather the superstructure on a substratum which has assumed a fixed form and persists unchanged.
>
> (p. 158)

In this part of her paper, Klein's criticisms of Anna Freud amount to critical supervision of her clinical work in writing and must have been a source of offence.

The complexity of the differences between Klein and Anna Freud is very evident in her discussion of the relationship between child analyst and the parents of child patients. Klein argues persuasively that analysing a child's relationships to parents and siblings is a core responsibility:

> The difference in our point of view is this: that I never attempt in any way to prejudice a child against those with whom he is associated. But if his parents have entrusted him to me to analyse, either in order to cure a neurosis or for other reasons, I think I am justified in taking the line which seems to me in the child's interest the most advantageous and the only possible one. I mean that of analysing without reservation his relation to those about him, and therefore in particular to his parents and brothers and sisters.
>
> (p. 163)

What her own rigorous pursuit of Oedipal themes – jealousy and hatred of younger siblings, rivalry with mother and so on – seems to omit is any focus on the pain and anxiety involved in separation. The 'going-away mother' is taken to be the Oedipal mother. Deeper investigation of the meaning of early experiences of loss was to come in Klein's later work on mourning and depressive anxieties.

But she is confident in her assertion that a 'capacity for love is liberated by analysis' and therefore sure of her ground in her belief that analysing the child's ambivalence will be of benefit to on-going family relationships and thus fulfil her duty to his parents as well as the child himself. She allows for the situation in which the child 'remains in surroundings wholly adverse to analysis' (that is, lives with a family who do not support the pursuit of psychic truth) thus: 'Even in such cases I have found that the children were enabled by analysis to adapt themselves better and therefore better to stand the test of an unfavourable *milieu* and to suffer less than before being analysed' (p. 165). In taking this view Klein is bolder than Anna Freud, who suggested that child analysis was only appropriate in circumstances where parents had some knowledge of and respect for psychoanalysis. Klein's argument that conscious and unconscious convictions among parents may be out of kilter is clearly right, but she does not give the weight to the problem of the containment of parental ambivalence or the intrusion of parental psychopathology into the setting for child analysis that contemporary clinicians have found necessary. This is one of the domains of clinical practice in which significant change in technique is most evident, since child psychotherapy is now rarely undertaken without some on-going parallel work with parents.

The idea that analysis can open up a child's capacity to love anticipates her later work, 'Envy and gratitude' (1957). There is both the infant's innate love and hate to take account of, and the love which arises from the deep pleasure of being understood, and the gratitude and love evoked by the generous responsiveness of the thinking, feeling, understanding object.

In her concluding paragraphs there is a definition of her approach to child (and adult) analysis which prefigures the oft-quoted injunction by Bion (1970) to abjure 'memory and desire'. She writes:

> [A] children's analyst must have the same Ucs attitude as we require in the analyst of adults, if he is to be successful. It must enable him to be really willing *only to analyse* and not to wish to mould and direct the minds of his patients. If anxiety does not prevent him, he will be able calmly to wait for the development of the correct issue, and in this way that issue will be achieved.
>
> ('Symposium on child-analysis', 1927; p. 167)

The 'issue' she has in mind is psychic development and the role of psychoanalysis in enabling it to take place. Her conviction in the strength of the developmental drive in psychic life is the bedrock of her boldness and capacity for discovery.

Chapter 3

Epistemophilia

The love of understanding and its inhibition

Klein's recognition of the intensity of the child's desire to understand him- or herself, the other people who mattered in their worlds and indeed the world itself was one of her most original contributions. The origin of this strand in her work is often located in the extraordinary paper about 'Dick', an autistic boy she encountered and wrote about in her 1930 paper ('The importance of symbol-formation in the development of the ego'). But her interest in the child's natural curiosity (the curiosity which, after all, enables Lewis Carroll's Alice (Empson, 1935) to manage and survive her bewildering experiences in dream-Wonderland) links in a deep way with her investigation of the growth of the mind in her early papers. She was convinced that a psychoanalytic attitude to children should embrace their cognitive development. She had a profound love and respect for the child's mind in its intellectual, social, moral and aesthetic dimensions.

In this domain of her thinking, one is reminded of Freud's fascination with Little Hans, whose combination of curiosity and inhibition was so revealing. Freud's understanding from his analysis of Little Hans's phobias was that the blocked desire to comprehend how babies were made was the heart of the matter. Klein's investigation led her to focus on the child's earlier preoccupation with what happens inside mother's body, and the severe inhibition of mental life that followed when anxiety impeded this fundamental object of inquiry. What they were both impressed by was the importance of taking seriously the young child's intellectual struggles to grasp what we usually refer to as 'the facts of life', despite the emotional turbulence this necessitated. Freud noted of Little Hans that he was 'attributing a great deal to the mental capacity of a child between four and five years of age' (1909, p. 135), and when Klein met Dick it was the very atrophy of these mental capacities that so caught her attention. The theory she developed reached back into a much earlier phase of mental life and provided an account of what could prevent the growth of the source of phantasy and rich imagination and of intimate relationships between child and parents which had enabled Little Hans to communicate so vividly what went on in his mind. The contrast between Hans's internal landscape, teeming with life, and Dick's impoverished mind must have been very striking to her alongside the experience of her own children and her other child patients. This was a very new phenomenon for analytic scrutiny.

There are three major papers written between 1928 and 1931 which develop her thinking about intellectual inhibition which she sees as the consequence of anxieties interfering with the ordinary expression of the epistemophilic instinct, most strikingly visible in the numerous 'why' questions with which normal young children badger any grown-up willing to listen.

The first of these, 'Early stages of the Oedipus conflict' (1928), offers a clear statement of her view of the early superego and the guilt associated with the severe conscience of the young child as a consequence of pre-genital Oedipal phantasies.

The analysis of little children reveals the structure of the super-ego as built up of identifications dating from very different periods and strata in the mental life. These identifications are surprisingly contradictory in nature, excessive goodness and excessive severity existing side by side. We find in them, too, an explanation of the severity of the super-ego, which comes out especially plainly in these infant analyses. It does not seem clear why a child of, say, four years old should set up in his mind an unreal, phantastic image of parents who devour, cut and bite. But it *is* clear why in a child of about *one year* old the anxiety caused by the beginning of the Oedipus conflict takes the form of a dread of being devoured and destroyed. The child himself desires to destroy the libidinal object by biting, devouring and cutting it, which leads to anxiety, since awakening of the Oedipus tendencies is followed by introjection of the object, which then becomes one from which punishment is to be expected. The child then dreads a punishment corresponding to the offence: the super-ego becomes something which bites, devours and cuts.

The connection between the formation of the super-ego and the pregenital phases of development is very important from two points of view. On the one hand, the sense of guilt attaches itself to the oral- and anal-sadistic phases, which as yet predominate; and, on the other, the super-ego comes into being while these phases are in the ascendant, which accounts for its sadistic severity.

('Early stages of the Oedipus conflict', 1928; p. 187)

Klein's metaphor of the 'strata' of mental life, reminding us of Freud's analogy between the work of the psychoanalyst and the archaeologist, has proved very fertile in tackling issues of clinical technique. Whether the patient is child or adult, the analyst has to find a way to communicate about the complex layers of the personality – the baby within the young child, the young child within the schoolboy or girl, the child within the adolescent, and so on.

The experience of guilt and the child's belief that frustrations are a form of punishment go together. Klein developed this crucial idea in connection with the child's curiosity and the frustrating nature of what cannot yet be understood, and the long-term consequences of the hatred this engenders.

Another reason why the direct connection between the pregenital phase of development and the sense of guilt is so important is that the oral and anal frustrations, which are the prototypes of all later frustrations in life, at the same time signify *punishment* and give rise to anxiety. This circumstance makes the frustration more acutely felt, and this bitterness contributes largely to the hardship of all subsequent frustrations.

We find that important consequences ensue from the fact that the ego is still so little developed when it is assailed by the onset of the Oedipus tendencies and the incipient sexual curiosity associated with them. The infant, still undeveloped intellectually, is exposed to an onrush of problems and questions. One of the most bitter grievances which we come upon in the unconscious is that these many overwhelming questions, which are apparently only partly conscious and even when conscious cannot yet be expressed in words, remain unanswered. Another reproach follows hard upon this, namely, that the child could not understand words and speech. Thus his first questions go back beyond the beginnings of his understanding of speech.

In analysis both these grievances give rise to an extraordinary amount of hate. Singly or in conjunction they are the cause of numerous inhibitions of the epistemophilic impulse: for instance, the incapacity to learn foreign languages, and, further, hatred of those who speak a different tongue. They are also responsible for direct disturbances in speech, etc. The curiosity which shows itself plainly later on, mostly in the fourth or fifth year of life, is not the beginning, but the climax and termination, of this phase of development, which I have also found to be true of the Oedipus conflict in general.

The early feeling of *not knowing* has manifold connections. It unites with the feeling of being incapable, impotent, which soon results from the Oedipus situation. The child also feels this frustration the more acutely because he *knows nothing* definite about sexual processes. In both sexes the castration complex is accentuated by this feeling of ignorance.
(pp. 187–188)

This emphasis on the pain of ignorance is related here to the child's sexual immaturity, but is of course experienced and expressed by children in numerous other spheres of life. The painfulness of littleness, impotence and not being able to understand is what the child's wish to know unleashes. Klein shows how the rage that can be evoked means that the desire to know has an intrinsically aggressive edge:

The early connection between the epistemophilic impulse and sadism is very important for the whole mental development. This instinct, activated by the rise of the Oedipus tendencies, at first mainly concerns itself with the mother's body, which is assumed to be the scene of all sexual processes and developments. The child is still dominated by the anal-sadistic libido-position which impels him to wish to *appropriate* the contents of the body. He thus begins to be curious about what it contains, what it is like, etc. So the epistemophilic instinct and the desire to take possession come quite early to be most intimately connected with one another and at the same time with the sense of guilt aroused by the incipient Oedipus conflict.
(p. 188)

She goes on to describe the differential development of the boy and girl with respect to the link between early identification with mother and the concomitant strong desire for a baby of one's own, and the direction of the epistemophilic instinct:

The amalgamation of the desire for a child with the epistemophilic impulse enables a boy to effect a displacement on to the intellectual plane; his sense of being at a disadvantage is then concealed and over-compensated by the superiority he deduces from his possession of a penis, which is also acknowledged by girls. This exaggeration of the masculine position results in excessive protestations of masculinity.
(pp. 190–191)

> The little girl's epistemophilic impulse is first roused by the Oedipus complex; the result is that she discovers her lack of a penis. She feels this lack to be a fresh cause of hatred of the mother, but at the same time her sense of guilt makes her regard it as a punishment. This embitters her frustration in this direction, and, in its turn, exercises a profound influence on the whole castration complex.
>
> (p. 193)

Klein is impressed by the impact on intellectual orientation of the diverging predominant anxieties in the early sexual development of the child. At the height of the Oedipal period, when all children are sorting out feelings about father and mother, while the boy fears castration, the girl fears damage to her internal organs. She suggests this enables the boy more easily to turn his mental energies outwards to the 'conquering' of the world through understanding it, supported by the reality of his possession of a penis, while the girl is more likely to be preoccupied with the uncertainties involved in her desire for motherhood and thus imaginatively drawn to represent what might be taking place inside her. Although Klein herself does not make this point in her explication of the early Oedipus conflict, we can usefully bear in mind Freud's emphasis on human bisexuality, and thus bring together the 'male' and 'female' trajectories she describes as each contributing to the personality as a whole in any individual.

The relevance of early sexual development and the Oedipus complex for intellectual development is at root that it gives rise to so many profound questions for the child – about the nature of sexual difference, about generational difference, about the origins of life, and indeed the fact of death, as Money-Kyrle elaborated in his paper, 'Cognitive development' (1968). These questions can either be struggled over, sometimes with great anxiety, as for Little Hans and many of Klein's young patients, or avoided. This takes us to her next major paper, 'The importance of symbol-formation in the development of the ego' (1930), which includes the case study of Dick, a child in whom anxiety had caused an almost complete shut-down in development.

In tackling the topic of symbol formation, Klein starts with a restatement of her observations of the sadistic aspects of the child's early phantasies towards mother, and their impact in the pre-genital phase of Oedipal development. Here is her summary of the baby's unconscious picture of the world:

> The child expects to find within the mother (a) the father's penis, (b) excrement, and (c) children, and these things it equates with edible substances. According to the child's earliest phantasies (or 'sexual theories') of parental coitus, the father's penis (or his whole body) becomes incorporated in the mother during the act. Thus the child's sadistic attacks have for their object both father and mother, who are in phantasy bitten, torn, cut or stamped to bits. The attacks give rise to anxiety lest the subject should be punished by the united parents, and this anxiety also becomes internalized in consequence of the oral-sadistic introjection of the objects and is thus already directed towards the early super-ego. I have found these anxiety-situations of the early phases of mental development to be the most profound and overwhelming. It is my experience that in the phantasied attack on the mother's body a considerable part is played by the urethral and

> anal sadism which is very soon added to the oral and muscular sadism. In phantasy the excreta are transformed into dangerous weapons: wetting is regarded as cutting, stabbing, burning, drowning, while the faecal mass is equated with weapons and missiles. At a later stage of the phase which I have described, these violent modes of attack give place to hidden assaults by the most refined methods which sadism can devise, and the excreta are equated with poisonous substances.
>
> ('The importance of symbol-formation in the development of the ego', 1930; pp. 219–220)

This dangerous state of affairs is a source of severe anxiety for the self from within and without. Klein makes two suggestions about what happens at this point with respect to identification. Her earlier idea was that 'symbolic equations', in which all sorts of things (activities, interests, etc.) could become a source of interest and pleasure were the building blocks for symbolism with its potential for sublimation. She now adds that it is the early forms of anxiety which set in motion the mechanisms of identification, 'he is impelled constantly [by anxiety] to make other and new equations, which form the basis of his interest in the new objects and of symbolism' (p. 220).

> Thus, not only does symbolism come to be the foundation of all phantasy and sublimation but, more than that, it is the basis of the subject's relation to the outside world and to reality in general. I pointed out that the object of sadism at its height, and of the desire for knowledge arising simultaneously with sadism, is the mother's body with its phantasied contents. The sadistic phantasies directed against the inside of her body constitute the first and basic relation to the outside world and to reality. Upon the degree of success with which the subject passes through this phase will depend the extent to which he can subsequently acquire an external world corresponding to reality . . . A sufficient quantity of anxiety is the necessary basis for an abundance of symbol-formation and of phantasy; an adequate capacity on the part of the ego to tolerate anxiety is essential if anxiety is to be satisfactorily worked over, if this basic phase is to have a favourable issue and if the development of the ego is to be successful.
>
> (p. 221)

She goes on to present a clinical account of her patient Dick, aged 4, and describes him thus:

> This case, of which I will now give some details, is that of a four-year-old boy who, as regards the poverty of his vocabulary and of his intellectual attainments, was on the level of a child of about fifteen or eighteen months. Adaptation to reality and emotional relations to his environment were almost entirely lacking. This child, Dick, was largely devoid of affects, and he was indifferent to the presence or absence of mother
>
> *(continued)*

(continued)

or nurse. From the very beginning he had only rarely displayed anxiety, and that in an abnormally small degree. With the exception of one particular interest, to which I will return presently, he had almost no interests, did not play, and had no contact with his environment. For the most part he simply strung sounds together in a meaningless way, and constantly repeated certain noises. When he did speak he generally used his meagre vocabulary incorrectly. But it was not only that he was unable to make himself intelligible: he had no wish to do so. More than that, Dick's mother could at times clearly sense in the boy a strong negative attitude which expressed itself in the fact that he often did the very *opposite* of what was expected of him. For instance, if she succeeded in getting him to say different words after her, he often entirely altered them, though at other times he could pronounce the same words perfectly. Again, sometimes he would repeat the words correctly, but would go on repeating them in an incessant, mechanical way until everyone round him was sick and tired of them . . .

. . . Then too, when he hurt himself, he displayed very considerable insensibility to pain and felt nothing of the desire, so universal with little children, to be comforted and petted. His physical awkwardness, also, was quite remarkable. He could not grip knives or scissors, but it was noteworthy that he could handle quite normally the spoon with which he ate.

The impression his first visit left on me was that his behaviour was quite different from that which we observe in neurotic children. He had let his nurse go without manifesting any emotion, and had followed me into the room with complete indifference. There he ran to and fro in an aimless, purposeless way, and several times he also ran round me, just as if I were a piece of furniture, but he showed no interest in any of the objects in the room. His movements as he ran to and fro seemed to be without co-ordination. The expression of his eyes and face was fixed, far-away and lacking in interest.

(pp. 221–222)

Klein notes the absence of real parental affection in Dick's first two years of life due particularly to his mother's excessive anxiety, and the marked improvement in his development between two and three when an attentive nurse and his loving grandmother came on the scene. Feeding, however, remained very difficult, echoing the very painful feeding history of his early months when he had almost starved. Most disturbing to Klein was the fact that Dick had 'failed to establish emotional contact' (p. 223) with either nurse or grandmother despite their tenderness.

Klein suggests that his condition of 'lacking object relation' had its roots in his incapacity to tolerate anxiety, together with premature genital excitement which caused an increase in anxiety about any expression of aggression. We might suggest this premature genitality was linked to the extreme deprivation of oral gratification. She continues thus:

The ego had ceased to develop phantasy-life and to establish a relation with reality. After a feeble beginning, symbol-formation in this child had come to a standstill. The early attempts had left their mark in one interest, which, isolated and unrelated to

> reality, could not form the basis for further sublimations. The child was indifferent to most of the objects and playthings around him, and did not even grasp their purpose or meaning. But he was interested in trains and stations and also in door-handles, doors and the opening and shutting of them.
>
> (p. 224)

Klein interprets these interests as 'to do with the penetration of the penis into the mother's body', that is, as evidence of a recurrent symbolic equation. His own and his father's penis are equated, both felt to be imbued with dangerous aggression towards mother.

> Moreover, his defences against his destructive impulses proved to be a fundamental impediment to his development. He was absolutely incapable of any act of aggression, and the basis of this incapacity was clearly indicated at a very early period in his refusal to bite up food. At four years old he could not hold scissors, knives or tools, and was remarkably clumsy in all his movements. The defence against the sadistic impulses directed against the mother's body and its contents – impulses connected with phantasies of coitus – had resulted in the cessation of the phantasies and the standstill of symbol-formation. Dick's further development had come to grief because he could not bring into phantasy the sadistic relation to the mother's body.
>
> (p. 224)

Klein describes how difficult it was to institute an analytic relationship with Dick not so much because of the poverty of his speech but because of his enormous inhibition in play. Alongside his extreme limitation in fantasy expression, she observed tremendous sensitivity to the awareness of a damaged object. He would, for example, say of pencil shavings, 'poor Mrs Klein'. She characterised this as 'premature empathy', a phenomenon linked to what she would later describe as 'depressive' anxiety and guilt but which had in Dick's life appeared at a much earlier period. This observation has proved to be replicated in much recent clinical work with children with a diagnosis of autism, a diagnosis not in use at the time of Dick's treatment but one which he would have been given in later years, as has been widely noted. Some of these children seem to suffer from a devastating form of early anxiety about the solidity of themselves and their objects, which leads to the closing down of links to the outside world, much in the way that Klein described in Dick. She writes in close detail of the emergence and vicissitudes of his capacity to be interested in things:

> [T]he working-over of this anxiety was beginning by way of the establishment of a symbolic relation to things and objects, and at the same time his epistemophilic and aggressive impulses were set in action. Every advance was followed by the releasing of fresh quantities of anxiety and led to his turning away to some extent from the things with which he had already established an affective relation and which had
>
> *(continued)*

(continued)

> therefore become objects of anxiety. As he turned away from these he turned towards new objects, and his aggressive and epistemophilic impulses were directed to these new affective relations in their turn. Thus, for instance, for some time Dick altogether avoided the cupboard, but thoroughly investigated the wash-basin and the electric radiator, which he examined in every detail, again manifesting destructive impulses against these objects. He then transferred his interest from them to fresh things or, again, to things with which he was already familiar and which he had given up earlier. He occupied himself once more with the cupboard, but this time his interest in it was accompanied by a far greater activity and curiosity and a stronger tendency to aggression of all kinds. He beat on it with a spoon, scratched and hacked it with a knife and sprinkled water on it. He examined in a lively way the hinges of the door, the way in which it opened and shut, the lock, etc., climbed up inside the cupboard and asked what the different parts were called. Thus as his interests developed he at the same time enlarged his vocabulary, for he now began to take more and more interest not only in the things themselves but in their names. The words which before he had heard and disregarded he now remembered and applied correctly.
>
> (pp. 227–228)

As his analysis proceeded, affectionate and ordinarily needy feelings for his nurse and parents began to appear. The link between this interest in other people and a desire for communication led to other changes.

> The desire to make himself intelligible, which was lacking before, is now in full force. Dick tries to make himself understood by means of his still meagre but growing vocabulary which he diligently endeavours to enlarge. There are many indications, moreover, that he is beginning to establish a relation to reality.
>
> (p. 228)

In reflecting on the unusual challenge of working with a child like this, Klein comments:

> Events proved that even this very imperfectly developed ego was adequate for establishing connection with the unconscious. From the theoretical point of view I think it is important to note that, even in so extreme a case of defective ego-development, it was possible to develop both ego and libido only by analysing the unconscious conflicts, without bringing any educational influence to bear upon the ego. It seems plain that, if even the imperfectly developed ego of a child who had no relation at all with reality can tolerate the removal of repressions by the aid of analysis, without being overwhelmed by the id, we need not fear that in neurotic children (i.e. in very much less extreme cases) the ego might succumb to the id. It

> is also noteworthy that, whereas the educational influence exercised by those about him previously glided off Dick without any effect, now, when owing to analysis his ego is developing, he is increasingly amenable to such influence, which can keep pace with the instinctual impulses mobilized by analysis and quite suffices to deal with them.
>
> (p. 229)

She adds a note to the effect that psychosis in childhood is a phenomenon capable of investigation through child analysis. This was, of course, a very bold claim but one which has been the inspiration for an important dimension of child analytic research in the last 50 years (Alvarez, 1992; Rustin *et al.*, 1997).

It is important to note here Klein's focus on the complexity of the impact of anxiety on young children. On the one hand, it has the creative potential to stir phantasy and curiosity. The very intensity of the child's longings for, and the consequent intensity of, his anxieties about his mother's body is bound up with the growth of the mind, which has to find a way to contain such powerful emotional experiences. At the same time, too much anxiety, as she demonstrates in her analysis of Dick, can overwhelm the ego and lead to a closing down of development. We might see this as the internal correlate of her point in the 1928 paper ('Early stages of the Oedipus conflict') that the external blocking of early curiosity can breed intense bitterness. The child whose desire to understand is not met with sympathetic support is at risk of being flooded with hatred when faced with such frustration, because the pain and humiliation of ignorance are too hard to bear. It is felt to be inflicted knowingly and hatefully. Aggression which is a necessary element in the child's instinctual resources in the first case becomes unavailable, replaced by absence of meaning, passivity and absence of relationships. In the second, aggression is mobilised to express hate and to defend the self in a world experienced as hostile, but is not available for creative engagement with the world.

Klein's appreciation of just how difficult it is for a young child to deal with such feelings is evident in her experimentation with techniques to make contact with her little patients. Just as she found her method of play analysis almost by accident (though the accident of genius, one is tempted to say), so with Dick, who could not play, she adapted her technique, becoming very active in her way of talking and showing him what he was feeling. Far indeed from the idea of the analyst as the cool observer of her patient. The sessions she describes leap off the page and Dick's capacity to make use of an object comes to life through the powerful pull which her understanding of him exerts. It is interesting to note that some of the contemporary psychoanalytic work with children on the autistic spectrum (Tustin, 1972; Alvarez and Reid, 1999) echoes this idea of the child's urgent need for an object with a lively mind – someone who can ask questions, take risks in suggesting links, hold on to the idea that behaviour has meaning, and refuse to be put off by repetitive resistance and avoidance.

In the year following this work on symbol formation, Klein wrote a paper exploring intellectual inhibition ('A contribution to the theory of intellectual inhibition', 1931). She used material from the analysis of a 7-year-old she called John, who had already had two years of treatment and was able to bring his difficulties very directly to her. This gives us a vivid glimpse of Klein's technique of a child more ordinary than Dick, in which the patient's freedom to play, expressed both by drawing and by physical activities in the room, is combined with her inviting his verbal associations. Here is an excerpt:

> The boy complained to me that he could not distinguish certain French words from one another. There was a picture in the school of various objects to help the children to understand the words. The words were: *poulet*, chicken; *poisson*, fish; *glace*, ice. Whenever he was asked what any of these words meant he invariably answered with the meaning of one of the other two – for instance, asked *poisson*, he would answer ice; *poulet*, fish; and so on. He felt quite hopeless and despairing about it, saying he would never learn it, etc. I obtained the material from him by ordinary association, but at the same time he was also playing about idly in the room.
>
> I asked him first to tell me what *poulet* made him think of. He lay on his back on the table, kicking his legs about and drawing on a piece of paper with a pencil. He thought of a fox breaking into a chicken-house. I asked him when this would happen and instead of saying 'in the night,' he answered, 'At four o'clock in the afternoon,' which I knew to be a time when his mother was often out. 'The fox breaks in and kills a little chicken,' and while he said this he cut off what he had drawn. I asked him what it was and he said, 'I don't know.' When we looked at it, it was a house, of which he had cut off the roof. He said that was the way the fox got into the house. He realized that he was himself the fox, that the chicken was his little brother and that the time at which the fox broke in was precisely when his mother was out.
>
> ('A contribution to the theory of intellectual inhibition', 1931; pp. 236–237)

Later on they talked about fish and ice, and John's anxiety became more evident and things got stuck. The following day he reported a bad dream:

> The fish was a crab. He was standing on a pier at the seaside where he has often been with his mother. He was supposed to kill an enormous crab which came out of the water on to the pier. He shot it with his little gun and killed it with his sword, which was not very efficient. As soon as he killed the crab, he had to kill more and more of them which kept on coming out of the water.
>
> (p. 237)

The analysis of this material and John's many associations led to Klein describing to him the beliefs he had about his parents' sexual relationship. She told him that his intrusive aggressive phantasies towards his parents and his consequent paranoid anxieties about the 'more and more crabs' which threatened him arose because he saw the paternal penis as dangerous and killing as a consequence of his projecting into it his own hostile feelings. John was relieved at her understanding of how terrified he was of the injured maternal body by which he felt tormented. She comments:

> After this he began in the same hour to draw parallel lines getting narrower and wider. It was the clearest possible vagina symbol. He then put his own little engine on it and let it go up the lines to the station. He was very relieved and happy. He felt now that he

could symbolically have intercourse with his mother; whereas before this analysis her body was a place of horrors. This seems to show what one can see confirmed in every man's analysis, that his dread of the woman's body as a place full of destruction might be one of the main causes of impaired potency. This anxiety is also, however, a basic factor in inhibitions of the desire for knowledge, since the inside of the mother's body is the first object of this impulse; in phantasy it is explored and investigated, as well as attacked with all the sadistic armoury, including the penis as a dangerous offensive weapon, and this is another cause of subsequent impotence in men: penetrating and exploring are to a great extent synonymous in the unconscious. For this reason, after the analysis of his anxiety relating to his own and his father's sadistic penis – the piercing yellow pencil equated with the burning sun – John was much more able to represent himself symbolically as having coitus with his mother and investigating her body. The next day he could look attentively and with interest at the picture on the wall at school and could distinguish the words from one another easily.

J. Strachey (1930) has shown that reading has the unconscious significance of taking knowledge out of the mother's body, and that the fear of robbing her is an important factor for inhibitions in reading. I should like to add that it is essential for a favourable development of the desire for knowledge that the mother's body should be felt to be well and unharmed. It represents in the unconscious the treasure-house of everything desirable which can only be got from there; therefore if it is not destroyed, not so much in danger and therefore not so dangerous itself, the wish to take food for the mind from it can more easily be carried out.

(pp. 240–241)

Klein argues that the unconscious preoccupation with a damaged maternal body also evokes the child's anxiety about his own body:

Just as the excessive anxiety in regard to the destruction wrought in the mother's body inhibits the capacity to obtain any *clear conception* of its contents, so in an analogous way the anxiety in regard to the terrible and dangerous things that are happening inside one's own body can suppress all investigation into it; and this again is a factor in intellectual inhibition . . .

. . . But what I wish to draw attention to here, in addition to this fact, is the connection, which is observable over and over again in analysis, between a diminution of anxiety on the part of the ego in respect of the super-ego and an increased capacity in the child to become acquainted with its own intrapsychic processes and to control them more efficiently through its ego.

(pp. 242–243)

Klein links the underlying basis for sexual potency and the free play of the epistemophilic instinct: intellectual discovery involves penetration into things, and is thus unconsciously equated with sexual intercourse. She summarises what John's analysis demonstrated as follows, linking changes in his character, and ego development.

> To sum up what has been said: While the improvement in John's capacity to conceive the condition of the inside of his *mother's body* led to a greater ability to understand and appreciate the outer world, the reduction of his inhibition against really knowing about the inside of his *own* body at the same time led to a deeper understanding and better control over his own mental process; he could then clear up and bring order into his own mind. The first resulted in a greater capacity to take in knowledge; the second entailed a better ability to work over, organize and correlate the knowledge obtained, and also to give it out again, i.e. return it, formulate it or express it – an advance in ego-development. These two fundamental contents of anxiety (relating to one's mother's body and one's own body) condition each other and react on each other in every detail, and in the same way the greater freedom of the two functions of introjection and extrajection (or projection), resulting from a reduction in the anxiety from these sources, allows both to be employed in a more appropriate and less compulsive way . . .
>
> . . . The degree to which a reduction of the sadism and anxiety and of the operation of the super-ego can be achieved, so that the ego acquires a broader basis on which to function, determines the degree of improvement in the patient's accessibility to influence by the external world, together with a progressive resolution of his intellectual inhibitions.
>
> (pp. 244–245)

This case study focuses particularly on links between paranoid characteristics (fearfulness, distrust, secrecy, etc.) and inhibitions of the intellect. Much more briefly, she also mentions another striking conjunction, between obsessional anxiety and 'an inability to distinguish between what is valuable and what is worthless', expressed in a desire for indiscriminate accumulation of things or bits of knowledge. Klein suggests that such compulsive behaviour is based on anxious seeking after 'good' things which might counteract the 'bad' things inside, and also protect the self from 'bad' things which might attack from outside. We can see here an instance of the way she moves from consideration of more neurotic features such as John's original worries about muddling up words, to more psychotic levels of anxiety. In fact, her investigation of the basis for intellectual inhibition encompasses the whole range of mental states, including what would ordinarily be deemed intellectual disability of the sort illustrated by her patient Dick.

These three papers represent her continuing interest in the growth of the child's mind and her view that analysis offered a way to free a child from the block to creative thought, and to foster the independence of mind she so much valued. The experience within child analysis of watching over the growth of a mind can be particularly poignant, as is also shown in many of her other papers and at greater length in *Narrative of a Child Analysis*.

As she turned her attention to the study of manic-depressive states, a different kind of anxiety about the damaged state of the internal mother came to the fore. John's inhibited epistemophilic impulses were a consequence of persecutory fears of retaliation for phantasied sadistic attacks, but Dick's anxiety about anything which hinted at damage had already alerted her to the intensity of pained feelings for the suffering of the damaged object. In her 1935 paper ('A contribution to the psychogenesis of manic-depressive states'; see Chapter 5) she extended her thinking about how deeply a mind can be impeded in a lively exploration of the world, impeded in learning, thinking, imagining, by despairing feelings in the face of damaged objects in the internal world.

The later development of her view of the central importance of the epistemophilic instinct is most fully represented in the work of Wilfred Bion on thinking (Bion, 1962a, 1962b). His definition of the most fundamental form of thinking is that it involves the attempt to get to know the nature of oneself and others. His theory thus addresses precisely the phenomena Klein was exploring in the papers discussed in this chapter, though by the time of his writing he had the additional resource of the concept of projective identification which first appeared in her 1946 paper, 'Notes on some schizoid mechanisms'.

Bion was working with severely ill adult schizophrenic patients whose intellectual deficit he tried to understand. There is perhaps a continuity here with Klein's conviction that psychoanalysis needed to attend to the failure of cognitive development as she did with her patient Dick. Bion elaborated a theory of the necessary conditions for the emergence of thinking. What makes it possible for the infant to start on the lifelong process of trying to relate to reality? He suggested that the baby conveys his profound anxieties to his mother through somatic non-verbal communication which the theory of projective identification enables us to understand. The mother's openness to her baby's state of feeling enables her to receive and give meaning to the infant's behaviour through her emotional response. Bion named the mother's mental activity in trying to understand her baby 'reverie'. Her understanding enables her to respond in a way which gives shape and coherence to the baby's experience, so that, for example, the pains of hunger are both relieved by the baby being fed but also over time come to be recognisable as such to the baby, distinguishable from other somatic states. The infant's capacity for thought, discrimination and, in the broadest sense, rationality thus grows from the experience of being thought about (mother's reverie), from being 'contained' (Bion's word) by the mature mind of his mother. He thus takes in not only food and other forms of infant care but simultaneously an idea of meaningfulness, meaning that has been given to him in the maternal response.

This theory led Bion to suggest that the epistemophilic instinct should be given an equivalent importance in psychoanalysis to the impulses of love and hate. There is an enormous literature exploring his theory and its implications for our conception of the mind, our understanding of psychic development and for clinical technique. Some of the worldwide interest generated by Bion's thinking tends to overlook its origins in Klein's earlier extension of Freud's metapsychology, but there is also a strong tradition of writing based on the close links between Freud, Klein and Bion. This is too extensive to explore here, but it seems appropriate to give one example to show how much Klein's papers contributed to set in motion this research into the conditions for thought and to sustain Freud's fundamental investigation into the human capacity for understanding ourselves, that is, the importance of insight for psychological health.

One example which captures these strands are two papers by Money-Kyrle (1968, 1971) which discuss the individual's struggle to engage with some fundamental features of reality which he called the 'facts of life'. This usage includes but goes much beyond the everyday sense of this phrase. Money-Kyrle defines three tasks which face us if we are to succeed in using our minds to the full. The first concerns the acknowledgement of generational difference and our dependence as infants on parental care. He follows Klein in attributing fundamental importance to our relationship to our first object, the breast, the feeding mother, who sustains life and protects us from the fear of death. The second is the recognition of sexual difference, the idea that the parental intercourse which creates life depends on the complementarity of the sexes. The contemporary potential of cloning might seem to present a challenge to this at a scientific level, but the evidence from the psychoanalytic study of the inner world suggests that whatever the actual composition of a child's family, the idea of there being two different elements (the maternal and the paternal, we might say) that together make up the nature of the world seems to recur at every level of development. The third is the recognition of the linearity of time and of our inevitable mortality.

Money-Kyrle is interested in the distortions of thinking which enable us to evade facing these facts. These include, for example, the infantile omnipotent phantasy of parthenogenesis, the belief in circular time which denies the reality of change, ageing and loss, and the various forms of confusion between external and internal and between self and object. Here we may note particularly the ways these questions echo some of Klein's great interests: infantile omnipotent defences against early anxieties, our dependence on the quality of our internal objects, the differential development of the sexes, the lifelong significance of loss and mourning initiated at the time of weaning. What Money-Kyrle's papers discuss is how we become able to think truthfully about ourselves and, like Klein, he sees both the impulse to inquire and understand and the power of the desire to avoid this because of the inescapable painfulness of reality and its limitations. The greatest limit is of course the fact of mortality, and this will take us on to Klein's study of mourning.

Chapter 4

Technique in child analysis

Klein wrote three papers explicitly on this topic, relating to work with young children, latency children and adolescents. These gather together the practice implied in many others of the clinical examples included in almost all her writings and spell out the rationale for her approach. Much later she also wrote a series of as-yet unpublished lectures on technique in adult analysis which are likely soon to be available in book form. The three papers on child analysis were all included as chapters in her first book, *The Psycho-Analysis of Children,* published in 1932 and dedicated to Karl Abraham. The completion of this book was a significant achievement and represents the clinical and theoretical conclusions she drew from her extensive work as a child analyst. It is also full of down-to-earth descriptions of the setting required for child analysis and this suggests that Klein viewed the book as one which could guide future generations of child analysts in practical ways, as well as inspire them with the desire to practise her craft. In 1932 this was still a very new field, though one which had attracted the support and keen interest of very senior psychoanalytic figures, including Freud. The book was surely intended to be read as an authoritative statement of the approach to child analysis which Klein had developed in Berlin (Frank, 2009) – and was continuing to develop in London – and which she intended to serve as a foundational text in this new field. Her enthusiastic reception in London, where child patients were referred on her arrival, must have seemed like good evidence of a space waiting to be filled. Klein's foreword to the first English edition was full of hope. At this point she was surrounded by generous intellectual and professional support at the highest level.

In this chapter we shall review these three papers, but it is appropriate to begin by quoting the vigorous opening lines of this book:

> Psycho-analysis has led to the creation of a new child psychology. Psycho-analytic observations have taught us that even in their earliest years, children experience not only sexual impulses and anxiety, but also great disappointments. Along with the belief in the asexuality of the child has gone the belief in the 'Paradise of Childhood'. These are the conclusions which were gained from both analysis of adults and direct observation of children, and which are confirmed and supplemented by the analysis of small children.
>
> (*The Psycho-Analysis of Children*, 1932; p. 3)

It is absolutely characteristic of Klein's thinking that she immediately turns to clinical detail to demonstrate her view that children's deep anxieties are linked to strong feelings of guilt, arising from aggressive phantasies originating in Oedipal preoccupations, and also important to note that her first example is a child she began to see at age 2¾. At once therefore she is claiming that the Oedipal complex begins very early in a child's life, an important divergence from Freud's initial view. She also spells out at the outset the psychoanalytic roots of her technique:

> The very differences between the infantile mind and the grown-up one showed me, in the first instance, the way to get at the associations of the child and to understand its unconscious. These special characteristics of the child's psychology have furnished the basis of the technique of play analysis which I have been able to work out. The child expresses its phantasies, its wishes and its actual experiences in a symbolic way through play and games. In doing so, it makes use of the same archaic and phylogenetically acquired mode of expression, the same language, as it were, that we are familiar with in dreams; and we can only fully understand this language if we approach it in the way Freud has taught us to approach the language of dreams. Symbolism is only a part of it. If we wish to understand the child's play correctly in relation to its whole behaviour during the analytic session we must not be content to pick out the meaning of the separate symbols in the play, striking as they often are, but must take into consideration all the mechanisms and methods of representation employed by the dream-work, never losing sight of the relation of each factor to the situation as a whole. Early analysis of children has shown again and again how many different meanings a single toy or a single bit of play can have, and that we can only infer and interpret their meaning when we consider their wider connections and the whole analytic situation in which they are set . . .
>
> . . . For play is the child's most important medium of expression. If we make use of this play technique we soon find that the child brings as many associations to the separate elements of its play as adults do to the separate elements of their dreams. These separate play-elements are indications to the trained observer; and as it plays, the child talks as well, and says all sorts of things which have the value of genuine associations. (pp. 7–8)

She concludes this introductory chapter with this claim:

> In conclusion I should like to sum up briefly what has been said in this chapter. The more primitive nature of the child's mind makes it necessary to find an analytic technique especially adapted to the child, and this we find in play analysis. By means of play analysis we gain access to the child's most deeply repressed experiences and fixations and are thus able to exert a radical influence on its development. The difference between this method of analysis and that of adult analysis, however, is purely one of technique and not of principle. The analysis of the transference-situation and of the resistance, the removal of the early infantile amnesia and of the effects of repression,

> as well as the uncovering of the primal scene – all these things play analysis does. It can be seen that all criteria of the psycho-analytic method apply to this technique too. Play analysis leads to the same results as the adult technique, with only one difference, namely, that the technical procedure is adapted to the mind of the child.
>
> (pp. 14–15)

How is this to be achieved with young children? Klein gives us a lively glimpse of what it might have been like to have been taken to see her:

> On a low table in my analytic room there are laid out a number of small and simple toys – little wooden men and women, carts, carriages, motor-cars, trains, animals, bricks and houses, as well as paper, scissors and pencils. Even a child that is usually inhibited in its play will at least glance at the toys or touch them, and will soon give me a first glimpse into its complexes by the way in which it begins to play with them or lays them aside, or by its general attitude towards them.
>
> (p. 16)

As the chapter progresses we read of all sorts of vital practical things the child analyst has to sort out – to find out in the initial consultations with parents the child's words for body parts, urine, faeces and so on, and any special private family words which may be relevant; to have in mind how to deal with the situation if the child is too anxious to come alone to the consulting room; to decide whether the child may need help when going to the lavatory. Descriptions of several child patients' play then set out the ground for discussion of her technique. The outstanding point is her conviction about the place and pace of interpretation, and this usually comes as a shock to her readers since she does not hold back. Here is her justification for this bold approach:

> I have brought forward the above examples in order to support my view, based on empiric observation, that the analyst should not shy away from making a deep interpretation even at the start of the analysis, since the material belonging to a deeper layer of the mind will come back again later and be worked through. As I have said before, the function of deep-going interpretation is simply to open the door to the unconscious, to diminish the anxiety that has been stirred up and thus to prepare the way for analytic work.
>
> I have repeatedly laid emphasis upon the child's capacity for making a spontaneous transference.
>
> (p. 24)

Klein therefore uses her immediate observation of the child's behaviour and puts into words the response to herself and the whole situation, relating it to the feelings towards the parental figures in the child's life. The point is, she argues, to see the mobilisation of the central anxiety which the analytic setting unleashes and to take hold of it, thus offering the child the feeling of being understood and invited to recognise that his analyst is someone available to help with what upsets him.

How one gets this across to the child is spelt out in a number of examples. There is a particularly interesting description of the initial work with Ruth, aged 4¼, whose extreme anxiety demanded a flexible approach from Klein, since she refused to come into the consulting room on her own. As her older sister had been brought along, Klein invited her to join Ruth, and her presence, as Klein had hoped, allowed Ruth to begin to play. But one day a few weeks later the sister was unwell. Klein judged that she could now take the risk of a session with Ruth alone. Here is what happened:

> With her parents' consent I took the second course. The nurse handed the little girl over to me outside my room and went away in spite of her tears and screams. In this very painful situation I again began by trying to soothe the child in a non-analytical, motherly way, as any ordinary person would. I tried to comfort her and cheer her up and make her play with me, but in vain. When she saw herself alone with me, she just managed to follow me into my room, but once there I could do nothing with her. She went quite white, and screamed, and showed all the signs of a severe attack of anxiety. Meanwhile I sat down at the toy-table and began to play by myself, all the while describing what I was doing to the terrified child, who was now sitting in a corner. Following a sudden inspiration, I took as the subject of my game the material which she herself had produced in the previous session. At the end of it she had played round the wash-basin and had fed her dolls and given them huge jugfuls of milk, etc. I now did the same kind of thing. I put a doll to sleep and told Ruth I was going to give it something to eat and asked her what it should be. She interrupted her screams to answer 'milk', and I noticed that she made a movement towards her mouth with her two fingers (which she had a habit of sucking before going to sleep) but quickly took them away. I asked her whether she wanted to suck them and she said: 'Yes, but properly.' I recognized that she wanted to reconstitute the situation as it happened at home every evening, so I laid her down on the sofa and, at her request, put a rug over her. Thereupon she began to suck her fingers. She was still very pale and her eyes were shut, but she was visibly calmer and had stopped crying. Meanwhile I went on playing with the dolls, repeating her game of the session before . . .
>
> All the while I began by applying my interpretations to the doll – showing her as I played with it that it was afraid and screaming, and telling her the reason – and then I proceeded to repeat the interpretations which I had given for the doll by applying them to her own person. In this way I established the analytical situation in its entirety. While I was doing this Ruth grew visibly quieter, opened her eyes and let me bring the table on which I was playing to the sofa and continue my game and my interpretations close beside her. Gradually she sat up and watched the course of the play with growing interest, and even began to take an active part in it herself.
>
> (pp. 27–28)

As is evident in this example, Klein used the technique of 'displacement' when talking to Ruth, attributing the child's terrible worries to the doll, as a first step, and explaining gently what it was that made the doll so frightened. She is very attentive not only to the pace at which children can cope with facing their fears but also to the form of words which are appropriate. 'I take the way in which the children think and speak using their own images as my model' (p. 32). She noted, for example, that a little boy said of the toy swing, 'look how it dangles and bumps' and then utilised his word 'bump' in talking to him about parental intercourse, and found that this made immediate sense to him.

The playroom Klein advises for the analysis of young children has to provide other opportunities for play in addition to the small toys she gave them. She suggests it should have a small basin and running water, and items for water play (beakers, sponge, cloth, etc.) and describes how all the furniture of the room will be pressed into use at times and needs to be serviceable for such purposes. She also gave children material for making things as well as drawing – paper, card, pencils, scissors, string, bits of wood, even a knife (!) – and was tolerant of children choosing to bring their own toys. The search is for a way in which the child will be able to express himself as freely as possible. On the whole Klein's patients were inhibited in play rather than wild and difficult to control, which would be more often an issue with the patients seen in contemporary psychotherapy with children, but what comes alive is her sense of freedom in finding out what will work with a particular chid, and her willingness to experiment.

Once the child patient is a little older, games of make-believe often come to the fore, as in the case history of Erna, a very depressed 6-year-old girl with severe sleeping difficulties and obsessional thumb sucking and masturbation. Klein found she needed to play the parts assigned to her by Erna in many scenarios, in which the child's intense rivalry with her, representing mother, was at the heart of every game. The ferocity of Erna's phantasies and play was extreme, and in her work with this severely ill child Klein did have to place severe limits on her behaviour, making it plain that she was not to attack her analyst physically, although she was permitted to express her destructive rage freely in other ways. Klein formulates the appropriate technique for dealing with emotional outbursts as having three elements: the child is only required to control expression of his feeling in so far as there is a necessity in reality (e.g. not to flood the whole room, not to injure the analyst); expression of destructive messy impulses within the room is accepted; the analyst's task is to interpret the meaning of the child's abusive and violent behaviour in the session in the context of earlier developmental difficulties, and to tolerate the child's destructiveness meanwhile.

Moving on to discuss analysis in the latency period Klein first describes the marked change in children's relationship to themselves and others as the passions of early childhood recede, though we may note here that the notion of 'latency' has undergone considerable revision in the light of today's children's earlier development, a sexualised and generally uninhibited cultural context and changed family and educational mores.

> The analysis of children in the latency period presents special difficulties. Unlike the small child, whose lively imagination and acute anxiety enables us to gain access to and contact with its unconscious more easily, children in the latency period have a very limited imaginative life, in accordance with the strong tendency to repression which is characteristic of their age; while, in comparison with the grown-up person, their ego is
>
> *(continued)*

(continued)

still undeveloped, and they neither have insight into their illness nor a desire to be cured, so that they have no incentive to start analysis and no encouragement to go on with it . . .

. . . children of this age group do not play like small children nor give verbal associations like adults. Nevertheless I have found it possible to establish the analytic situation without delay if I approach their unconscious from a point of departure that corresponds to the nature of the older child. The small child is still under the immediate and powerful influence of its instinctual experiences and phantasies and puts them in front of us straight away; it is therefore appropriate, as I found in early analyses, to interpret, even in the first sessions, the small child's representations of coitus and its sadistic phantasies; whereas the child in the latency period has already desexualized those experiences and phantasies much more completely and worked them over in a different form.

(p. 58)

Children's games in this later phase of childhood tend to be much more connected with everyday reality and there is more repression in evidence, as in Klein's description of Inge's play:

For a considerable time she played an office game with me, in which she was the manager who gave orders of every sort and dictated letters and wrote them, in contrast to her own severe inhibitions in learning and writing. In this her desires to be a man were clearly recognizable. One day she gave up this game and began to play at school with me. It is to be noted that she not only found her lessons difficult and unpleasant but had a great dislike for school itself. She now played at school with me for quite a long time, by taking the part of the mistress while I represented the pupil; the kind of mistakes she made me make gave me important clues to the reasons for her own failure at school. Inge, as a youngest child, had, in spite of all appearances to the contrary, found the superiority of her elder brothers and sisters very hard to put up with, and when she went to school she had felt that the old situation was being reproduced. As the details of the lessons which she gave in the role of a mistress revealed, in the last resort and at a very early age, her own desire for knowledge had not been satisfied and was repressed . . .

(pp. 61–62)

While Inge was a failure in reality, in imagination she played every role. Thus in the game I have described, in which she played the part of office-manager, she represented her successes in the role of father; as the school mistress she had numerous children, and at the same time exchanged her role of the youngest child for that of the oldest and most intelligent; while in the game of being a seller of toys and food, admittedly by a double displacement of roles, she reversed the oral frustrations.

(p. 63)

We can note here Klein's emphasis on the damaging impact of the blocking of Inge's desire to find things out. Instead of being able to express her longing to understand the world and to feel enabled to explore reality, she has turned to a phantasy of already being in possession of all knowledge.

Sometimes children of this age are able to bring dreams to their analysis, but their associations are more likely to be expressed through simultaneous physical or play activity rather than in verbal form. The developmental maturation of the child is of course considerably supported by the analytic work and in latency children the transition from action-based communication through play into more purely verbal expression can often be observed.

> This boy [a nine-year-old], who behaved in many respects like an adult obsessional and in whom morbid brooding was a marked symptom, also suffered from severe anxiety which was, however, chiefly exhibited in great irritability and in fits of rage. A great part of this analysis was carried on by means of toys and with the help of drawing. I was obliged to sit beside him at the play-table and to play with him even to a greater extent than I usually have to with most small children. Sometimes I had even to carry out the actions involved in the game alone by myself under his direction. For instance, I had to build up the bricks, move the carts about and so on, while he merely supervised my actions. The reason he gave for this was that his hands sometimes trembled very much, so that he could not put the toys in their places or might upset or damage them. This trembling was a sign of the onset of an anxiety attack. I could in most cases cut the attacks short by carrying out the game as he wanted it, at the same time interpreting, in connection with his anxiety, the meaning of the actions (in the game). His fear of his own aggressiveness and his disbelief in his capacity to love had made him lose all hope of restoring the parents and brothers and sisters, whom, in his phantasy, he had attacked. Hence his fear that he might accidentally knock down the bricks and things which had already been put up. This distrust of his own constructive tendencies and of his ability to make restitution was one of the causes of his severe inhibition in learning and playing.
>
> After his anxiety had been resolved to a large extent, Werner played his games without assistance from me. He did a great many drawings and gave abundant associations to them. In the last part of his analysis he produced his material chiefly in the form of free associations. Lying on the couch – a position in which he, like Kenneth, preferred to give his associations – he would narrate continuous phantasies of adventure in which apparatus, mechanical contrivances and so on played a large part. In these stories the material that had before been represented in his drawings appeared again, but enriched in many details.
>
> (pp. 66–67)

The vast range of cases on which Klein draws in this chapter is remarkable, and testifies to the extent of her clinical experience. The number of examples also serves to demonstrate the imaginative flexibility in her techniques. When writing about one very cut-off 9½-year-old boy, whose play was profoundly monotonous, she described how not only did she need to play with him as one might with a very small child and follow his rarely verbalised instructions, but she also realised that in order to establish rapport and avoid replicating the behaviour of his intrusive father she had to remain silent herself. To offer interpretations, she surmised, would have provoked further retreat. This boy's inhibition in speaking persisted for a long time, but in due course he began to be able to send her messages in writing, and then to whisper things to her as long as she too used a low voice, thus protecting them from the persecutors which she realised he believed had been ever present.

In this chapter Klein also tackles the question of the child analyst's relationship to her patient's parents. She puts it like this:

> I refer to the analyst's dealings with the parents of his patients. In order for him to be able to do his work there must be a certain relation of confidence between himself and the child's parents. The child is dependent on them and so they are included in the field of the analysis; yet it is not they who are being analysed and they can therefore only be influenced by ordinary psychological means. The relationship of the parents to their child's analyst entails difficulties of a peculiar kind, since it touches closely upon their own complexes. Their child's neurosis weighs very heavily upon the parents' sense of guilt, and at the same time as they turn to analysis for help, they regard the necessity of it as a proof of their guilt with regard to their child's illness. It is, moreover, very trying for them to have the details of their family life revealed to the analyst. To this must be added, particularly in the case of the mother, jealousy of the confidence which is established between the child and its (woman) analyst.
>
> (p. 75)

A couple of pages later, however, she writes of the potentially benign effect of a child's analysis on family relationships:

> The removal or lessening of a child's neurosis has a good effect upon its parents. As the mother's difficulties in dealing with her child diminish, her sense of guilt diminishes too, and this improves her attitude towards the child.
>
> (p. 78)

Yet she is cautious in considering what can be achieved in the direct contact between a child's analyst and his parents:

> Nevertheless, I do not, in the light of my own experiences, put much faith in the possibility of affecting the child's environment. It is better to rely upon the results achieved in the child itself, for these will enable it to make a better adaptation even to a difficult environment and will put it in a better position to meet any strains which that environment may lay upon it.
>
> (p. 78)

These suggestions arise from a context in which the parents seeking help for their child from Klein were often quite well informed about psychoanalysis and indeed committed to it intellectually. Although a number of the case histories she reports involve a child's treatment being ended prematurely from a psychoanalytic perspective, this was usually due not to a breakdown of support from the parents, suggesting how well Klein was able to calibrate the kinds of links she made with them, but to external factors such as a family move. Making space in children's lives for several sessions a week did not seem to pose great difficulties, and many families had nannies who could bring the children to their sessions. Few of the mothers were themselves working outside the home. All of this is a far cry from contemporary life, but it is also the case that, while Klein found she could work successfully on the basis of quite limited meetings between herself and her patients' parents, child analysts and psychotherapists now most often find that some separate arrangements for regular parental consultation in addition to review meetings with the child's therapist prove necessary. The complexity of professional networks which do not appear in Klein's account of her work also tend to require a good deal of liaison. However, the stance Klein takes with regard to the privacy of the child's sessions remains fundamental, and she offers a wise reminder of the primary duty of the child analyst in her reflections on the way that parents (and one might add, other adults significant in the child's life) can often find it difficult to keep track of the child's behaviour and relationships during the course of his treatment:

> I think we shall be well content to forgo our full due of recognition from that quarter [parents] so long as we bear in mind that the foremost aim of our work is to secure the well-being of the child and not the gratitude of its mother and father.
>
> (p. 79)

Such a prescription sits rather uncomfortably with the contemporary emphasis in public health provision on tracking outcome closely, and judging this in major part by the views of parents and teachers. Klein is by no means uninterested in how the children she has treated develop and she quite often includes information about their later trajectory when she has been able to ascertain details. She is committed to helping her patients to relate to the demands of external reality, and is clearly satisfied when this is brought about, but she is primarily concerned to protect the child's private space within the analysis, which is needed if the problems of his inner world are to be given proper attention.

In the third of the chapters on technique Klein tackles the changes ushered in by the child's experience of puberty. The cases she presents range in age from 12 to 15, so as the age of puberty has moved forward over the last 80 years, it is probably helpful to think of her technical recommendations as applying to the early years of adolescence somewhat more broadly.

Here is her opening statement:

> Typical analyses at the age of puberty differ in many essentials from analyses in the latency period. The instinctual impulses of the child are more powerful, the activity of his phantasy greater, and his ego has other aims and a different relation to reality. On the other hand there are points of similarity with the analysis of the
>
> *(continued)*

(continued)

small child, owing to the fact that at the age of puberty, we once again meet with a greater dominance of the instinctual impulses and the unconscious, and a much richer phantasy life. Moreover, in puberty manifestations of anxiety and affect are very much more acute than in the latency period, and are a kind of recrudescence of anxiety which is so characteristic of small children.

Warding off and modifying anxiety, which is also an essential function of the ego in the case of the small child is, however, carried out with greater success by the more developed ego of the adolescent. For he has developed his various interests and activities (sports and so on) to a great extent with the object of mastering that anxiety, of over-compensating for it and of masking it from himself and from others. He achieves this in part by assuming the attitude of defiance and rebelliousness that is characteristic of puberty. This provides a great technical difficulty in analysis at puberty; for unless we very quickly gain access to the patient's affects – strong as they are at this age – which he principally manifests in a defiant transference, it may very well happen that the analysis will suddenly be broken off.

(p. 80)

She goes on to note the continuity in many respects in the presentation of young adolescents with the preoccupations visible in the play of small children:

The material of the adolescent closely resembles that presented by the small child. At the ages of puberty and pre-puberty boys busy themselves in their phantasy with people and things in the same way as small children play with toys. What Peter, aged three years and nine months, expressed by means of little carts and trains and motors, the fourteen-year-old Ludwig expressed in long discourses, lasting for months, on the constructional differences between various kinds of motors, bicycles, motor-cycles, and so on. Where Peter pushed along carts and compared them with one another, Ludwig would be passionately interested in the question of which cars and which drivers would win some race; and whereas Peter paid a tribute of admiration to the toy man's skill in driving and made him perform all sorts of feats, Ludwig for his part, was never tired of singing the praises of his idols of the sporting world.

(p. 81)

While the more normal adolescent will tend to display a vivid conflictful world peopled by admired heroes (sporting heroes in Klein's cases, perhaps figures from popular culture too, nowadays) in contrast to the scornful dismissal of teachers, relatives, the 'uncool', more inhibited characters maintain a retreat from disturbing feelings more akin to what is ordinary during the latency years. Klein suggests that when latency sets in too soon or continues too long, that is, occupies an extended period of years, it is an indication of a severe developmental disturbance. This grounding of her observations in an understanding of normal patterns of child development is most important, and it is a feature of the way she introduces us to the many children whose material she presents that she makes quite a clear assessment of their degree of disturbance. Some are described as fundamentally normal children who could nonetheless benefit from analysis in terms of the development of character and the lifting of subtle restrictions in their relationships. Others are children whose neurotic difficulties were all too obvious, whose lives were blighted by their anxieties and whose problems made them a source of deep concern for their parents.

In discussing her technique with adolescents, Klein presents several cases in which guilt and anxiety about sexual activities, either past or present, are a central feature. Here is an example:

> In the analysis of the fourteen-year-old Ludwig . . . I was able to discover . . . the reason for his strong feelings of guilt about his younger brother. When, for instance, Ludwig spoke about his steam-engine being in need of repair, he at once went on to give associations about his brother's engine which would never be any good again. His resistance in connection with this and his wish that the session would soon come to an end turned out to be caused by his fear of his mother, who might discover the sexual relations which had existed between him and his younger brother and which he partly remembered. These relations had left behind them severe unconscious feelings of guilt in him, for he, as the elder and stronger, had at times forced his brother into them. Since then he had felt responsible for the defective development of his brother, who was seriously neurotic.
>
> (pp. 83–84)

The centrality of anxiety about masturbation, sexual fantasy and sexual activity with other children is quite striking. This feature perhaps has its origins in the relatively repressive upbringing of children in the early twentieth century with respect to sexual knowledge and also to auto-erotic activity, but it meant that in order to help these patients Klein had to think deeply about the sexual development of the boy and girl, and this led her to revise aspects of Freudian theory. Here is her approach to the pubertal girl:

> I now turn to the analysis of girls at the age of puberty. The onset of menstruation arouses strong anxiety in the girl. In addition to the various other meanings which it has and with which we are familiar, it is, in the last resort, the outward and visible sign that the interior of her body and the children contained there have been totally destroyed. For this reason the development of a complete feminine attitude in the girl takes longer and is beset by more difficulties than is the case with the boy in establishing his masculine position. This greater difficulty in the woman's development results in a reinforcement of the masculine component of the girl at puberty. In other cases only a partial development, mostly on the intellectual side, sets in at that time, while her sexual life and personality remain in a protracted latency which in many cases may last beyond the age of puberty . . .
>
> . . . Even girls in whom the feminine position predominates have anxiety during puberty which is more severe and more acute in its expression than in the adult woman.
>
> (pp. 85–86)

Klein goes on to give a long account of her work with Ilse, aged 12 at the start of her treatment. After realising that Ilse was a most reluctant patient, quite unable to talk with any freedom, Klein suggested that she might like to draw.

> During the months that followed, Ilse's associations consisted in the main of drawing – apparently without any phantasy – done with compasses, according to exact measurements. These measurements and calculations of parts of things was the main activity, and the compulsive nature of this occupation became increasingly clear. After much slow and patient work it emerged that the various forms and colours of these parts represented different people. Her compulsion to measure and count proved to be derived from the impulse, which had become obsessive, to find out for certain about the inside of her mother's body and the number of children there, the differences between the sexes, and so forth. In this case, too, the inhibition of her whole personality and intellectual growth had arisen from a very early repression of her powerful instinct for knowledge, which had changed into a defiant rejection of all knowledge. With the help of this drawing, measuring and counting we made considerable progress and Ilse's anxiety became less acute.
>
> (p. 88)

Ilse became able to talk about her despair over her failure at school and her tormenting belief that her clothes were all wrong and that she never looked right. The account continues:

> As Ilse's difficulties in learning continued to diminish, a very great change took place in her whole nature. She became capable of social adaptation, made friends with other girls and got on much better with her parents and her brothers and sisters. One could now call her a normal girl and her interests now approximated to what was adequate to her age; and as she was now good at school, a favourite with her mistresses and had become an almost too-obedient daughter, her family were completely satisfied with the success of her analysis and saw no reason for its continuance. But I did not share their opinion. It was obvious that at this point, when she was thirteen and physical puberty had already begun, Ilse had psychically only just accomplished a really successful transition to the latency period. By means of resolving anxiety quantities and reducing her sense of guilt, the analysis had enabled her to adapt herself socially, and to progress psychically to the latency period. However gratifying these changes might be, the person I saw before me was still a rather dependent child who was still excessively fixated to her mother. Though her circle of interests was greatly widening she was still hardly capable of having any ideas of her own. She usually prefaced her expressions with such words as 'Mother thinks'. Her wish to please, the great care that she now took of her appearance in contrast to her former total indifference to it, her need for love and recognition – all these sprang predominantly from her desire to please her mother and her mistresses; the same purpose served her desire to do better than her schoolmates. Her homosexual attitude was predominant and there were as yet scarcely any heterosexual impulses visible in her.

> The continuation of the analysis, which now proceeded in a normal fashion, led to far-reaching changes not only in this respect, but in the whole development of Ilse's personality. In this she was very much helped by the fact that we were able to analyse the anxiety which menstruation aroused in her . . . . It was only now that her psychological puberty really set in. Before this, she had not been in a position to criticize her mother and form her own opinions, because this would have signified making a violent sadistic attack upon her mother. The analysis of this sadism enabled Ilse – in keeping with her age – to achieve a greater self-reliance which became visible in her way of thinking and acting.
>
> (pp. 90–91)

Klein concludes her discussion of this case with this comment:

> In this case, we see how the girl's failure to work over her over-strong sense of guilt was able to disturb not only her transition to the latency period but the whole course of her development. Her affects, which found an outlet in outbursts of rage, had been displaced; the modification of her anxiety went wrong. Ilse, who had the appearance of an unhappy and discontented individual, was not aware of her own anxiety nor of her dissatisfaction with herself. It was a great advance in her analysis when I was able to make her understand that she was unhappy and to show her that she felt inferior and unloved and that she was in despair about it and, in her hopelessness, would make no attempt to gain the love of others.
>
> (p. 91)

She goes on to suggest that the analysis of pubertal children requires an understanding of the technique of adult analysis, that is, the use of free association and the couch. Indeed, she argues that training in adult psychoanalysis is a prerequisite for the 'more difficult field of child analysis'. This expectation remains the practice in some psychoanalytic societies but has been subject to sustained challenge over the last 60 years, during which child psychoanalytic training has successfully established itself as an independent pathway. Given Klein's own theoretical advances in understanding that the roots of our psychological difficulties go back to our very early lives, it can certainly be cogently argued that the psychoanalytic study of the child's mind is an excellent point of departure. It is also the case that some children do show themselves to be very responsive to the psychoanalytic method, getting to the emotional heart of the matter more readily than some adult patients. What child analysis does tend to protect is the combination of the centrality of clinical observation and a psychoanalytic theory attuned to development, and such attention to the potential growth of the mind is a useful counterbalance to a focus on pathology.

Klein follows up the chapters on technique with some observations on indications for treatment in children which are extraordinarily wide-ranging. The difficulties she mentions include eating disorders ('derangements in eating', she calls them); sleep disturbances; phobias and excessive timidity; inhibitions in play and/or a capacity for physical expression; self-harm and accident-proneness; hyperactivity ('overliveliness and fidgetiness' are her words); tics; inhibitions in learning; over-reliance on material possessions and gifts; and unusual vulnerability to physical illness. This list attests to both her enormous range of experience and to the unifying power of her model of the role of early anxiety and guilt in shaping the mind. It is also remarkably prescient in terms of the difficulties presented to contemporary child and adolescent mental health services.

She also offers some considered comments on normality, pathology and health in children. First, a reminder as to what is specific to child analysis:

> Finally I would like to draw attention to the technique employed in the treatment of this case. In the first part of it I used the technique belonging to the latency period, and in the second that belonging to puberty. I have repeatedly referred to the connecting links between the various forms of psycho-analytic technique appropriate to different stages. Let me emphasize that I regard the technique of early analysis as the basis of the technique applicable to children of every age. In the last chapter I have said that my method of analysing children of the latency period was based on the play technique I had worked out for small children. But as the cases discussed in the present chapter show, the technique of early analysis is indispensable for many patients at the age of puberty as well; for we shall fail with many of these often very difficult cases if we do not sufficiently take into account the adolescent's need for action and for expression of phantasy and are not careful to regulate the amount of anxiety liberated and, in general, do not adopt an exceedingly elastic technique.
>
> (pp. 92–93)

And now, a portrait of healthy development:

> Comparison with the neuroses of adults cannot serve as a yard-stick, since the child who most approximates to a non-neurotic adult is by no means the child who is least neurotic. Thus, for instance, a small child which fulfils all the requirements of its upbringing and does not let itself be dominated by its life of phantasy and instinct, which is in fact, to all appearances completely adapted to reality and, moreover, shows little sign of anxiety – such a child would assuredly not only be precocious and quite devoid of charm, but would be abnormal in the fullest sense of the word. If this picture is completed by the extensive repression of phantasy which is a necessary pre-condition of such a development, we should certainly have cause to regard that child's future with concern. A child whose development has been of this kind suffers, not from a quantitatively minor neurosis but from a symptomless neurosis; and as we know from the analysis of adults, such a neurosis is usually a serious one.
>
> (p. 101)

She continues:

> The question now to be considered is: how does a child show that it is fairly well adapted internally? It is a favourable sign if it enjoys playing and gives free rein to its

> phantasy in doing so, being at the same time, as can be recognized from certain definite indications, sufficiently adapted to reality, and if it has really good – not over-affectionate – relations to its objects. Another good sign is if, together with this, it shows a relatively undisturbed development of its instinct for knowledge, which freely turns in a number of different directions, yet without having that character of compulsion and intensity which is typical of an obsessional neurosis. The emergence of a certain amount of affect and anxiety is also, I think, a pre-condition of a favourable development. These and other indications of a favourable prognosis have in my experience, however, only a relative value and are no absolute guarantee of the future; for it often depends on the unforeseeable external realities, favourable or unfavourable, which the child encounters as it grows up whether its neurosis of the child will reappear in the life of the adult or not.
>
> (p. 103)

And:

> The adult individual may succumb to a neurosis, to characterological defects, to disturbances of his capacity for sublimation or to disorders of his sexual life. An infantile neurosis can be detected at an early age, as I have endeavoured to show, by various slight but characteristic signs; the cure of the infantile neurosis is the best prophylaxis against the neurosis of the adult. Later characterological defects and difficulties are best prevented by being eliminated in childhood. The play of children, which enables us to penetrate so deeply into their minds, gives us a clear indication when their analysis can be considered as being completed in respect of their future capacity for sublimation. Before we can consider the analysis of a small child as completed, its inhibitions in playing must have been largely reduced. This has been accomplished when its interest in play appropriate to its age has become not only deeper and more stable but has also been extended in various directions.
>
> When, as a result of the analytic work, a child who starts with a single obsessive interest in play gains an ever-widening interest in games, this process is equivalent to the expansion of interests and the increase of capacity for sublimation which is the aim of the analysis of an adult. In this way, by understanding the play of children we can estimate their capacity for sublimation in future years; and we can also tell when an analysis has sufficiently guarded against future inhibitions of their capacity to learn and to work.
>
> Finally, the development of the child's interest in play, and the variations in quantity and kind which they show, also permit reliable conclusions about its future sexual development.
>
> (pp. 104–105)

This is what Klein aimed for with her young patients.

Klein's technique, usually represented as seeking to make contact with a child's deeper anxieties as soon as possible, can easily be overstated. As documented in this chapter, she took sensitive account of children's individual ways of holding anxieties at bay and would try out different ways of enabling them to begin to trust her. Nonetheless, debate on matters of technique and underlying theory was intense, and in *The Freud–Klein Controversies 1941–45* (King and Steiner, 1991) are recorded the divergent views of Klein and her co-workers and the group led by Anna Freud in the form of papers presented to the British Psychoanalytical Society in a long series of meetings between October 1942 and February 1944.

There have been significant developments in psychoanalytic technique in subsequent years. Of central relevance in these changes is the theory of the early shaping of the mind developed by W.R. Bion and the new understanding of the relationship between the minds of mother and baby, and by analogy, analyst and patient. The model of containment of infantile anxiety through maternal receptiveness and reverie opened up the potential understanding of very early unintegrated forms of experience, and also of broken-down psychotic states in which mental structure and an awareness of reality have become unavailable. Analysts began to recognise how important was the function of containment with respect to these fragmented forms of experience. Before interpretation could be useful to the patient, the unthinkable-about experiences had to become recognised, known to a mind capable of bearing them and transformed through the thinking activity of the analyst.

This expanded understanding of early forms of human communication was particularly relevant for child analysis, and more so in the light of changes in the population of children being referred for analytic help. The by-and-large stable families in which Klein's patients grew up are now often replaced by very troubled backgrounds, high levels of trauma, loss and deprivation. The growing complexity of the contemporary globalised world has been accompanied by a sharply increased incidence of mental health problems among children and adolescents, including very serious levels of difficulty.[1]

A second major theoretical discovery impinging on technique was the revised understanding of countertransference. Heimann's suggestion (1950), that the analyst's countertransference sometimes reflected not the continuing personal problems of the analyst, as Freud and Klein had believed, but an unconscious response to an aspect of the patient, has been very influential. In fact, Klein's own theory of projective identification (see Chapter 6) was vital in making this new perspective possible.

Technique in analytic work with children and adolescents has changed in the light of these ideas. The gathering in of the anxieties evoked by the analytic setting remains the starting point, but what and when to interpret to the child are less clear-cut. Exploring the distinction between deficit and disturbance (Alvarez, 1992) is one aspect of this development. Allowing for the idea that the analyst's feelings in the session provide vital clues to the child's deeper emotional state, particularly when the levels of mental pain are very high, is another (Hoxter, 1983). 'Kleinian' technique now encompasses a considerable range, though the focus on the centrality of anxiety and on the importance of finding words to describe emotion and the inner world remains central.

1 It is only in recent decades that reliable epidemiological data has become available in the UK. This indicates that the incidence of serious mental ill health among children and young people doubled between 1974 and 1999. For boys aged 15–16, the proportions of young people reporting frequent feelings of depression or anxiety increased from 1 in 30 to 2 in 30; for girls from 1 in 20 to 2 in 20. In 2004, one in ten children and young people (10 per cent) aged 5–16 had a clinically diagnosed mental disorder. See http://www.hscic.gov.uk/catalogue/PUB06116/ment-heal-chil-youn-peop-gb-2004-rep2.pdf, and Green *et al.* (2005). Data gathered in 2009 suggests that this increase levelled off after 1999, although worsening economic prospects on a European scale, particularly for young people's employment, may lead to renewal of this upward trend. On this, see http://www.nuffieldfoundation.org/time-trends-adolescent-well-being and Hagell (2012).

Chapter 5

Mourning, the discovery of the depressive position and its implications for the theory of Oedipal development

Klein's understanding of loss and the mourning process is perhaps the most widely cited and admired of her contributions to psychoanalysis. Just as Freud's paper on mourning and melancholia captured and ordered immediately comprehensible and universal aspects of human experience, so do Klein's 1935–1940 papers on depression and mourning illuminate hitherto mysterious or unrecognised features of our responses to loss. Freud's personal bereavements and a world at war were the context for his thinking, and Klein's work too has the background of both tragic personal loss and the deeply troubled Europe of the 1930s, suffering the impact of severe economic depression and the rise of Fascism. Klein's writing does not make reference to any of this, and is closely focused on psychoanalytic theory and clinical observation, but perhaps some of the powerful resonance of her writing is nonetheless linked to the reader's awareness of her personal losses and the unbearable world events of the time.

She begins her investigation of depressive states by contrasting them to both paranoia and mania, and poses the question as to the importance and nature of the early introjective processes which underlie melancholia, emphasising that the greater coherence of the ego and the gradually more integrated nature of the objects within the infant's mind bring about a vital development.

> In paranoia the characteristic defences are chiefly aimed at annihilating the 'persecutors', while anxiety on the ego's account occupies a prominent place in the picture. As the ego becomes more fully organized, the internalized imagos will approximate more closely to reality and the ego will identify itself more fully with 'good' objects. The dread of persecution, which was at first felt on the ego's account, now relates to the good object as well and from now on preservation of the good object is regarded as synonymous with the survival of the ego.
>
> Hand in hand with this development goes a change of the highest importance; namely, from a partial object-relation to the relation to a complete object. Through this step the ego arrives at a new position, which forms the foundation of the situation called the loss of the loved object. Not until the object is loved *as a whole* can its loss be felt as a whole.
>
> ('A contribution to the psychogenesis of manic-depressive states', 1935; p. 264)

Klein goes on to describe how concern for the safety of the object affects not only introjection, as Abraham had suggested, but also the subject's feelings about what happens to the introjected object. How is it then to be preserved and protected? She links the increased desire for the presence of an internal good object to the process of restoration, which she now terms reparation or restitution. Through reparative efforts, both the good object and the self can be felt to be safer from destructive impulses, but the need for the ongoing support of the good object is paramount.

> It now becomes plain why, at this phase of development, the ego feels itself constantly menaced in its possession of internalized good objects. It is full of anxiety lest such objects should die. Both in children and adults suffering from depression, I have discovered the dread of harbouring dying or dead objects (especially the parents) inside one and an identification of the ego with objects in this condition.
>
> From the very beginning of psychic development there is a constant correlation of real objects with those installed within the ego. It is for this reason that the anxiety which I have just described manifests itself in a child's exaggerated fixation to its mother or whoever looks after it. The absence of the mother arouses in the child anxiety lest it should be handed over to bad objects, external and internalized, either because of her *death* or because of her return in the guise of a *'bad'* mother.
>
> Both cases mean to the child the loss of the loved mother, and I would particularly draw attention to the fact that dread of the loss of the 'good', internalized object becomes a perpetual source of anxiety lest the real mother should die. On the other hand, every experience which suggests the loss of the real loved object stimulates the dread of losing the internalized one too.
>
> (pp. 266–267)

At the same time as the growing awareness of this need for the presence of this good object both within and without comes the recognition of the dangers posed by the hostility of the self towards this needed object:

> It seems to me that only when the ego has introjected the object as a whole, and has established a better relationship to the external world and to real people, is it able fully to realize the disaster created through its sadism and especially through its cannibalism, and to feel distressed about it . . .
>
> . . . The ego then finds itself confronted with the psychic reality that its loved objects are in a state of dissolution – in bits – and the despair, remorse and anxiety deriving from this recognition are at the bottom of numerous anxiety-situations. To quote only a few of them: there is anxiety how to put the bits together in the right way and at the right time; how to pick out the good bits and do away with the bad ones; how to bring the object to life when it has been put together; and there is the anxiety of being interfered with in this task by bad objects and by one's own hatred, etc.
>
> (p. 269)

Klein notes the overwhelming nature of the reparative task felt to confront the child at this point, but also suggests that here we have the roots of mature love:

> [T]he ego comes to a realization of its love for a good object, a whole object and in addition a real object, together with an overwhelming feeling of guilt towards it. Full identification with the object based on the libidinal attachment, first to the breast, then to the whole person, goes hand in hand with anxiety for it (of its disintegration), with guilt and remorse, with a sense of responsibility for preserving it intact against persecutors and the id, and with sadness relating to expectations of the impending loss of it. These emotions, whether conscious or unconscious, are in my view among the essential and fundamental elements of the feelings we call love.
>
> (p. 270)

She contrasts this with a paranoid state of mind, to which the individual can be 'thrust back' because of the degree of suffering that guilt and remorse entail, and we here begin to grasp Klein's understanding of the inevitable oscillation between the depressive and paranoid positions taken up later by Bion in particular. This concept of 'position' conveys a whole complex interplay of anxieties and defences, and Klein suggests this enables us to think across the whole life cycle rather than to locate these problems as 'phases' of child development:

> It seems to me characteristic of the paranoiac that, though, on account of his persecution-anxiety and his suspicions, he develops a very strong and acute power of observation of the external world and of real objects, this observation and his sense of reality are nevertheless distorted, since his persecution-anxiety makes him look at people mainly from the point of view of whether they are persecutors or not. Where the persecution-anxiety for the ego is in the ascendant, a full and stable identification with another object, in the sense of looking at it and understanding it as it really is, and a full capacity for love, are not possible . . .
>
> . . . the sufferings connected with the depressive position thrust him back to the paranoiac position. Nevertheless, though he has retreated from it, the depressive position has been reached and therefore the liability to depression is always there. This accounts, in my opinion, for the fact that we frequently meet depression along with severe paranoia as well as in milder cases.
>
> If we compare the feelings of the paranoiac with those of the depressive in regard to disintegration, we can see that characteristically the depressive is filled with sorrow and anxiety for the object, which he would strive to unite again into a whole, while to the paranoiac the disintegrated object is mainly a multitude of persecutors, since each piece is growing again into a persecutor.
>
> (pp. 271–272)

She gives vivid clinical examples to elaborate these points which throw light on eating disorders, hypochondriachal anxieties and suicide. Here is her description of a patient with somatic anxieties which could be traced in his dream life:

> For instance, patient X, who had been told as a child that he had tapeworms (which he himself never saw) connected the tapeworms inside him with his greediness. In his analysis he had phantasies that a tapeworm was eating its way through his body and a strong anxiety of cancer came to the fore. The patient, who suffered from hypochondriacal and paranoid anxieties, was very suspicious of me, and, among other things, suspected me of being allied with people who were hostile towards him. At this time he dreamt that a detective was arresting a hostile and persecuting person and putting this person in prison. But then the detective proved unreliable and became the accomplice of the enemy. The detective stood for myself and the whole anxiety was internalized and was also connected with the tapeworm phantasy. The prison in which the enemy was kept was his own inside – actually the special part of his inside where the persecutor was to be confined. It became clear that the dangerous tapeworm (one of his associations was that the tapeworm is bisexual) represented the two parents in a hostile alliance (actually in intercourse) against him.
>
> (p. 273)

She goes on to argue that omnipotent mania is not only an escape from melancholic depression but also from the paranoid anxieties about internal persecution. The denial of psychic reality which mania entails precipitates a tendency to deny external reality. At the same time the manic state involves compulsive efforts to control matters, particularly with respect to the internal objects whose death is dreaded but denied. These anxieties lead to manic efforts at resuscitation which Klein terms manic reparation, to distinguish it from reparation based on awareness of destructive impulses and concern about their consequences. Another characteristic of mania is pervasive contempt for objects which strip them of their value. When the objects are allowed their importance, Klein argues that the overcoming of depression is dependent on reparation. This idea of 'overcoming' is a variant of the concept of working through, though it does perhaps suggest a once-and-for-all achievement, in contrast to the idea of repeated revisiting of conflicts during an analysis and throughout life suggested by Freud's original formulation. Perhaps that is why Klein prefers 'working through' in some of her later writing on these themes, such as in 'Our adult world and its roots in infancy' (1959).

In the 1935 paper she provides a very clear summary of her picture of normal infantile development:

> The object-world of the child in the first two or three months of its life could be described as consisting of hostile and persecuting, or else of gratifying parts and portions of the real world. Before long the child perceives more and more of the whole person of the mother, and this more realistic perception extends to the world beyond the mother. (The fact that a good relation to its mother and to the external world helps the baby to overcome its early paranoid anxieties throws a new light on the importance of its earliest experiences. From its inception analysis has always laid stress on the importance of the child's early experiences, but it seems to me that only since we know more about the nature and contents of its early anxieties, and the continuous interplay between

its actual experiences and its phantasy-life, can we fully understand *why* the external factor is so important.) But when this happens its sadistic phantasies and feelings, especially its cannibalistic ones, are at their height. At the same time the child now experiences a change in its emotional attitude towards its mother. Its libidinal fixation to the breast develops into feelings towards her as a person. Thus feelings both of a destructive and of a loving nature are experienced towards one and the same object and this gives rise to deep and disturbing conflicts in the child's mind.

In the normal course of events the ego is faced at this point of its development – roughly between four and five months of age – with the necessity to acknowledge psychic reality as well as the external reality to a certain degree. It is thus made to realize that the loved object is at the same time the hated one; and, in addition to this, that the real objects and the imaginary figures, both external and internal, are bound up with each other. I have pointed out elsewhere that in the very young child there exist, side by side with its relations to real objects – but on a different plane, as it were – relations to its unreal imagos, both as excessively good and excessively bad figures, and that these two kinds of object-relations intermingle and colour each other to an ever-increasing degree in the course of development. The first important steps in this direction occur, in my view, when the child comes to know its mother as a whole person and becomes identified with her as a whole, real and loved person. It is then that the depressive position – the characteristics of which I have described in this paper – come to the fore. This position is stimulated and reinforced by the 'loss of the loved object' which the baby experiences over and over again when the mother's breast is taken away from it, and this loss reaches its climax during weaning . . .

. . . The whole situation and the defences of the baby, which obtains reassurance over and over again in the love of the mother, differ greatly from those in the adult melancholic. But the important point is that these sufferings, conflicts, and feelings of remorse and guilt, resulting from the relation of the ego to its internalized object, are already active in the baby . . .

It seems that at this stage of development the unification of external and internal, loved and hated, real and imaginary objects is carried out in such a way that each step in the unification leads again to a renewed splitting of the imagos. But as the adaptation to the external world increases, this splitting is carried out on planes which gradually become increasingly nearer and nearer to reality. This goes on until love for the real and the internalized objects and trust in them are well established. Then ambivalence, which is partly a safeguard against one's own hate and against the hated and terrifying objects, will in normal development again diminish in varying degrees.

Along with the increase in love for one's good and real objects goes a greater trust in one's capacity to love and a lessening of the paranoid anxiety of the bad objects – changes which lead to a decrease of sadism and again to better ways of mastering aggression and working it off.

('A contribution to the psychogenesis of manic-depressive states', 1935; pp. 285–288)

Paranoid and manic anxieties dominate when the infant 'fails to establish its loved object within', but, Klein concludes, 'the infantile depressive position is the central position in the child's development'. Here is the cornerstone of her theory of the evolution of the child's internal world, rooted in her vision of the object-relatedness of the human infant.

It is interesting to read her short paper on 'Weaning' written in the following year and in more everyday language, probably envisaging a wider public readership, especially of mothers, as it was written for a book edited by Rickman (1939) entitled *On the Bringing-Up of Children*. This paper links her theoretical conclusions to observations about children in everyday family circumstances. This different orientation demands a different tone of voice. Here is Klein's explanation of early splitting and of part objects and their evolution:

> It may seem curious that the tiny child's interest should be limited to a part of a person rather than to the whole, but one must bear in mind first of all that the child has an extremely undeveloped capacity for perception, physical and mental, at this stage, and then we must remember the all-important fact that the tiny child is only concerned with his immediate gratification or the lack of it; Freud called this the 'pleasure–pain principle'. Thus the breast of the mother which gives gratification or denies it becomes, in the mind of the child, imbued with the characteristics of good and evil. Now, what one might call the 'good' breasts become the prototype of what is felt throughout life to be good and beneficent, while the 'bad' breasts stand for everything evil and persecuting . . .
>
> . . . The object world of the child in the first two or three months of its life could be described as consisting of gratifying or of hostile and persecuting parts or portions of the real world. At about this age he begins to see his mother and others about him as 'whole people', his realistic perception of her (and them) coming gradually as he connects her face looking down at him with the hands that caress him and with the breast that satisfies him, and the power to perceive 'wholes' (once the pleasure in 'whole persons' is assured and he has confidence in them) spreads to the external world beyond the mother.
>
> ('Weaning', 1936; pp. 290–291)

She continues with an account of the interplay of internal and external:

> In the earliest stage of mental development every unpleasant stimulus is apparently related in the baby's phantasy to the 'hostile' or denying breasts, every pleasant stimulus on the other hand to the 'good', gratifying breasts. It seems that here we have two circles, the one benevolent and the other vicious, both of which are based on the interplay of external or environmental and internal psychical factors; thus any lessening of the amount or intensity of painful stimuli or any increase in the capacity to adjust to them should help to diminish the strength of phantasies of a frightening nature, and a decrease of frightening phantasies in its turn enables the child to take steps towards a better adaptation to reality, and this helps to diminish the frightening phantasies.

> It is important for the proper development of the mind that the child should come under the influence of the benevolent circle I have just outlined; when this happens he is greatly assisted in forming an image of his mother as a person; this growing perception of the mother as a whole implies not only very important changes in his intellectual, but also in his emotional development.
>
> (p. 292)

Reiterating her view that depression has its 'deepest source' in the failure to deal with early conflicts between feelings of love and hate, she again states that when guilt can be tolerated it has 'far-reaching effects on the child's future mental well-being, his capacity for love and his social development', and adds 'I wanted to indicate that aggressive feelings, which lead to so much disturbance in the child's mentality, are at the same time of the highest value for his development' (p. 294). The tremendous importance of balance in all the major ideas that inform Klein's thinking is visible here: love and hate go together, as do guilt and repair, anxiety as a painful affect and as a stimulus to development.

The final function of the good internal object and the threat of losing it, so terrifying to the small child, is described thus and linked to weaning conceived as an incremental process:

> If the child succeeds in establishing within himself a kind and helpful mother, this internalized mother will prove a most beneficial influence throughout his whole life. Though this influence will normally change in character with the development of the mind, it is comparable with the vitally important place that the real mother has in the tiny child's very existence . . .
>
> . . . [Because] the child feels any frustration very acutely . . . we find that the child feels, when the breast is wanted but is not there, as if it were lost for ever; since the conception of the breast extends to that of the mother, the feelings of having lost the breast lead to the fear of having lost the loved mother entirely, and this means not only the real mother, but also the good mother within . . .
>
> . . . The actual experience of weaning greatly reinforces these painful feelings or tends to substantiate these fears; but in so far as the baby never has uninterrupted possession of the breast, and over and over again is in the state of lacking it, one could say that, in a sense, he is in a constant state of being weaned or at least in a state leading up to weaning. Nevertheless, the crucial point is reached at the actual weaning when the loss is complete and the breast or bottle is gone irrevocably.
>
> (p. 295)

At this point Klein's writing is somewhat uncharacteristic, as she translates her tender appreciation of the acute sufferings of the infant into descriptions of how mothers can and should help their babies. It is as if the urge to give 'expert' advice, so foreign to Klein's analytic convictions, briefly takes over. Here is an example of this kind of thing, and more follows, including advice about the desirability of breast feeding, the frequency of feeds, the use of a dummy, methods of toilet training and attitudes to infantile sexual activity:

> Mothers often do not realize that a tiny baby is already a human being whose emotional development is of highest importance. A good contact between mother and child may be jeopardized at the first or at the first few feeds by the fact that the mother does not know how to induce the baby to take the nipple; if, for example, instead of dealing patiently with the difficulties as they arise, the nipple is pushed rather roughly into the baby's mouth, he may fail to develop a strong attachment to the nipple and to the breast, and become a difficult feeder. On the other hand, one can observe how babies who show this initial difficulty develop under patient assistance into quite as good feeders as those who have no initial difficulty at all.
>
> (p. 297)

Klein's capacity for imagining the world of mothers and babies in detail is imbued with a great desire to help the baby with what she now understands are the huge psychic demands of mental development. There is a delightful ending to this paper which probably does convey in a more benign way what she has in mind in her injunctions to parents and her repeated references to the importance of slow and gradual changes in the everyday care of babies:

> I understand that in old English the word weaning was used not only in the sense of 'weaning from' but also of 'weaning to'. Applying these two senses of the word, we may say that when real adaptation to frustration has taken place, the individual is weaned not only from his mother's breasts, but towards substitutes – towards all those sources of gratification and satisfaction which are needed for building up a full, rich and happy life.
>
> (p. 304)

It might be useful here to note that, although Klein writes at length about the infant's relation to mother's breast in many papers, and does indeed believe the baby's experience of being fed to be pivotal in the nature of his fundamental object relations, she makes it repeatedly clear that she viewed the 'breast relationship' as including many other aspects of the mother. After all, it is the whole mother who feeds the child, and the baby at the breast is held in mother's arms, can look at her face (and eye-to-eye contact is especially important), smell her skin as well as the milk, can feel mother's heart beat and the warmth of her body, and hear the rhythm of her breathing and the sound of her voice. As the paragraph quoted above illustrates, the breast is used by Klein to refer to the whole body and mind relationship to the mother. It starts with the newborn's search for the nipple, but expands in richness and complexity along with the baby's development. This wider sense of persons (baby, mother and, indeed, father and siblings) is of a piece with Klein's concept of the total transference being the focus in an analysis. All aspects of the analytic situation are what make up the total picture and all require attention.

Klein expanded her account of mourning in her 1940 paper 'Mourning and its relation to manic-depressive states'. She argues that early experiences of mourning (the loss of the baby's feeding relationship to mother) are revived whenever grief is experienced in later life, and that 'normal mourning' depends on the individual having successfully resolved the infantile depressive position. She underlines that this loss is a double one, not only of the lost external object but also of the internalised object felt to reside in the inner world. Here is her description of the interaction of internal and external:

> All the enjoyments which the baby lives through in relation to his mother are so many proofs to him that the loved object *inside as well as outside* is not injured, is not turned into a vengeful person. The increase of love and trust, and the diminishing of fears through happy experiences, help the baby step by step to overcome his depression and feeling of loss (mourning). They enable him to test his inner reality by means of outer reality. Through being loved and through the enjoyment and comfort he has in relation to people his confidence in his own as well as in other people's goodness becomes strengthened, his hope that his 'good' objects and his own ego can be saved and preserved increases, at the same time as his ambivalence and acute fears of internal destruction diminish.
>
> Unpleasant experiences and the lack of enjoyable ones, in the young child, especially lack of happy and close contact with loved people, increase ambivalence, diminish trust and hope and confirm anxieties about inner annihilation and external persecution; moreover they slow down and perhaps permanently check the beneficial processes through which in the long run inner security is achieved.
>
> ('Mourning and its relation to manic-depressive states', 1940; pp. 346–347)

In summarising her theory of the depressive position Klein proposes a new and highly evocative word to characterise the anxieties about loss:

> I now propose to use for these feelings of sorrow and concern for the loved objects, the fears of losing them and the longing to regain them, a simple word derived from everyday language – namely the 'pining' for the loved object. In short – persecution (by 'bad' objects) and the characteristic defences against it, on the one hand, and pining for the loved ('good') object, on the other, constitute the depressive position.
>
> (p. 348)

The pain of 'pining' gives rise to manic defensive efforts. Klein adds an important new emphasis to her earlier understanding of mania:

> The desire to control the object, the sadistic gratification of overcoming and humiliating it, of getting the better of it, the *triumph* over it, may enter so strongly into the act of reparation (carried out by thoughts, activities or sublimations) that the 'benign' circle started by this act becomes broken. The objects which were to be restored change again into persecutors, and in turn paranoid fears are revived. These fears reinforce the paranoid defence mechanisms (of destroying the object) as well as the manic
>
> *(continued)*

(continued)

> mechanisms (of controlling it or keeping it in suspended animation, and so on). The reparation which was in progress is thus disturbed or even nullified – according to the extent to which these mechanisms are activated. As a result of the failure of the act of reparation, the ego has to resort again and again to obsessional and manic defences . . .
>
> . . . In this connection I wish to stress the importance of *triumph*, closely bound up with contempt and omnipotence, as an element of the manic position.
>
> (p. 351)

She links the significance of triumph to the fluctuation between idealisation and contempt characteristic of manic states, and then goes on to explain the importance of reparative impulses in the evolution of the depressive position in childhood:

> Returning to the course of early development, we may say that every step in emotional, intellectual and physical growth is used by the ego as a means of overcoming the depressive position. The child's growing skills, gifts and arts increase his belief in the psychical reality of his constructive tendencies, in his capacity to master and control his hostile impulses as well as his 'bad' internal objects. Thus anxieties from various sources are relieved, and this results in a diminution of aggression and, in turn, of his suspicions of 'bad' external and internal objects. The strengthened ego, with its greater trust in people, can then make still further steps towards unification of its imagos—external, internal, loved and hated—and towards further mitigation of hatred by means of love, and thus to a general process of integration.
>
> (p. 353)

What follows from this naturally is the link to the normal course of mourning:

> The pain experienced in the slow process of testing reality in the work of mourning thus seems to be partly due to the necessity, not only to renew the links to the external world and thus continuously to re-experience the loss, but at the same time and by means of this to rebuild with anguish the inner world, which is felt to be in danger of deteriorating and collapsing. Just as the young child passing through the depressive position is struggling, in his unconscious mind, with the task of establishing and integrating his inner world, so the mourner goes through the pain of re-establishing and re-integrating it.
>
> (p. 354)

Klein gives a vivid clinical example of dreams from the analysis of a woman whose young son died suddenly to explore how the two sets of feelings which make up the depressive position can be worked through. The case example also serves to show how concrete in nature are experiences in the internal world. She then adds the very interesting reflection on the wider significance of mourning in mental life:

> Thus, while grief is experienced to the full and despair at its height, the love for the object wells up and the mourner feels more strongly that life inside and outside will go on after all, and that the lost loved object can be preserved within. At this stage in mourning, suffering can become productive. We know that painful experiences of all kinds sometimes stimulate sublimations, or even bring out quite new gifts in some people, who may take to painting, writing or other productive activities under the stress of frustrations and hardships. Others become more productive in a different way – more capable of appreciating people and things, more tolerant in their relation to others – they become wiser. Such enrichment is in my view gained through processes similar to those steps in mourning which we have just investigated. That is to say, any pain caused by unhappy experiences, whatever their nature, has something in common with mourning. It reactivates the infantile depressive position; the encountering and overcoming of adversity of any kind entails mental work similar to mourning.
>
> (p. 360)

She concludes by contrasting normal and abnormal mourning in this way:

> The fundamental difference between normal mourning on the one hand, and abnormal mourning and manic-depressive states, on the other, is this: the manic-depressive and the person who fails in the work of mourning, though their defences may differ widely from each other, have this in common, that they have been unable in early childhood to establish their internal 'good' objects and to feel secure in their inner world. They have never really overcome the infantile depressive position. In normal mourning, however, the early depressive position, which had become revived through the loss of the loved object, becomes modified again, and is overcome by methods similar to those used by the ego in childhood. The individual is reinstating his actually lost loved object; but he is also at the same time re-establishing inside himself his first loved objects – ultimately the 'good' parents – whom, when the actual loss occurred, he felt in danger of losing as well. It is by reinstating inside himself the 'good' parents as well as the recently lost person, and by rebuilding his inner world, which was disintegrated and in danger, that he overcomes his grief, regains security, and achieves true harmony and peace.
>
> (p. 369)

Klein has thus set out to make clear her view that the roots of manic-depressive illness lie in failures of early development, a particularly striking example of the way in which her work with young children shaped her approach to the analysis of adults and to fundamental psychoanalytic theory. This feature of her work is also very present in the topic that she next tackled.

In her paper of 1945, Klein sets out to link the theory of the depressive position with the central psychoanalytic idea of the Oedipus complex. She also states much more clearly at this point in her writings the ways in which her clinical discoveries led her to revise Freud's view of Oedipal phenomena, just as she had revised aspects of his theory of mourning. She gave a title to this paper – 'The Oedipus complex in the light of early anxieties' – which makes it plain that she thinks that the new knowledge of the anxieties of the depressive position entails some rethinking. The most important change hinges on the much greater emphasis she now places on the power of loving feelings to propel the child's sexual development. Klein gives an account of the analysis of two children to lay the basis for her revised views: Richard, to be the subject of the later *Narrative of a Child Analysis*, and Rita, discussed in an earlier chapter in *The Psycho-Analysis of Children*. Both these children suffered from severe states of anxiety.

In the case history of Richard, she concentrates on material aroused by her absence on a brief visit to London. This event conjoined his loss of some sessions and his great anxiety about her well-being since London was under air-raid attack. Here is her account of his distressed state when the analysis resumed:

> On my return I found Richard very worried and depressed. During the whole first hour he hardly looked at me, and alternated between sitting rigidly on his chair without lifting his eyes and wandering out restlessly into the adjoining kitchen and into the garden. In spite of his marked resistance he did, however, put a few questions to me: Had I seen much of 'battered' London? Had there been an air-raid while I was there? Had there been a thunderstorm in London?
>
> One of the first things he told me was that he hated returning to the town where the analysis took place, and called the town a 'pigsty' and a 'nightmare'. He soon went out into the garden, where he seemed more free to look round. He caught sight of some toadstools which he showed to me, shuddering and saying they were poisonous. Back in the room, he picked up a book from the shelf and particularly pointed out to me a picture of a little man fighting against an 'awful monster'.
>
> On the second day after my return Richard told me with great resistance about a conversation he had had with his mother while I was away. He had told his mother that he was very worried about his having babies later on and had asked her whether it would hurt very much. In reply she had, not for the first time, explained the part played by the man in reproduction, whereupon he had said he would not like to put his genital into somebody else's genital: that would frighten him, and the whole thing was a great worry to him.
>
> ('The Oedipus complex in the light of early anxieties', 1945; p. 374)

Klein links Richard's aggressive feelings and phantasies towards his parents' sexual relationship to his tremendous fears but goes on to refer to the inner struggle this hostility provoked because of his deep affection for his mother, and indeed for herself in the transference. How could he deal with this? She suggests that regression to oral rather than genital preoccupations is one way out, though it has only limited success.

Richard's anxiety about his aggression, and particularly about his oral-sadistic tendencies, was very great and led to a sharp struggle in him against his aggression. This struggle could at times be plainly seen. It is significant that in moments of anger he ground his teeth and moved his jaws as if he were biting. Owing to the strength of his oral-sadistic impulses he felt in great danger of harming his mother. He often asked, even after quite harmless remarks to his mother or to myself: 'Have I hurt your feelings?' The fear and guilt relating to his destructive phantasies moulded his whole emotional life. In order to retain his love for his mother, he again and again attempted to restrain his jealousy and grievances, denying even obvious causes for them.

However, Richard's attempts to restrain his hatred and aggressiveness and to deny his grievances were not successful. The repressed anger about frustrations in the past and present came out clearly in the transference situation – for instance, in his response to the frustration imposed on him by the interruption of the analysis. We know that by going to London I had become in his mind an injured object. I was not, however, injured only through being exposed to the danger of bombs, but also because by frustrating him I had aroused his hatred; in consequence he felt unconsciously that he had attacked me. In repetition of earlier situations of frustration, he had become – in his phantasied attacks on me – identified with the bombing and dangerous Hitler-father, and he feared retaliation. I therefore turned into a hostile and revengeful figure.

The early splitting of the mother figure into a good and bad 'breast mother' as a way of dealing with ambivalence had been very marked in Richard. This division developed further into a division between the 'breast mother' who was 'good' and the 'genital mother' who was 'bad'. At this stage of the analysis, his actual mother stood for the 'good breast mother', while I had become the 'bad genital mother', and I therefore aroused in him the aggression and fears connected with that figure. I had become the mother who is injured by the father in sexual intercourse, or is united with the 'bad' Hitler-father . . .

. . . While I was in London, Richard was more than ever inseparable from his mother. As he put it to me, he was 'Mum's chick' and 'chicks do run after their Mums'. This flight to the breast mother, as a defence against anxiety about the genital mother, was not successful. For Richard added: 'But then chicks have to do without them, because the hens don't look after them any more and don't care for them.'

(pp. 376–377)

Richard's subsequent play with his fleet of battleships then allowed Klein to see a different defence taking shape as Richard revealed his reparative wishes. After a collision between the ships that represented himself and mother, Richard reordered the ships, placing the mother and father ships together and the others, representing the other members of the family, 'in order of age'.

Here the fleet game was expressing his wish to restore harmony and peace in the family, by allowing his parents to come together and by giving way to his father's and brother's authority. This implied the need to restrain jealousy and hatred, for only then,

(continued)

> *(continued)*
>
> he felt, could he avoid the fight with his father for the possession of his mother. In that way he warded off his castration fear and moreover preserved the good father and the good brother. Above all, he also saved his mother from being injured in the fight between his father and himself.
>
> Thus Richard was not only dominated by the need to defend himself against the fear of being attacked by his rivals, his father and brother, but also by concern for his good objects. Feelings of love and the urge to repair damage done in phantasy – damage which would be repeated if he gave way to his hatred and jealousy – came out in greater strength.
>
> Peace and harmony in the family, however, could only be achieved, jealousy and hatred could only be restrained, and the loved objects could only be preserved if Richard repressed his Oedipus wishes. The repression of his Oedipus wishes implied a partial regression to babyhood, but this regression was bound up with the *idealization* of the mother-and-baby relationship. For he wished to turn himself into an infant free from aggression, and in particular free from oral-sadistic impulses. The idealization of the baby presupposed a corresponding idealization of the mother, in the first place of her breasts: an ideal breast which never frustrates, a mother and child in a purely loving relation to each other. The bad breast, the bad mother, was kept widely apart in his mind from the ideal mother.
>
> (p. 378)

She summarises the effect of the depressive anxieties on his development in this way:

> These fears contributed again and again to his flight to the 'breast' mother. He could achieve relative stability only on a predominantly pre-genital level. The forward movement of the libido was impeded, because anxiety and guilt were too great and the ego was unable to evolve adequate defences. Thus the genital organization could not be sufficiently stabilized, which implied a strong tendency to regression. The interplay between the phenomena of fixation and regression could be seen at every step of his development.
>
> (p. 380)

Working through this regressive trend allowed Richard's anxiety to be modified by Klein's interpretations, and his hopefulness and a more normal level of Oedipal competition to emerge.

> In playing with the fleet, Richard allocated one ship to me and one to himself; I was going on a pleasure trip in my ship and so was he in his. At first he moved his ship away, but soon brought it round and put it quite close to mine. This touching of ships had in former material – particularly in relation to his parents – repeatedly symbolized sexual intercourse. In this play, therefore, Richard was expressing his genital desires as well as his hope for potency . . .

> . . . Because of this hope of restoring and reviving his good object, which implied his belief that he could cope more successfully with his aggression, Richard was able to experience his genital desires more strongly. Also, since his anxiety was lessened, he could turn his aggression outwards and take up in phantasy the fight with his father and brother for the possession of his mother.
>
> (pp. 381–382)

In his next drawing Richard stated that he was not one of the babies. He now saw himself instead as a boy who could become a potent man and his aggression as creative rather than destructive. In a further session, Richard's drawings came to represent more of the internal situation, and the relationship to his internal family to be now similarly under the sway of his friendly feelings.

> When Richard had become able during his analysis to face the psychological fact that his loved object was also his hated object and that the light-blue mother, the queen with the crown, was linked in his mind with the horrid bird with the beak, he could establish his love for his mother more securely. His feelings of love had become more closely linked with his feelings of hatred, and his happy experiences with his mother were no longer kept so widely apart from his experiences of frustration. He was therefore no longer driven on the one hand to idealize the good mother so strongly and on the other hand to form such a terrifying picture of the bad mother. Whenever he could allow himself to bring the two aspects of the mother together, this implied that the bad aspect was mitigated by the good one. This more secure good mother could then protect him against the 'monster' father. This again implied that at such times she was not felt to be so fatally injured by his oral greed and by the bad father, which in turn meant that he felt that both he and his father had become less dangerous. The good mother could come to life once more, and Richard's depression therefore lifted.
>
> (p. 396)

In her discussion of 2½-year-old Rita, Klein again highlights that the highly conflictual relationship to her mother was not only a consequence of persecutory fears, but also of depressive anxiety. Rita's states of sadness and constant questions about whether she was loved were poignant indications of her near despair about being lovable and being able to love in turn.

> In one aspect her mother represented a terrifying and retaliating figure. In another aspect she was Rita's indispensable loved and good object, and Rita felt her own aggression as a danger to this loved mother. She was therefore overwhelmed by the fear of losing her. It was the strength of these early anxieties and feelings of guilt which largely determined Rita's incapacity to tolerate the additional anxiety and guilt arising from the Oedipus feelings – rivalry and hatred against her mother. In defence she repressed her hatred and over-compensated for it by excessive love, and this necessarily implied a regression to earlier stages of the libido.
>
> (p. 400)

Klein notes the particular anxiety that hatred of mother brings in its train for the girl child:

> Rita's depressive anxieties about the death of her mother were bound up with persecutory fears relating to attacks on her own body by a retaliating mother. In fact such attacks always appear to a girl not only as a danger to her body, but as a danger to everything precious which in her mind her 'inside' contains: her potential children, the good mother and the good father.
>
> The incapacity to protect these loved objects against external and internal persecutors is part of the most fundamental anxiety situation of girls . . .
>
> . . . Rita could not allow herself the wish for a child from her father, and the identification with her mother in the Oedipus situation could not be established, until her anxieties and guilt in relation to both parents had lessened.
>
> (pp. 405–406)

The two cases thus explore the consequences of the conflict between love and hate for the differential sexual development of boy and girl. Klein gives this clear summary.

After restating her understanding of the shared experience of gratification and frustration of boy and girl baby in the feeding relationship with mother, and the way their disappointment in finding out about the non-ideal mother leads both towards an interest in father, she points out:

> Owing to the dominance of anxiety and guilt there is an over-strong fixation to the early stages of libidinal organization and, in interaction with this, an excessive tendency to regress to those early stages. In consequence, the Oedipus development is interfered with and the genital organization cannot be securely established. In the two cases referred to in this paper, as well as in others, the Oedipus complex began to develop on normal lines when these early anxieties were diminished . . .
>
> . . . My experience has led me to believe that, from the very beginning of life, libido is fused with aggressiveness, and that the development of the libido is at every stage vitally affected by anxiety derived from aggressiveness. Anxiety, guilt and depressive feelings at times drive the libido forward to new sources of gratification, at times they check the development of the libido by reinforcing the fixation to an earlier object and aim.
>
> (p. 407)

This is then elaborated with respect to the different position of the sexes and linked to the problem of aggression, guilt and the depressive position:

> This movement to and fro between the various aspects of the primary imagos implies a close interaction between the early stages of the inverted and positive Oedipus complex . . .

. . . Early genital desires, as well as oral ones, are directed towards mother and father. This is in line with my assumption that in both sexes there is an inherent unconscious knowledge of the existence of the penis as well as of the vagina. In the male infant, genital sensations are the basis for the expectation that his father possesses a penis which the boy desires according to the equation 'breast = penis'. At the same time, his genital sensations and impulses also imply the search for an opening into which to insert his penis, i.e. they are directed towards his mother. The infant girl's genital sensations correspondingly prepare the desire to receive her father's penis into her vagina . . .

. . . The course of libidinal development is thus at every step stimulated and reinforced by the drive for reparation, and ultimately by the sense of guilt. On the other hand, guilt which engenders the drive for reparation also inhibits libidinal desires. For when the child feels that his aggressiveness predominates, libidinal desires appear to him as a danger to his loved objects and must therefore be repressed.

(pp. 409–410)

She suggests that, while the deepest anxieties of the boy focus on fears of castration, the girl's are directed towards her future fertility, the well-being of her internal reproductive organs and the fate of her imagined babies. Referring to bisexuality she draws attention to the element of what is missing for each gender:

The girl's desire to possess a penis and to be a boy is an expression of her bisexuality and is as inherent a feature in girls as the desire to be a woman is in boys.

(p. 414)

In the bold final section of the paper Klein brings together the revisions to classical theory she is making, particularly her views on the early phases of the Oedipus complex, the early development of the superego and the importance of love and reparative impulses.

I shall now summarize my own views on these essential issues. As I see it, the boy's and girl's sexual and emotional development from *early infancy onwards* includes genital sensations and trends, which constitute the first stages of the inverted and positive Oedipus complex; they are experienced under the primacy of oral libido and mingle with urethral and anal desires and phantasies. The libidinal stages overlap from the earliest months of life onwards. The positive and inverted Oedipus tendencies are from their inception in close interaction. It is during the stage of genital primacy that the positive Oedipus situation reaches its climax.

In my view, infants of both sexes experience genital desires directed towards their mother and father, and they have an unconscious knowledge of the vagina as well as

(continued)

(continued)

of the penis. For these reasons Freud's earlier term 'genital phase' seems to me more adequate than his later concept of the 'phallic phase'.

The super-ego in both sexes comes into being during the oral phase. Under the sway of phantasy life and of conflicting emotions, the child at every stage of libidinal organization introjects his objects – primarily his parents – and builds up the super-ego from these elements.

Thus, though the super-ego corresponds in many ways to the actual people in the young child's world, it has various components and features which reflect the phantastic images in his mind. All the factors which have a bearing on his object relations play a part from the beginning in the building-up of the super-ego.

The first introjected object, the mother's breast, forms the basis of the super-ego. Just as the relation to the mother's breast precedes and strongly influences the relation to the father's penis, so the relation to the introjected mother affects in many ways the whole course of super-ego development. Some of the most important features of the super-ego, whether loving and protective or destructive and devouring, are derived from the early maternal components of the super-ego.

The earliest feelings of guilt in both sexes derive from the oral-sadistic desires to devour the mother, and primarily her breasts (Abraham). It is therefore in infancy that feelings of guilt arise. Guilt does not emerge when the Oedipus complex comes to an end, but is rather one of the factors which from the beginning mould its course and affect its outcome . . .

. . . Freud, as we know, arrived at the theoretical conclusion that the father, as well as the mother, is an object of the son's libidinal desires. (Cf. his concept of the inverted Oedipus complex.) Moreover, Freud in some of his writings (among his case histories particularly in the 'Analysis of a Phobia in a Five-Year-Old Boy', 1909) has taken account of the part which love for his father plays in the boy's positive Oedipus conflict. He has, however, not given enough weight to the crucial role of these feelings of love, both in the development of the Oedipus conflict and in its passing. In my experience the Oedipus situation loses in power not only because the boy is afraid of the destruction of his genital by a revengeful father, but also because he is driven by feelings of love and guilt to preserve his father as an internal and external figure . . .

. . . Penis envy and the castration complex play an essential part in the girl's development. But they are very much reinforced by frustration of her positive Oedipus desires. Though the little girl at one stage assumes that her mother possesses a penis as a male attribute, this concept does not play nearly as important a part in her development as Freud suggests. The unconscious theory that her mother contains the admired and desired penis of the father underlies, in my experience, many of the phenomena which Freud described as the relation of the girl to the phallic mother.

The girl's oral desires for her father's penis mingle with her first genital desires to receive that penis. These genital desires imply the wish to receive children from her

> father, which is also borne out by the equation 'penis = child'. The feminine desire to internalize the penis and to receive a child from her father invariably precedes the wish to possess a penis of her own.
>
> While I agree with Freud about the prominence of the fear of loss of love and of the death of the mother among the girl's anxieties, I hold that the fear of having her body attacked and her loved inner objects destroyed essentially contributes to her main anxiety situation.
>
> (pp. 416–419)

As was pointed out in the notes to the 1975 edition of Klein's work, she was much more direct in this paper in stating the areas of difference between her developmental theory and Freud's. The account given is in essence the same as in her 1928 paper ('Early stages of the Oedipus conflict'), though the extensive clinical examples at the start of the paper introduce the material in a quite different way – perhaps a recognition through her experience of how important the presentation of clinical evidence had been in the discussions in the British Psychoanalytical Society ('The Controversial Discussions') in influencing the outcome of those debates. The clinical grounding of the ideas Klein and her co-workers put forward in those meetings impressed many of the independent-minded among the membership. The painful process of realising how much she was seen as non-Freudian by her opponents may have contributed to being able to clarify more openly the important differences there were between Freud's original formulations and the views which she now held, however loyal she might be in acknowledging the roots of psychoanalysis.

The radical departure from a theory of psychological development rooted in physiological drives is now evident. For Klein the motivational forces at work are the emotions of love and hate which the infant experiences from the start of life in his relationship with others, beginning with the absolute dependence on mother and expanding outwards from that core. The discovery of the constellation of anxieties which she gathered into her concept of the depressive position was what enabled her to describe with clarity the central conflict of love and hate and the guilt which this conflict entailed. This, she showed, is what determines the nature of the child's internal world, the evolution of his character and his relationship to other people.

Klein's linking of the Oedipus complex, as described by Freud and later revised by her, with her new concept of the depressive position is quite central to her clinical thinking, but the two frameworks nonetheless did not prove easy to integrate for her successors. The Oedipus complex of Freud's 'Three essays' (1905) and case histories has a very different atmosphere from Klein's writing about depressive anxieties and the defences they give rise to. Clinicians found this puzzling and could find themselves moving between two kinds of theory rather than grasping their interrelationship.

A significant collection of papers by contemporary Kleinian analysts published as a book, *The Oedipus Complex Today* (Steiner, 1989), addressed current understandings of the Oedipus complex, drawing on clinical experience and demonstrating the ongoing theoretical development of Klein's model. The background of Bion's ideas is also clearly present throughout. Britton's paper, 'The missing link: parental sexuality in the Oedipus complex' (1989), was extremely helpful in spelling out a way in which these paradigms could be brought together. He argued that being able to relate to reality is grounded in recognition of the relationship between parents. Oedipal illusions defend the self against this recognition but unfortunately prevent working through the rivalry with each parent and the closing of what Britton terms the Oedipal triangle. The triangle implies the capacity to observe and to be observed, to be a witness of the link between mother and father and to achieve objectivity through the awareness of being seen by others. This is also the precondition for a sense of mental space, required for thinking to develop. If parental intercourse is seen in a destructive light the mind's development is greatly compromised. Britton suggests that early maternal containment is a precondition for successful working through of the early Oedipal complex. Too early (too early for the child's mental capacities) awareness of parental intercourse can be catastrophic. It threatens the child's still vulnerable link to mother, thus evoking fears of survival and psychotic levels of anxiety. Oedipal illusions belong to a later development when mourning the loss of the exclusive infantile link to mother is possible, however painful. In her introduction to the book, Hanna Segal points out that the triangular space also refers to the space for an imagined new baby in the family (Steiner, 1989).

Feldman's paper, 'The Oedipus complex: manifestations in the inner world and the therapeutic situation' (1989), explores the implications of Oedipal struggles for the development of thought. Being able to conceive of a creative parental couple fosters the growth of thinking, while a destructive image of parental intercourse is associated with damaged or inhibited thinking. He therefore suggests that the nature of the Oedipal couple in phantasy affects not only the potential for thinking, but also the quality of thought. The difficult Kleinian concept of the combined object is elucidated in clinical examples which differentiate problems which can arise from the painful confrontation with a creative parental couple – a couple combined in a way which allows for their being together and also apart – and the quite different situation when the couple are experienced as combined but impenetrable, that is, refusing any awareness of the excluded other. Feldman also discusses the fact that projections of the model of the couple in the mind go in both directions, from child to internal parents, but also from the parents' internal parental imagos into the child.

O'Shaughnessy's (1989) paper explores the 'invisible' Oedipus complex, that is, the clinical situation where no triangular structures seem to be in place. She suggests this invisibility masks an absolutely unbearable situation – the invisibility is an outcome of an unmanageable experience in which feelings of exclusion, of being 'cast out', are dominant. Singleness and separateness are rendered unbearable as a consequence of what she calls fracturing of objects (a particular form of very early splitting) and the unavailability of any good internal object to which the child can turn when confronted by a couple.

These papers are quoted here not only because they are such significant examples of the ongoing development of theory and clinical practice which Klein's 1945 paper ushered in, but also because they contribute so helpfully to understanding the conceptual integration this paper represents.

Chapter 6

Splitting, the paranoid-schizoid position and the concept of projective identification

In 1946, Klein returned to a consideration of the very first stages of mental development which she had studied in her analysis of the many young children she wrote about in her early papers. The working out of her view of the constellation of anxieties and defences which she had named the depressive position stimulated a re-theorisation of the very early infantile mental processes which preceded the more integrated emotional states she placed broadly in the second half of the first year of life. The more paranoid and schizoid anxieties of the beginning of life she now gathered in a unified concept of a paranoid-schizoid position. This more fully delineated range of psychic phenomena also made possible powerful links to severe forms of mental illness in adults, in the same way that the theory of the depressive position had illuminated manic-depressive and obsessional states. The roots of psychotic disorder, she suggested, are to be found in those anxieties and defences which are normal in early infancy but can become a source of major illness if development stalls.

Klein's account of early ego development foregrounds a number of features, including her view that the baby's experience is characterised by lack of cohesion, a 'tendency towards integration [alternating with a tendency towards disintegration]'. She agrees with Winnicott in emphasising this initial state of unintegration, and her colleague Esther Bick (1964, 1968) later developed an account of the importance of the infant's fear of falling to pieces and described the defences mobilised against this very early anxiety. Klein's own central thesis concerns the ego's function in dealing with anxiety and she describes the processes of splitting, projection and introjection as follows:

> We are, I think, justified in assuming that some of the functions which we know from the later ego are there at the beginning. Prominent amongst these functions is that of dealing with anxiety. I hold that anxiety arises from the operation of the death instinct within the organism, is felt as fear of annihilation (death) and takes the form of fear of persecution. The fear of the destructive impulse seems to attach itself at once to an object – or rather it is experienced as the fear of an uncontrollable overpowering object. Other important sources of primary anxiety are the trauma of birth (separation anxiety) and frustration of bodily needs; and these experiences too are from the beginning felt as being caused by objects. Even if these objects are felt to be external, they become through introjection internal persecutors and thus reinforce the fear of the destructive impulse within.
>
> *(continued)*

(continued)

The vital need to deal with anxiety forces the early ego to develop fundamental mechanisms and defences. The destructive impulse is partly projected outwards (deflection of the death instinct) and, I think, attaches itself to the first external object, the mother's breast . . .

. . . In states of frustration and anxiety the oral sadistic and cannibalistic desires are reinforced, and then the infant feels that he has taken in the nipple and the breast *in bits*. Therefore in addition to the divorce between a good and a bad breast in the young infant's phantasy, the frustrating breast – attacked in oral-sadistic phantasies – is felt to be in fragments; the gratifying breast, taken in under the dominance of the sucking libido, is felt to be complete. This first internal good object acts as a focal point in the ego. It counteracts the processes of splitting and dispersal, makes for cohesiveness and integration, and is instrumental in building up the ego. The infant's feeling of having inside a good and complete breast may, however, be shaken by frustration and anxiety. As a result, the divorce between the good and bad breast may be difficult to maintain, and the infant may feel that the good breast too is in pieces . . .

. . . It is in phantasy that the infant splits the object and the self, but the effect of this phantasy is a very real one, because it leads to feelings and relations (and later on, thought-processes) being in fact cut off from one another . . .

. . . Introjection and projection are from the beginning of life also used in the service of this primary aim of the ego. Projection, as Freud described, originates from the deflection of the death instinct outwards and in my view it helps the ego to overcome anxiety by ridding it of danger and badness. Introjection of the good object is also used by the ego as a defence against anxiety.

('Notes on some schizoid mechanisms', 1946; pp. 4–6)

In this account, Klein links the infant's earliest anxiety, which is the fear of dying in the absence of the sustaining good object, with the existence of a death instinct alongside the instinct for life. Debate about the meaningfulness and clinical value of the conception of a death instinct remains a live issue in psychoanalysis, but for Klein the integration of Freud's instinct theory with her emphasis on early object relationships was vital. She wished to affirm that her understanding of early projective processes was an elaboration of Freud's view of the instinctive basis of the human mind. What is, however, new and distinctive is the place she accords to the infant's initial awareness of an object, mother's breast, into which the terrifying forces which arise from the death instinct can be projected. Alongside this expulsion of dangers to the self's survival is the taking in of all the good nurturing aspects of maternal care through which the baby feels a sense of peace and safety. Also enormously important in consequence of the absolute dependence on the external object is separation anxiety. Klein mentions this here with reference to the separation from mother's body at birth, the transition from being inside to living outside. Her concept of projective identification, to be discussed later in this chapter, was closely linked to the distinction between inside and outside, the awareness of separateness of self and object, since this concept describes an unconscious phantasy in which this separateness is obliterated, and aspects of the self are projected into mother.

Attention to the anxieties evoked by separation has, of course, also played a central role in the development of attachment theory (Bowlby, 1969, 1973, 1980) and the extensive contemporary awareness of varieties of attachment (e.g. Main, 1995; Fonagy, 2001) which track with formal research methods some of the subtleties of the psychoanalytic understanding of the early mother–child relationship (Fonagy and Target, 2003; Mayes *et al.*, 2007).

What follows from the urgent need to project the threat to survival is the necessity to keep apart the bad object, which now contains what is feared, from the good object, on which the baby depends. Here Klein elucidates her understanding of the early defence of splitting, that is, sharply dividing good and bad. She suggests that in order to maintain the splitting of the object the infant resorts to idealisation of the good object (breast) as a protection against the feared persecution from the bad object (breast). Klein goes on to show how the splitting of this first object also involves a split in the ego, and describes the omnipotent nature of this splitting process, which she sees as the central early defensive mechanism, analogous to the role which repression plays at a later stage of development. The omnipotent aspect of this account of mental functioning underlines the fact that we are in the realm of phantasy, needed by an immature ego not yet equipped to face the demands of reality, which include an awareness of dependence and the anxieties consequent on such knowledge. In omnipotent thinking, the mind can invent its own version of how things are.

> The frustrating and persecuting object is kept widely apart from the idealized object. However, the bad object is not only kept apart from the good one but its very existence is denied, as is the whole situation of frustration and the bad feelings (pain) to which frustration gives rise. This is bound up with denial of psychic reality. The denial of psychic reality becomes possible only through strong feelings of omnipotence – an essential characteristic of early mentality. Omnipotent denial of the existence of the bad object and of the painful situation is in the unconscious equal to annihilation by the destructive impulse. It is, however, not only a situation and an object that are denied and annihilated – it is *an object relation* which suffers this fate; and therefore a part of the ego, from which the feelings towards the object emanate, is denied and annihilated as well.
>
> In hallucinatory gratification, therefore, two interrelated processes take place: the omnipotent conjuring up of the ideal object and situation, and the equally omnipotent annihilation of the bad persecutory object and the painful situation. These processes are based on splitting both the object and the ego.
>
> In passing I would mention that in this early phase splitting, denial and omnipotence play a rôle similar to that of repression at a later stage of ego-development.
>
> (p. 7)

Restating her early account of the infant's oral, urethral and anal attacks in phantasy which express the infant's efforts to take possession of the desired good aspects of mother, and to get rid of the bad aspects of the self by expelling them into mother, Klein goes on to define her new concept of projective identification. She initially links this with the infant's hostile projections, but then adds that a similar process takes place with respect to the projection of loving feelings. Her contention is that these early concrete projective processes are an absolutely necessary and normal aspect of normal babyhood, and enable us to understand this first object relationship, from which developments can then proceed. A risk to mental health arises, however, if these projections are 'excessive'. The bodily concreteness of the phantasy is underlined by Klein's suggestion that the projection takes place into mother. This is the background to her detailed account of the infant's phantasies about the interior of mother's body, based on the baby's own bodily experiences and accompanying phantasies about bodily processes. After describing the infant's greedy oral assault, she continues thus:

> The other line of attack derives from the anal and urethral impulses and implies expelling dangerous substances (excrements) out of the self and into the mother. Together with these harmful excrements, expelled in hatred, split-off parts of the ego are also projected on to the mother or, as I would rather call it, *into* the mother. These excrements and bad parts of the self are meant not only to injure but also to control it and to take possession of the object. In so far as the mother comes to contain the bad parts of the self, she is not felt to be a separate individual but is felt to be *the* bad self.
>
> Much of the hatred against parts of the self is now directed towards the mother. This leads to a particular kind of identification which establishes the prototype of an aggressive object-relation. I suggest for these processes the term 'projective identification'. When projection is mainly derived from the infant's impulse to harm or to control the mother, he feels her to be a persecutor. In psychotic disorders this identification of an object with the hated parts of the self contributes to the intensity of the hatred directed against other people. As far as the ego is concerned the excessive splitting off and expelling into the outer world of parts of itself considerably weaken it. For the aggressive component of feelings and of the personality is intimately bound up in the mind with power, potency, strength, knowledge and many other desired qualities.
>
> It is, however, not only the bad parts of the self which are expelled and projected, but also good parts of the self. Excrements then have the significance of gifts; and parts of the ego which, together with excrements, are expelled and projected into the other person represent the good, i.e. the loving parts of the self. The identification based on this type of projection again vitally influences object-relations. The projection of good feelings and good parts of the self into the mother is essential for the infant's ability to develop good object-relations and to integrate his ego. However, if this projective process is carried out excessively, good parts of the personality are felt to be lost, and in this way the mother becomes the ego-ideal; this process too results in weakening and impoverishing the ego. Very soon such processes extend to other people, and the result may be an over-strong dependence on these external representatives of one's own good parts. Another consequence is a fear that the capacity to love has been lost because the loved object is felt to be loved predominantly as a representative of the self.
>
> The processes of splitting off parts of the self and projecting them into objects are thus of vital importance for normal development as well as for abnormal object-relations.
>
> (pp. 8–9)

A parallel account is given of introjective processes with the same point being emphasised, namely that while the introjection of a good object provides the core of the developing ego, too great a dependence on taking in goodness from outside is a danger to the vitality of the developing ego. The potential for complex confusion between self and object is what Klein's theory throws light on. Confusional states become more capable of being understood once the concept of projective identification is taken into account.

It is important to bear in mind that Klein's account of the various forms of disturbance linked to excessive splitting and projective identification (depersonalisation, schizophrenic disintegration, excessive withdrawal, paranoia, claustrophobia, some forms of failure of development) contrasts these with the normal course of events. It is interesting to note that the contemporary emphasis on 'resilience' and 'emotional regulation' as prime achievements in a child's development is already present in Klein's picture of the normal evolution of the mind.

> In normal development, the states of disintegration which the infant experiences are transitory. Among other factors, gratification by the external good object again and again helps to break through these schizoid states. The infant's capacity to overcome temporary schizoid states is in keeping with the strong elasticity and resilience of the infantile mind. If states of splitting and therefore of disintegration, which the ego is unable to overcome, occur too frequently and go on for too long, then in my view they must be regarded as a sign of schizophrenic illness in the infant, and some indications of such illness may already be seen in the first few months of life. In adult patients, states of depersonalization and of schizophrenic dissociation seem to be a regression to these infantile states of disintegration.
>
> (p. 10)

What follows from the recognition that projective identification involves the splitting of the self and the loss of parts of the self now felt to reside within and be part of the object, is that object relations are narcissistic in character. This is a difficult idea to grasp. It involves the recognition that some relationships with other people are fundamentally shaped not by any recognition of difference and separateness but by projective processes which impede the awareness of otherness. Klein demonstrates how this narcissistic form of object relations leads to a perception of objects as not only sources of danger which the self tries to deal with by controlling behaviour, but also as bearing the guilt for the aggression they now contain. One is reminded here of the toddler's angry complaint against furniture on which he has hurt himself, that it is the table's fault. This has its equivalent in the fury that adults are prone to direct at their computers or other equipment when they experience them as malfunctioning.

It is also worth noting here that Klein's account of early infant development anticipates contemporary views of the crucial importance of early intervention when there is disturbance in the infant–mother relationship. As she writes, the risk is that states of disintegration in the infant which signal an incapacity to regulate emotion become a disabling and pivotal feature of the mind. Without help, such an infant is indeed left to cope with anxieties overwhelming to his mental capacity. This situation may arise as a consequence of particularly high levels of anxiety in the baby (Klein thinks of these as sometimes having a constitutional basis) or difficulties on the mother's side in being able to respond to her baby helpfully, or of course some combination of the two. It is not difficult to amplify these points when we bear in mind the range of experiences during pregnancy and at birth for mother and baby, and the crucial impact of the level of support for the mother–baby couple in the early months. Here, however,

Klein is focusing attention on the ways in which infant's and mother's anxieties intersect, and the particular problem that arises when the baby's anxiety and hostile feelings are strong.

The breadth of the impact on relationships which are dominated by projective identification is enormous. Klein illustrates this with further discussion of separation anxiety:

> The projection of split-off parts of the self into another person essentially influences object-relations, emotional life and the personality as a whole. To illustrate this contention I will select as an instance two universal phenomena which are interlinked: the feeling of loneliness and fear of parting. We know that one source of the depressive feelings accompanying parting from people can be found in the fear of the destruction of the object by the aggressive impulses directed against it. But it is more specifically the splitting and projective processes which underlie this fear. If aggressive elements in relation to the object are predominant and strongly aroused by the frustration of parting, the individual feels that the split-off components of his self, projected into the object, control this object in an aggressive and destructive way. At the same time the internal object is felt to be in the same danger of destruction as the external one in whom one part of the self is felt to be left. The result is an excessive weakening of the ego, a feeling that there is nothing to sustain it, and a corresponding feeling of loneliness. While this description applies to neurotic individuals, I think that in some degree it is a general phenomenon.
>
> (pp. 13–14)

We can see here an instance of the close connection Klein believed is always present between the observable relationships of the individual and others in his world and the structure of his internal world. This, of course, is what makes her belief in the possibility of change through psychoanalytic treatment: if the analysis can influence the shape of internal object relationships, the individual's capacity for relating to others will be open to change and development.

In the later part of the paper Klein considers the interrelationships of the paranoid-schizoid and depressive positions. She summarises her overall view in this way:

> During the second half of the first year the infant makes some fundamental steps towards working through the depressive position. However, schizoid mechanisms still remain in force, though in a modified form and to a lesser degree, and early anxiety-situations are again and again experienced in the process of modification. The working through of the persecutory and depressive positions extends over the first few years of childhood and plays an essential part in the infantile neurosis. In the course of this process, anxieties lose in strength; objects become both less idealized and less terrifying, and the ego becomes more unified. All this is interconnected with the growing perception of reality and adaptation to it.
>
> If development during the paranoid-schizoid position has not proceeded normally and the infant cannot – for internal or external reasons – cope with the impact of depressive anxieties a vicious circle arises. For if persecutory fear, and correspondingly schizoid mechanisms, are too strong, the ego is not capable of working through the depressive position. This forces the ego to regress to the paranoid-schizoid position and reinforces

the earlier persecutory fears and schizoid phenomena. Thus the basis is established for various forms of schizophrenia in later life; for when such a regression occurs, not only are the fixation-points in the schizoid position reinforced, but there is a danger of greater states of disintegration setting in. Another outcome may be the strengthening of depressive features . . .

. . . Some fluctuations between the paranoid-schizoid and the depressive positions always occur and are part of normal development. No clear division between the two stages of development can therefore be drawn; moreover, modification is a gradual process and the phenomena of the two positions remain for some time to some extent intermingled and interacting.

(pp. 15–16)

The idea of two such fundamental structures of mind has come to be seen by later Kleinian thinkers as having immense explanatory power in understanding the individual's on-going struggles for integration, and the mind's response to the challenges of new experience. Bion conceived this as a continuum in which oscillation between a more paranoid-schizoid and more depressive relationship to the world was the normal human condition. Klein's account at times is more suggestive of a temporal sequence in which depressive anxieties replace the paranoid-schizoid fears of early infancy, though the clinical examples she offers in this paper and elsewhere make it abundantly clear that in analytic work the dynamic to and fro was what she encountered. In writing about a patient who was expressing detachment from feeling, speaking in a deadened voice after she had spoken to him about his hostile attitude to her, which had been conveyed very forcefully, she was struck by the powerful changes in his mood as the sources of his anxiety became clearer. Recovering from his temporary annihilation of feeling, he spoke of feeling upset, but also hungry. Klein comments on this sequence as follows:

The feeling of hunger indicated that the process of introjection had been set going again under the dominance of the libido. While to my first interpretation of his fear of destroying me by his aggression he had responded at once with the violent splitting off and annihilation of parts of his personality, he now experienced more fully the emotions of grief, guilt and fear of loss, as well as some relief of these depressive anxieties. The relief of anxiety resulted in the analyst again coming to stand for a good object which he could trust. Therefore the desire to introject me as a good object could come to the fore. If he could build up again the good breast inside himself, he would strengthen and integrate his ego, would be less afraid of his destructive impulses; in fact he could then preserve himself and the analyst.

(p. 20; footnote 1)

I have repeatedly found that advances in synthesis are brought about by interpretations of the specific causes for splitting. Such interpretations must deal in detail with the transference-situation at that moment, including of course the connection with the past, and must contain a reference to the details of the anxiety-situations which drive the

(continued)

> *(continued)*
>
> ego to regress to schizoid mechanisms. The synthesis resulting from interpretations on these lines goes along with depression and anxieties of various kinds. Gradually such waves of depression – followed by greater integration – lead to a lessening of schizoid phenomena and also to fundamental changes in object-relations.
>
> (p. 21)

This leads her to reflect on the apparent absence of anxiety and emotion which is so problematic a feature of schizoid patients. She suggests that powerful anxieties are nonetheless at the root of such mental states:

> This lack of anxiety in schizoid patients is only apparent. For the schizoid mechanisms imply a dispersal of emotions including anxiety, but these dispersed elements still exist in the patient. Such patients have a certain form of latent anxiety; it is kept latent by the particular method of dispersal. The feeling of being disintegrated, of being unable to experience emotions, of losing one's objects, is in fact the equivalent of anxiety. This becomes clearer when advance in synthesis has been made. The great relief which a patient then experiences derives from a feeling that his inner and outer worlds have not only come more together but back to life again. At such moments it appears in retrospect that when emotions were lacking, relations were vague and uncertain and parts of the personality were felt to be lost, everything seemed to be dead.
>
> (p. 21)

Klein always placed anxiety at the centre of her theory of mental development, anxiety about survival being what propels the infant into the first crucial relationship. The forms and nature of the dominant anxieties and the defences mobilised to protect the self become the core of the paranoid-schizoid and depressive positions she had now elaborated so clearly. The immediate recognisability of these constellations of emotion and form of relationship to self and others is surely what has rendered these concepts so fruitful in clinical psychoanalysis and indeed in some of the wider applications of psychoanalytic ideas beyond the consulting room.

In her paper 'On identification' (1955), Klein added further thoughts on projective identification and its relationship to the individual's struggle between the life and death instincts. These enrich the clinical significance of the concept. After reviewing her earlier depiction of projective processes in which in phantasy not only destructive and bad parts of the self are split off, but also good and loving parts, she restates that these projected aspects are ordinarily reintegrated in the course of development. What she is now concerned with is what happens to the individual's relationship to the world in consequence of the internalisation of a good relationship with the primary object. Klein suggests that integration 'which implies being alive, loving and being loved' grows under the auspices of the internal good object and that the chaos and disintegration arising from splitting by contrast represent its absence. She writes:

> I would suggest that a securely established good object, implying a securely established love for it, gives the ego a feeling of riches and abundance which allows for an outpouring of libido and projection of good parts of the self into the external world without a sense of depletion arising. The ego can then also feel that it is able to re-introject the love it has given out, as well as taking goodness from other sources, and thus be enriched by the whole process. In other words, in such cases there is a balance between giving out and taking in, between projection and introjection.
>
> Furthermore . . . the feeling of containing an unharmed nipple and breast—although coexisting with phantasies of a breast devoured and therefore in bits—has the effect that splitting and projecting are not *predominantly* related to fragmented parts of the personality but to more coherent parts of the self. This implies that the ego is not exposed to a fatal weakening by dispersal and for this reason is more capable of repeatedly undoing splitting and achieving integration and synthesis in its relation to objects.
>
> Conversely, the breast taken in with hatred, and therefore felt to be destructive, becomes the prototype of all bad internal objects, drives the ego to further splitting, and becomes the representative of the death instinct within.
>
> ('On identification', 1955; pp. 144–145)

In Klein's discussion of Julian Green's 1950 novel, *If I Were You*, she shows how the hero's massive and concrete projection of parts of himself into others depletes his vitality and knowledge of himself, and profoundly disturbs his capacity to relate to other people. She suggests that the end of the novel, in which the hero finally achieves a peaceful death, is a depiction of a process of re-integration. This follows a lifetime of failure to forgive parental objects for their failings and a painful and fruitless search for the recovery of contact with a good object. This, however, could only be achieved by a process of facing rather than evading fundamental early anxieties.

The concept of projective identification has also proved to have an immense potential for clinical and theoretical development. For example, in his theory of thinking Bion (1962a) elaborated the distinction implicit in Klein's own account between projective identification used for positive purposes, emphasising its function in mother–infant pre-verbal communication, and an aspect of the infant's necessary dependence, and other circumstances in which it is used to rid the self of unwanted emotion and to control the object in a hostile manner. The communicative potential of projective identification opened up fuller attention to the impact on the recipient of these projections. Are they to be given space within the mind, registered, pondered and given meaning, by mother for baby, or analyst for patient? If however there is no responsive mind available to the person who needs a place into which anxiety can be projected, transformation of unformed overwhelming anxiety ('nameless dread' in Bion's terms) into something meaningful and potentially nameable cannot take place.

This enlarged picture of the earliest object relationship is also linked to revised ideas about the countertransference. On the whole, Klein was suspicious of countertransference responses in the analyst, seeing them as likely to be evidence of the analyst's own concerns and not therefore relevant to understanding the patient. Heimann's rethinking countertransference phenomena (1950) as also including unconscious responsiveness in the analyst to the patient's communications received via projective identification, and experienced – through identification – as being part of the analyst's own mind was another development made possible as projective identification became a recognisable phenomenon in clinical practice. The 'here and now' aspect of the clinical technique referred to in the quotations from Klein given above, aspects which she felt to be so vital, could be more fully studied with the additional layers of understanding which Bion, Heimann and many others began to describe.

Projective identification, initially so puzzling a concept, has in fact spawned a huge literature, and has proved to be one that transcends many of the intense theoretical conflicts within psychoanalysis. While a good many of Klein's ideas have often provoked rejection, this concept has travelled exceptionally well and become a central part of much contemporary psychoanalytic theory. A recent edited volume, *Projective Identification: The Fate of a Concept* (Spillius and O'Shaughnessy, 2012) provides a rich picture of a process of theoretical and clinical development within diverse psychoanalytic contexts. In the authoritative introduction to the book Spillius explicates Klein's own ideas about projective identification, making use of unpublished material from the Klein Archives held in the Wellcome Trust which shows how she continued to work on the concept on the basis of her analytic practice. This archival evidence underlines how deeply rooted in clinical experience were all of Klein's theoretical contributions. The clinical examples quoted in Spillius's chapter fill out the points made here and give us some access to Klein's own way of thinking things over.

The book explores the 'fate' of this concept – what has happened to it as it has been used in psychoanalytic thinking over the last 70 years. However confusingly complex the notion of projective identification may at first appear, its fertility has been remarkable, and one of the interesting things is to see how the idea has stimulated creative independent thought in many analysts. We might almost suggest that as an understanding of the potentially constricting aspects of identification (the tendency to echo the authorities rather than say anything new) has grown, the freedom to develop fresh lines of inquiry has opened up. Klein can thus be seen as not only the originator of a great deal in psychoanalytic thought and practice but also as a source of inspiration for impressive succeeding generations of thinkers. The fate of good ideas is indeed to create space for more when they are offered in a spirit of openness. The epistemophilic instinct can thus be expressed within a thinking community.

Chapter 7

The unique status of *Narrative of a Child Analysis*

The *Narrative of a Child Analysis* (1961) puts one in touch with many aspects of Klein's way of working with child patients and reveals the complexity of the task of understanding the connections between her clinical observations and her theoretical development. It also highlights why interpretations of the fundamentals of her technique can be so diverse. The widespread belief in her lack of interest in the external facts of a child's life, in her excessive interest in destructive aggression, in her harshly challenging approach to interpretation and in a narrowing focus on the transference relationship is not sustainable from the texts. Yet it is not difficult to see why many readers become overwhelmed by the descriptions she offers of the internal dynamics of the distressed child's world and the rigour of her analytic exploration of the sources of anxiety. Particularly for those not familiar with encountering the extreme passions of early childhood it is disturbing territory – although we have all been children, not many of us have easy access to our early emotional life. If we become parents we certainly come up against these realities afresh, and in our own lives are likely to have periods of turbulence which reverberate at an infantile level, but the resistance to acknowledging the intensity of childhood anxieties remains profound, even though twenty-first-century child-rearing practices and understandings of children's mental capacities are substantially changed from the prevailing assumptions at the time of Klein's writing.

The *Narrative* is not very widely read within the psychoanalytic community. In the contemporary context of demands for empirical evidence it is extraordinary to have a book which describes in such detail almost every session of an analysis, together with the analyst's subsequent reflections on the material in the form of notes appended to sessional material which had set Klein's thinking in new directions. Here we have 93 sessions and reproductions of many drawings made by the child. Nearly all the sessions are written up in very close detail and even those she notes as more briefly recorded or slightly incomplete provide a substantial narrative of the session. Klein discusses in her preface the question of the accuracy of her notes and acknowledges the likelihood of some errors of sequence or precise wording but argues against both note taking in the session and mechanical recording, on the grounds that both undermine the analytic frame. She summarises:

> For all these reasons I am sure that notes taken as soon as possible after each session provide the best picture of the day-to-day happenings in the analysis, and therefore

(continued)

(continued)

of the course of the analysis. Hence I believe that . . . I am giving in this book a true account of my technique and of the material.

(pp. 11–12)[1]

The circumstances in which this four-month period of analysis took place were exceptional. In 1941, in the relatively early days of the war, Klein moved to Pitlochry, Scotland. Her patient, Richard, then aged 10, was a severely neurotic boy who was very frightened of other children and consequently unable to attend school. The outbreak of war had increased his anxieties. He was hypochondriacal about both his own and his mother's health and often depressed and manifestly unhappy. He was the younger of two boys, and his older brother seemed by contrast to take life easily. Richard had always been a delicate child and at the time Klein met him his personality was a combination of marked, even paranoid, anxiety and inhibition and rather precocious verbal and artistic capacities. He liked best the company of adult women, which no doubt played a part in his initial hopefulness about how Mrs Klein might help him. Richard and his mother came to live close to Klein in a hotel and they went home for weekends to the family's nearby war-time home away from London. Klein found a room she could rent as a playroom which also served the local Girl Guides. There was therefore a good deal of evidence of their activities in the room (books, pictures, maps, etc.). There was no waiting room available, and Richard would sometimes meet Mrs K. on the way to his session and watch her unlock the room or walk back to the village with her afterwards. All this made for differences in the analytic setting, which must have been difficult for her to adapt to, but which also attest to her flexibility of mind and her capacity to adapt technique to circumstance. Her evacuation away from her practice in London no doubt also gave her the greater time availability necessary for the very detailed recording of Richard's sessions.

For both patient and analyst, the progress of the war was a vital background preoccupation. Richard was very well informed and very anxious about the fate of British forces and about the bombing of London. Neither of them knew what would be the timescale of their stay in Pitlochry or what they might find on returning to London. For Klein, this temporary loss of her home and established surroundings must have stirred many complex memories of previous moves. For Richard, the external events of the war served to make terrifyingly real the internal conflicts which the analysis revealed. The intensity of their experience as well as Richard's unusually vivid and communicative abilities and profound involvement in the analysis must have been important in Klein's decision to devote much time to preparing the book for publication in the last months of her life. This final piece of writing had a special place in her life's work, since it records work done in 1941 and Klein's reflections of 1958–1960, many of which track some of the later theoretical developments she had written about.

For reasons both of the historical moment and the nature of the book, it remains a unique and unprecedented document. The very detailed presentation of clinical material always to some extent entails the specificity of a particular analyst's work with a particular patient at a

1 In recent years, clinical psychoanalytic researchers working with adolescents have decided, in order to meet criteria for research funding, to combine traditional process recording with the audio recording of psychotherapy sessions, both in an Adolescent Depression Study coordinated from the Tavistock Clinic (Trowell, 2007, 2011) and in the IMPACT study (Goodyer *et al.*, 2011). It has been found that the effects of audio recording on the clinical process have been much less disturbing and disruptive than was anticipated.

given time and place. This means that, however large the theoretical or technical discoveries which an analysis gives rise to, there will also be the reader's encounter with the quality of the analytic conversation that is taking place, the individual voice of both patient and analyst, and the powerful identifications with each that this stirs. Reading the *Narrative* sometimes has the effect of stirring the longing in the adult reader to have had analysis as a child. This is to do with the appreciation of the impact of Klein's attentiveness and imaginative understanding on Richard, and the growth of his mind and whole being over which she presided. Also impressive is his ready access to the psychic material necessary for the analysis to proceed. An adult in analysis by contrast is confronted with layers of complex and disabling defences, and the pain of recognising damage done to life already lived.

Klein's later reflections, which are appended as notes to the sessions, introduce her thinking to us in a different way – as a theorist, someone interested to find a position from which to observe the development of her own ideas, an analyst with a capacity to recognise the strength and limitations of what she could see and understand at any given moment.

The unique nature of the book concerns not only the matter of the complete clinical record it offers but also its one-off status from other angles. Just as one cannot really imagine anything quite like Freud's indirect analysis of Little Hans ever occurring again, so the possibility of a repetition of a five-times-a-week analysis of a child which lasts only a few months and takes place in wartime conditions is profoundly improbable. However, elements of its particularity throw light on contemporary work in settings comparable in some respect. We have an account of a child separated at times from his family, of a child living in very anxious times for the whole population, and exposed to awareness of death in the intensified atmosphere of war. Richard also had to cope with his father's serious illness during his treatment. Klein's weaving together of the meaning of these wider world and family events with their inner reverberations for Richard – the personal significance they had for him – is a remarkable example of her understanding of the nature of the internal world, continuously under development in consequence of the projective and introjective activity of the mind, and therefore always in a dynamic relationship to the world beyond the self.

The *Narrative* offers an opportunity to review Klein's technique and the evolution of her thinking over time, within the short timeframe of Richard's analysis, and the longer frame of her revisiting the material later for publication.

Introduction to excerpts from the *Narrative*

To contextualise some points for discussion, here is a brief summary of the analytic process and some excerpts from Klein's session notes and her later reflections.

Klein's first aim is to establish the analytic situation. To this end she pays attention to Richard's anxiety as something to explore and understand rather than to be diminished. She introduces him to his inner world of concrete unconscious phantasy. She is working with her recent theory of psychic positions at the back of her mind, the constellation of anxieties and defences which she believed determined crucial attitudes towards objects. In the *Narrative*, she writes of 'overcoming the depressive position', by which she means tolerating depressive anxieties, and she emphasises the experience of 'pining', which is the painful anxiety during separation about the state of the object following unconscious attacks. Pining includes feelings of guilt, remorse and loneliness. Klein's interest in loneliness was deep and long-lasting.

The playroom setting is understood as representing mother's body. Klein sees Richard's curiosity as both intrusive (aiming to control his object) and linked with his thirst for knowledge of the truth (the epistemophilic instinct). He is very vulnerable to overwhelming depressive anxiety, and during the analysis first an illness of his mother's, and later a much more serious one of his father's highlights this difficulty, and mobilises his search for help. He turns to drawings to show Klein what is happening in his mind. The iconography of war allows him to represent the internal conflicts which disturb and paralyse him. Klein brings him small toys as a further tool for communication, and Richard uses these and frequently adds a fleet of ships of his own to expand the range.

Klein tackles Oedipal themes from the start and speaks straightforwardly of Richard's curiosity, jealousy and envy in relation to his parents and his brother, and to herself. Gradually his more deeply disturbed, hypochondriacal and paranoid feelings become available for analysis. His inner persecution is relieved through this work, and more genuine reparative wishes emerge alongside depressive anxiety.

Probably because of the time-limited nature of the work, there is a sense of intense whirlwind in many of the later sessions. Klein interprets a huge amount of complex material to Richard. Sometimes we see him clearly growing in insight and tolerance of his nature and of reality, understanding, for example, the damaging consequences of his hostile projections into his object and of his greed. Despite the brevity and intense pace of the analysis, there is a powerful sense of some working through having been achieved, and some internalisation of the capacity for inquiry and understanding which Klein had provided.

From the *Narrative*

Klein on the importance of verbalising in child analysis

> On other occasions, too, although not always specifically referred to, Richard obtained marked relief through the lessening of the repression of his phantasies, and the ensuing increase in capacity to express them symbolically. In ordinary play, where the child remains largely unconscious of the content of his incestuous and aggressive phantasies and impulses, he nevertheless experiences relief through the very fact that he expresses them symbolically; and this is one of the factors which make play so important for the child's development. In analysis we should aim at getting access to deeply repressed phantasies and desires and thus helping the child to become conscious of them. It is important that the analyst should be able to convey to the child the meaning of his phantasies – whether they are deeply repressed or nearer consciousness – and to verbalize them. My experience has shown me that in doing so we meet closely the child's unconscious needs. I believe it to be a fallacy that there could be any harm to the child or to his relation to his parents from translating, as it were, his unconscious incestuous and aggressive desires and his criticism into concrete words.
>
> (session 8; p. 47)

Richard's capacity for symbolic expression and the immediacy of the transference

> Richard arrived a few minutes early and waited for Mrs K. on the doorstep. He seemed eager to start. He said he remembered something else he often worried about, but added that it was very different from the things he had talked about yesterday, altogether far away. He feared there might be a collision between the sun and the earth and the sun might burn up the earth; Jupiter and the other planets would be pulverized; and the earth,

the one planet with living people on it, was so important and precious . . . He again looked at the map and commented how awful it was what Hitler did to the world, the misery he caused. He thought Hitler was probably gloating in his room because others were suffering and he would enjoy having people whipped . . . He pointed at Switzerland on the map, saying it was a small neutral country that was 'encircled' by the huge Germany. There was also little Portugal, a friend. (He had mentioned, by the way, that he read three newspapers every day and listened to all the news on the wireless.) Brave little Switzerland had dared to shoot down planes, German or British, which flew over her territory.

Mrs K. interpreted that the 'precious earth' was Mummy, the living people her children, whom he wanted as allies and friends; hence his references to Portugal, the small country, and to the planets. The sun and earth in collision stood for something happening between his parents. 'Far away' meant near by, in the parents' bedroom. The pulverized planets stood for himself (Jupiter), and Mummy's other children, if they came between the parents.

(session 2; pp. 23–24)

Richard's first drawing: the nature of the analytic dialogue

Mrs K. had brought pencils, crayons, and a pad of writing-paper, and put them on the table. Richard asked eagerly what they were for, whether he could use them for writing or drawing. Mrs K. said he could do whatever he liked with them.

Richard had hardly begun the first drawing when he repeatedly asked whether Mrs K. minded that he was drawing. Mrs K. interpreted that he seemed to be afraid that by drawing he was doing something harmful to her. Richard, when he had finished Drawing 1, repeated his questions and suddenly noticed that he had made marks on the second page of the pad. Mrs K. interpreted that he was worried about the pencil marks because he was afraid that he was doing something destructive when he was drawing, and connected this with the fact that the drawing indicated a battle. Richard stopped when he had finished the first two drawings. Mrs K. asked him what they were about. Richard said there was an attack going on, but he did not know who would attack first, *Salmon* or the U-boat. He pointed at U102 and said that 10 was his own age; and to U16 he associated the age of John Wilson.[2] He was very surprised when he realized the unconscious meaning of these numbers and extremely interested to find that drawing could be a means of expressing unconscious thoughts.

Mrs K. pointed out that the numbers also indicated that he and John were represented by German U-boats, and were therefore hostile and dangerous to the British.

Richard was very much taken aback and disturbed by this interpretation, but after a silence agreed that it must be right. He said, though, that he surely could not wish to attack the British, for he was very 'patriotic'.

Mrs K. interpreted that the British represented his own family and that he had already recognized that he not only loved and wished to protect but also wished to attack them [split in the ego]; this appeared from the drawing where he was allied with John, who

2 John Wilson was an older boy living locally who was also a patient of Klein's and to whom Richard sometimes referred.

> also partly stood for his brother. But since John was being analysed by Mrs K., he appeared as an ally against her whenever Richard felt towards her the same hostility as he experienced towards his family.
>
> (session 12; pp. 56–57)

Movement between toys and drawing as modes of communication

> Richard made various groups of the little figures: there were two men together, then a cow and a horse in the first truck, and a sheep in the second. Then he arranged the little houses to form a 'village and a station'. He made the train run round and into the station. As he had left too little space, the train knocked over the houses, and he put them up again. He pushed the other train (which he called an 'electric' train) and a collision ensued. He became very upset and made the 'electric' train run over everything. The toys piled up and he spoke of it as a 'mess' and a 'disaster'. In the end only the 'electric' train was left standing up.

Mrs K. interpreted some earlier material about the children's sexual competition with the parents and the text then continues:

> In the end it all finished in 'disaster'. Mrs K. also interpreted his fear that the analysis might finish in disaster and that it would be his fault, in the same way as he felt he had done harm to Mummy. She reminded him as well of the dog which had to be destroyed and of his mentioning his granny's death . . .
>
> . . . Richard was extremely impressed by Mrs K.'s interpretation. He expressed his surprise that his thoughts and feelings could be shown in his play.
>
> Mrs K. interpreted that his recognizing that his play expressed his feelings also meant that Mrs K. made what went on in him clear to him. This proved to him that the analysis and Mrs K. were good and helpful. She now represented the good mother who would help him after all, in spite of the 'disaster' which he took to be his own fault.
>
> Richard asked Mrs K. if what happened in the end meant that the 'electric' train was himself and that he was the strongest of all. Mrs K. reminded him that he had been the biggest and most powerful of the family when he was represented by the big U-boat in Drawing 2.
>
> Richard, after a pause, pushed the toys aside and said he was 'tired' of them. He began to draw very elaborately and with great zest (Drawing 6). He said there were lots of babies, starfishes, there: they were in a 'blazing fury' and very hungry. They wanted to be near the plant (which he had not yet drawn), so they tore the octopus out from there. Richard then decided to make port-holes on the *Nelson*.
>
> (session 14; pp. 65–66)

Internalisation of a good object

Richard met Mrs K. on the way to the playroom. He was delighted to find that she had the key to the house. It now appeared that yesterday's incident [the room had been unavailable the day before] meant to him that the playroom might never again be available. He said with feeling, 'Good old room, I am very fond of it and glad to see it again.' He asked Mrs K. how long he had been with her.

Mrs K. replied that it was three and a half weeks. Richard was very surprised. He said it seemed so much longer; it seemed to have been going on for a very long time. He settled down contentedly to play with the fleet and said that he was happy.

Mrs K. interpreted his fear of losing the 'old playroom' as the fear of losing Mrs K. through death. She referred to the time (Ninth Session) when she and Richard had to fetch the key; after that he had told her his dreams about the black and deserted car, and switched the electric fire on and off which, as Mrs K. had pointed out, expressed his fear of Mrs K. and Mummy dying. The fear of losing the *old* room also expressed his grief about the death of his granny. Regaining the room meant to him that Mrs K. would remain alive and that Granny was revived.

Richard interrupted his play with the fleet and looked straight at Mrs K., saying quietly and with deep conviction, 'There is one thing I know and that is that you will be a lifelong friend of mine.' He added that Mrs K. was very kind, that he liked her very much, and that he knew that what she was doing with him was good for him, although sometimes it was very unpleasant. He could not say how he knew it was doing him good but he felt it.

Mrs K. interpreted that her explaining to him his fear of her death and his sorrow for his granny gave him the feeling that his granny was still alive in his mind – a lifelong friend of his – and that Mrs K., too, would remain alive for ever in this way, because he would contain her in his mind.

(session 21; pp. 93–94)

Klein's technique in linking to early infantile anxiety

Richard, while Mrs K. was interpreting, switched on the light and expressed great pleasure at seeing the room lit up. He said how very nice it all looked, and that it had been awful before. He again switched off the light. He then said how terrified he used to be at night. Nurse had to sit at his bedside until he went to sleep. He used to wake up in terror and yell until people came. This was four or five years ago. He added that it was not so nowadays, but he did not sound at all convinced.

Mrs K. interpreted his relief when he switched on the light in the playroom; the fears, which he had re-experienced, were lessened because Mrs K. was there with him and

(continued)

(continued)

because he could turn on the light when he wanted to, as well as discuss all his fears with her. Mrs K. therefore represented Nurse or Mummy at their best, as he would have wished them to be at night when he was alone. But it was not only in the past that he had felt these fears; they were still active; he had shown this in his play and in what he said.

Richard mentioned that his mother was better today than she had been yesterday. Mrs K. interpreted that yesterday he had felt that Mummy's bad throat meant that she, too, was poisoned, since so much of the material in that session had to do with his great fear of being poisoned and of being poisonous. Richard agreed that he might have felt this, but at once added, 'But poisoned by Bessie.'[3] Mrs K. reminded him that he had said he was looking after Mummy but had not said how he did it. Richard was very hesitant. Then he said he had bought something for her from the chemist's. It was something to sniff up her nose, and he added: probably some poisonous stuff. Mrs K. asked whether it was in a bottle. Richard said yes. Mrs K. interpreted that because he felt poisonous when he was angry and jealous he did not feel that he was able to help his mother, even when he wished to do so. The bottle he brought from the chemist turned to poison in his mind.

(session 28; p. 133)

Klein's note II

The analysis having revived Richard's early night-time anxieties . . . he remembered that when he was a little boy his nurse had to sit at his bedside until he went to sleep – a fact which he had not forgotten but had not told until then. It is of interest that this memory entered in the context of that particular session in which early anxieties, desires, and impulses had been revived in the analysis. This brings me also to the question of new memories coming up in the analysis. Their full value, in my view, consists in the possibilities they offer to the analyst to explore the experiences and emotions on which that memory is built. If this is not done, the coming-up of memories in the analysis loses in importance. The exploration of deep layers of the mind leads to the very vivid revival of early internal and external situations – a revival which I would describe as memories in feelings.

(session 28; pp. 135–136)

Richard's growing up

Richard was in a thoughtful but friendly mood. He showed Mrs K. his new cap and asked whether she liked it. He had mentioned once before that his old cap was too small and that the peak was broken. He also asked what she thought about his 'mixture' – his blazer, grey shorts, and tie. His mother did not think it was too good.

3 Bessie was the cook in the hotel where Richard and his mother were staying.

Mrs K. interpreted that the broken peak of his cap meant his damaged genital, that he hoped it was improving and growing, but that he wondered how the more grown-up penis would fit in with the rest of him, with his whole person; hence the 'mixture'. He wished Mrs K., standing for the good Mummy, to reassure him about his growing up, which implied permitting him to become an adult and have sexual desires, while he felt that his own mother did not trust him.

Richard replied that he had thought, while he was speaking to Mrs K., that she would explain it the way she did. Mrs K. asked whether he thought the explanation was correct. Richard said with conviction, 'Oh yes.' Then he added, with embarrassment, but obviously determined to speak out, that last night his genital had been very red and that he had been annoyed about this.

Mrs K. asked if he had done anything to make it red. Richard replied that he scratched it, but that it was sometimes red, in any case. Mrs K. interpreted that in one of his earlier drawings, red had already represented himself in the empire drawings. She suggested that red had also meant his injured and broken genital, damaged by his masturbation; he was very worried about this, not only annoyed. She asked what he thought about when touching or scratching his genital. Richard did not reply to this, but did not deny that he had been masturbating.

(session 36; pp. 171–172)

Richard's use of drawings

Then he made Drawing 35. He first drew the boat, which was meant to be a submarine, but turned it into a U-boat by crossing out the British flag. Underneath there were scribbles and Richard explained that he was bombing the U-boat, and that the little figure, which he said was behind the U-boat, was Hitler whom he was bombing as well. Farther down on the page there was also an 'invisible' Hitler whom he bombed. This Hitler was hidden behind scribbles. Richard pointed out where his face was, his tummy, and his legs. He said he had not realized while drawing that these scribbles were meant to be Hitler, but he saw it now . . . Mrs K. interpreted that Richard again showed that he felt his scribbles were bombs. She added that he now seemed to attack more openly with his faeces; these attacks were, moreover, more clearly directed against the bad Hitler-father, and in this way he avoided injuring the good Daddy and Mummy. But the 'invisible' Hitler also meant the bad Hitler inside him.

Richard agreed to these interpretations with conviction and said, 'This is true.'

(session 47; p. 224)

(continued)

(continued)

Richard then decided to draw a town and made Drawing 37. He said he would like to 'construct' it well, but he was so bad at drawing. He mentioned that there would have to be two railway tracks so as to avoid accidents. They joined farther on at the left, as they did at the station in 'X'. Then he drew some houses and the road which he called Albert Road. He said Albert was a name he liked, because it reminded him of Alfred, an older friend of Paul's [Richard's older brother] in the army; a very nice fellow, who was Richard's friend as well as Paul's. At the top left-hand corner of the drawing he wrote 'Buffer'; he said buffers were necessary. There was a level crossing, a bend, which was very dangerous for trains, and a siding to the right.

Mrs K. pointed out that the meaning of this drawing was similar to that of Drawing 36, namely, equality and agreement between him, Daddy, and Paul about their shares in Mummy's love. This was expressed by the two tracks branching off from the station which was Mummy; the buffers stood for an attempt to avoid collision. The goods yard, as formerly the convoy, was meant to feed all of them. Alfred also represented to him a better brother than Paul, not competing with him. In spite of all this, there was the dangerous bend which meant the dangers inside Mummy, mainly because of the fight between him, Daddy, and Paul. His wish to 'construct' a town well, and his regret that he was not good at drawing, expressed also his desire to rebuild the injured Mummy and give her babies, as well as to restore his own inside and make it safer.

Richard, while making the drawing just described, had been very absorbed and contented, and again said that he was happy. He was sniffing repeatedly although his cold had obviously gone, and remarked that he had not much mucus now.

Mrs K. interpreted that he was still concerned with the danger of poison inside him, the mucus represented the poisonous and poisoned stuff and by sniffing he tested whether it was still there.

(session 47; pp. 226–227)

Work towards integration

Richard arrived a few minutes late, but seemed unperturbed. He mentioned that he was going home by bus, and the bus ride played a large part in this session. His mood was very different from that of the previous day. This was partly due to his going home; he had been very homesick during that week. Also, as he told Mrs K., he had written to his mother and asked her to make different arrangements and felt that she would do so. Then he spoke a good deal about the chances of the bus being overcrowded. He said he had made inquiries and knew that he would travel with the pretty conductress, the one who always said 'half fares stand up' when the bus was crowded. The other conductress he liked was not so pretty, 'though by no means ugly', and did not say 'half fares stand up'; but she was due to go with the later bus. Obviously, in spite of his anxiety that he might have to stand, he also liked the idea of travelling with the pretty conductress, for he said repeatedly that she was very pretty and that he enjoyed looking at her.

Mrs K. interpreted that he liked her, although she was not altogether 'light blue' like the 'good' Mummy.

Richard repeated that she was very pretty and added, with amusement, no, she was not 'light blue', she was 'dark blue'. Her uniform was actually dark blue. What a pity it was that such a pretty girl should go about with a cap and collar and a tie. He had seen her once in girl's clothes and she looked so pretty. Then he added that he knew what Mrs K. meant about her not being altogether 'light blue'. It meant that she was not quite good and not quite bad. He went and drank some water from the tap and sat down at the table.

Mrs K. interpreted that his fears about the crowded bus, with the attractive conductress in it, also referred to the loved but suspect Mrs K. Recently he had felt that all the people on the busy road came to her and made her 'overcrowded' like the bus.

(session 77; pp. 393–395)

Klein's note I

His regret that the pretty conductress wore a uniform also expressed his wish that his mother, and now the analyst, should remain feminine, that is to say not containing her husband (Daddy), the male uniform standing for the internal male object. In his mind only the breast-mother could give him the feeling that she was by herself, unmixed with the father. His fear and dislike of the female genital connected with the feeling that the male genital was inside it. Such feelings play an important role in impotence and in disturbance of potency.

(session 77; pp. 398–399)

The threat posed by the end of the analysis

Richard then made Drawing 66 . . . Mrs K. interpreted Richard's struggle between his loving and hating her. He was trying to think that she was nice; beside the drawing representing her at the top of the page he had written 'lovely Mrs K.'. Nevertheless, he did not actually think that she was lovely, and therefore drew her without arms and hair, and evidently had no intention of making her look nice. He hated her for leaving him and joining other patients and her son and grandson.

Richard insisted that Mrs K. was lovely on the drawing because her tummy was heart-shaped and the arrow in the middle of it meant love. (His face was flushed and he often put his finger into his mouth; the struggle between hate and the wish to control it, and the mixture of persecutory and depressive anxiety, were expressed on his face.) He asked whether Mrs K. was sorry to go away. Was she going to stay with her son? She was not going to live in the heart of London, was she? Richard suddenly became aware of the word 'heart', looked surprised, and pointing at the drawing said, 'But here is the heart.'

> Mrs K. interpreted that her heart stood for the bombed London and was not only injured by love (the arrow) but also by bombs. Richard, who wished to love Mrs K., was afraid that, because she was leaving him, he might turn into Hitler who was going to bomb her. This increased his fear of her death, his loneliness, and his sadness about her departure.
>
> (session 80; pp. 412–413)

This material raises many interesting themes to consider. The first of these arises from the fact that so much detailed clinical material is available and thus enables us to investigate the common claim that analytic technique is unscientific because interpretations are not falsifiable. In session 3 Richard became interested in Klein's clock (brought to his first session because her watch had stopped) at an anxious moment following her interpretation of his greed, his hostility and aggression to Father, and his consequent fear of a nasty father monkey at the zoo. He then asked where the clock was, remarking that it was a nice clock and he liked looking at it.

> Mrs K. took the clock out of her bag. She pointed out that he felt worried and suggested that his reason for wanting to see the clock was that he wished to leave. Richard said no, he did not want to go, but he did wish to make sure that he would leave on time because he was going for a walk with Mummy. Also he liked the look of the clock. Mrs K. interpreted that he was anxious to see that Mummy was all right, not injured by his greedy attacks, and still loving him.
>
> (p. 30)

She went on to link this to the transference relationship to herself. In a later note, she discusses Richard's efforts to preserve the good relationship to mother and analyst through splitting off his hostile feelings, making clear her appreciation of his correction of her initial comment.

Two sessions later the clock theme returns, this time at the end of a session in which Klein had spoken of Richard's Oedipal competition with Father and his wish to replace Daddy with Mummy and Mr K. with Mrs K. and to be the 'charming little robin' whose picture he had admired, and thus to be the admired pet of Mummy and Mrs K. Richard responded that he had once had a robin and fed it but it flew away and did not return. Then he looked at the clock and wanted to know if his time was up. Klein spoke of his wish to leave and never return because he did not like what she had been saying to him about his wish for a sexual relationship with her. Richard demurred, but then agreed that he did want the time to be up but that he did not want to go before the end of the session. Klein's footnote comments on this mixture of resistance and the wish to maintain a friendly relationship with her.

What is evident here is the subtle balance in Klein's judgement about what is happening – she sees a fluid mix of fear and co-operation in Richard's attitude to her and she describes both his loving and his hostile feelings towards his parents. This analysis might be extended somewhat when one considers the meaning of Richard's preoccupation with Klein's clock and its relevance to Father Time. In session 3, the clock surely represents his link to a good father who will support and protect his good relationship to mother, and not be like the nasty frightening monkey. The clock which Mrs K. brings to the session also helps Richard to maintain a link to external reality while his inner anxieties are exposed within the confines of the analysis. He is not living in the timeless world of unconscious phantasy, but in a world bounded by differentiated times and spaces. In session 5, the clock's function as a representation of a good father is again evident. His comment about the robin who flew away could be thought of not only as a wish to escape, but also as a recognition of the unreality of his infantile Oedipal desires and his attachment to the reliable structures of his world. Time and generational difference are frustrating realities which we can omnipotently wish to ignore but they are also evidence of sources of safety and a bulwark against chaos (Money-Kyrle, 1968, 1971).

This small excerpt provides an example of Klein's careful recording of Richard's responses to her interpretations and also demonstrates the space her method creates for further exploration of the meaning of their exchanges. In much analytic writing the reader can feel that every interpretive base has been covered and that the omnipotent insight of the analyst is subtly implicit, but here the detail and enormous range of Richard's ways of responding to Klein as well as her subsequent reflective notes encourage readers to find their own response. Thus, Klein's book both shows us her own scientific attitude to her work and provides material for others to study and evaluate. Joseph's papers on technique, with their focus on the patient's response to the analyst's interpretation, pick up and develop this element in Klein's thinking (Joseph, 1989).

A second theme is the matter of Klein's flexibility and thoughtfulness in sustaining the setting in very unusual circumstances.

The playroom she used gave access to a little kitchen and to an outside space. Richard used all these spaces at different times and Klein followed him around, including joining him to look out of the window at people passing by, about whom he often talked. She did not mind assisting him with practical things that were difficult for him (the stiff taps in the kitchen, for example), she accepted the additional toys he brought with him, she apologised when she forgot to bring something with her, she answered quite a lot of his questions, including information about her visit to London in the course of the treatment. The rigidity often attributed to Kleinian technique seems markedly absent, but she is all the time pondering on the impact of all these events, sometimes feeling she made the wrong decision.

One striking episode is her agreeing to see him one Sunday to replace a session. The account of this session (no. 33) is fascinating because it records Richard's growing ease in owning his aggression – he vividly described various fights, real and imagined, with other boys, for example – and his enjoyment of the analysis and this special Sunday session. Klein interpreted his wish to have Mummy all to himself and his doubts that Daddy would agree to that. She notes: 'Richard was very amused at the idea' (p. 161). Interestingly, he asks her to date the drawings he had done, which perhaps picks up the theme of the importance of location in time and its link to father's role in the internal world.

Shortly after this Klein met his mother, who described a striking change in Richard after this session: at home he was both very aggressive but also more friendly and much easier to get on with. Richard's own way of putting this change to Klein in session 33 went like this:

> He said that when he woke up that morning he felt very happy in spite of not being at home on a Sunday. He thought that the work was doing him good after all. He felt so much more brave.
>
> (p. 157)

'He said all this with conviction', she writes. Klein does not specifically speculate on what this Sunday session meant to Richard, but the kindness in her attitude to him was surely part of it. Because he had previously been ill and missed several sessions and was now spending a weekend not at home, she was in effect offering to accompany him in dealing with the losses all this entailed. The generous quality of her concern for him is most evident, and one might suggest that his kinder attitude to himself is related to an internalisation of this more benign figure. Klein had reflected after session 15 on the despair and hatred of themselves which small children can feel when their lack of skill in constructive play hampers their efforts. Her appreciation of the pain children feel when a mess or 'disaster' or impasse in a game exposes them to fears of the power of their destructive impulses, and their helplessness to contain such forces or to put things right, made her very sensitive to the support that is necessary for development to take place. She saw that Richard often felt overwhelmed by 'loneliness, anxiety and guilt' at such moments, which provoked more frantic efforts to destroy the evidence of the internal catastrophe which the mess represented. Her work aims to relieve the savagery of the early superego which she had discovered in her first young child patients.

A third strand of interest, which represents a challenge to the recent psychoanalytic writers who have argued that their focus on siblings brings in a neglected theoretical vertex, is Klein's work with Richard on sibling relationships. Already in session 2 she adds a note about the importance of the child's relationship to members of the extended family, e.g. to grandparents and siblings. She suggests that these significant loved figures strengthen the growth of good internal objects because they are less closely involved in the Oedipal conflicts aroused by parental figures. In other words, the loving aspect of the relationship to brothers and sisters is highlighted. This develops in session 10 in the context of Richard's anxiety about conflicts between parental figures. (In reality there had been rows between Richard's nurse and the family cook which had led to this nurse leaving the family.) Klein spoke to him about his need for a younger brother or sister to help him when he was frightened about quarrelling grown-ups, that is, to help him by sharing his anxiety. She added that he was also afraid of brothers and sisters who turn against him when he felt aggressive towards or jealous of them. So here we have evidence of Klein's interest in both the familiar Freudian emphasis on sibling rivalry and hostility, but also her appreciation of the positive potential of sibling relationships, and her understanding of the feelings of a child who is the youngest in the family without the reassurance of the presence of younger children.

In session 12 she discusses with Richard his feelings about his older brother Paul. This arose from a drawing in which Richard had explored his wish to have more of his mother than father or Paul did. She suggested that when he wanted to take Mummy away from Paul he felt he then had to make up to him. In a note she clarifies that this might be a basis for homosexual feelings between brothers. They also talked about Richard's feelings about being the younger boy – on the one hand, the feeling that Paul is older, cleverer and thus more loved by mother, and on the other that Richard can comfort himself with the idea of being mother's baby. Richard had just checked that Mr Klein was dead, as he knew to be the case, and now asked if he was her youngest patient. Klein pointed out his wish to be her special baby. Her work with Richard on his real and imaginary relationships with siblings had a special urgency because of the symptomatic importance of his hatred and terror of other children and his great difficulty in tolerating any actual encounters with them, and his consequent isolation and loneliness.

Klein's attitude to Richard can often be discerned through studying the tone of her comments to him. From the first session, she treated him with absolutely direct seriousness, suggesting 'that he knew why he was coming to her: he had some difficulties with which he wanted to be helped' (p. 19). Responding to this profound respect for his intelligence and the seriousness of his problems, Richard launches in at once, describing his fear of boys in the street and of going out, his hatred of school and his preoccupation with the war. He spoke about Hitler's attack on Poland, looked at a map on the wall and commented that Mrs K. was Austrian, as Hitler was too. Her further enquiries about his worries clearly aimed to open up and mobilise his anxieties about his mother's health and safety, and Richard spoke about a nasty tramp he thought might come and kidnap Mummy at night. Klein immediately began to talk about parental sexual relations and Richard's worries about damage to Mummy. Richard's response included shock but also intense interest and he remarked at the end of the session that he liked 'talking and thinking'.

The assumption that this boy could engage in a profound psychoanalytic experience is at the heart of Klein's technique. They had many very grown-up conversations over the months, both about what was happening inside his mind and in their relationship and about external matters. For example, when he learned of her planned trip to London (session 38), he asked her to promise to go to a shelter at once if she heard the sirens. Klein did indeed promise to do so, and also agreed to give him her address when he said he wanted to write to her. He added that if she died, he would go to her funeral, and that he wanted Mrs K. to tell his mother who could continue this work with him if she died. She agreed to give his mother the name of another analyst.

A few weeks later, we get a glimpse of Richard's understanding of the analytic process. He had said that Mrs K.'s dress made him think of search lights, and he added, 'You search, don't you?' The mixture of his desire to be understood and his fear of what will be seen in the analytic search light is transparent in their subsequent exchanges. In session 69, they have an extended conversation about Richard's worries about going to school: he asked whether Mrs K. would tell his mother to send him to a big school? 'He could not stand that. He was still very frightened of bigger boys. He would be ill if he had to be frightened all the time' (p. 349). They discussed Richard's preference for a tutor, or maybe a small school, but Richard added sadly that what he would really like would be not even to have a tutor and not to have to learn at all. The absolute frankness of this is very touching. Klein's response gives weight both to the level of Richard's anxiety (she says she would not be in favour of a big school because he was so afraid of it) and to the idea of his development going forward and change in his state of mind being possible. She remarks that 'he might see how he got on during the next year; he might find that he liked being with children better than he used to do' (p. 350).

These exchanges make manifest something Klein felt sure of in her analytic work with children, namely the naturalness and solidity as well as the psychological complexity of the developmental process. Her work was oriented towards facilitating this development, to enabling her child patients to deal better with what was interfering with their engagement with life. In 'Envy and gratitude' (1957), which she had completed not long before she worked on the *Narrative*, she made the particular point that destructive envious feelings could be ameliorated and controlled through understanding and this insight confirmed her fundamentally hopeful analytic attitude. Richard's statement that he now felt more courageous is a particularly apt response to the courage which characterised Klein's own analytic attitude.

Chapter 8

Envy and gratitude

Klein published this short book in 1957. It is a very significant part of her contribution to psychoanalysis because of the originality of her understanding of the importance of the role of envy and gratitude in early object relations, and her contention of the ubiquitous presence of these emotions in infancy and throughout later life. This chapter will set out the main lines of her argument, illustrating this with quotations from the text, and providing some further commentary.

More than any other of her writings, it has been the source of profoundly divergent responses ever since. Her theory about the destructive potential of early infantile envy and its constitutional element divides her readers into two camps, those who believe that the light she throws on the dynamics of envy in our earliest relationships is of the greatest clinical and theoretical significance, and those who decry the idea that envious feelings can reasonably be attributed to infants and young children.

The disturbing impact of a focus on the phenomenon of envy has tended to outweigh the idea of emotional balance which Klein's title suggests. A recent collection of essays by major contemporary analysts responding to Klein's volume (Roth and Lemma, 2008) shows a great preponderance of attention to envy, the negative pole in her theory, and a consequent lesser emphasis on the phenomenon of gratitude. It is thus striking to read the footnote to the title and the first paragraphs Klein wrote, which each drew attention to Klein's own feelings of gratitude. In the footnote she writes movingly of the contribution of friends and colleagues to her writing (Lola Brook, Elliott Jacques and Judith Fay) and in the introductory section quoted below she outlines her debt to Abraham (her second analyst) and to Freud.

Klein's point of departure

> I have for many years been interested in the earliest sources of two attitudes that have always been familiar – envy and gratitude. I arrived at the conclusion that envy is a most potent factor in undermining feelings of love and gratitude at their root, since it affects the earliest relation of all, that to the mother. The fundamental importance of this relation for the individual's whole emotional life has been substantiated in a number of psycho-analytic writings, and I think that by exploring further a particular factor that can be very disturbing at this early stage, I have added something of significance to my findings concerning infantile development and personality formation.
>
> I consider that envy is an oral-sadistic and anal-sadistic expression of destructive impulses, operative from the beginning of life, and that it has a constitutional basis.

These conclusions have certain important elements in common with Karl Abraham's work, and yet imply some differences from it. Abraham found that envy is an oral trait, but – and this is where my views differ from his – he assumed that envy and hostility operate at a later period, which, according to his hypothesis, constituted a second, the oral-sadistic, stage. Abraham did not speak of gratitude, but he described generosity as an oral feature. He considered the anal elements as an important component in envy, and stressed their derivation from oral-sadistic impulses.

A further fundamental point of agreement is Abraham's assumption of a constitutional element in the strength of oral impulses, which he linked with the aetiology of manic-depressive illness.

Above all, both Abraham's work and my own brought out more fully and more deeply the significance of destructive impulses. In his 'A short history of the development of the libido, viewed in the light of mental disorders', written in 1924, Abraham did not mention Freud's hypothesis of the life and death instincts, although *Beyond the Pleasure Principle* had been published four years previously. However, in his book Abraham explored the roots of destructive impulses and applied this understanding to the aetiology of mental disturbances more specifically than had ever been done before. It appears to me that although he had not made use of Freud's concept of the life and death instincts, his clinical work, particularly the analysis of the first manic-depressive patients to be analysed, was based on insight which was taking him in that direction. I would assume that Abraham's early death prevented his realizing the full implications of his own findings and their essential connection with Freud's discovery of the two instincts.

As I am about to publish *Envy and Gratitude*, three decades after Abraham's death, it is a source of great satisfaction to me that my work has contributed to the growing recognition of the full significance of Abraham's discoveries.

('Envy and gratitude', 1957; pp. 176–177)

Here we see Klein's fundamental starting point clearly stated. Feelings of envy undermine the baby's loving relationship to mother. Such feelings she believes have a constitutional basis – that is, they are innate or prior to experience – and they are expressed in both oral and anal phantasies of attack on mother's body. She argues that vicissitudes of envy and gratitude are rooted in the operation of the life and death instincts, and explains that hate and envy are present in the earliest months. She goes on to describe how her analysis of young children provided her with new source material. Following a lengthy quote from Freud's 'Constructions in analysis', in which he explores the analogy of psychoanalysis and archaeology, she continues thus.

Earliest object relations

Experience has taught me that the complexity of the fully grown personality can only be understood if we gain insight into the mind of the baby and follow up its development into later life. That is to say, analysis makes its way from adulthood to infancy,

(continued)

(continued)

and through intermediate stages back to adulthood, in a recurrent to-and-fro movement according to the prevalent transference situation.

Throughout my work I have attributed fundamental importance to the infant's first object relation – the relation to the mother's breast and to the mother – and have drawn the conclusion that if this primal object, which is introjected, takes root in the ego with relative security, the basis for a satisfactory development is laid. Innate factors contribute to this bond. Under the dominance of oral impulses, the breast is instinctively felt to be the source of nourishment and therefore, in a deeper sense, of life itself. This mental and physical closeness to the gratifying breast in some measure restores, if things go well, the lost pre-natal unity with the mother and the feeling of security that goes with it. This largely depends on the infant's capacity to cathect sufficiently the breast or its symbolic representative, the bottle; in this way the mother is turned into a loved object. It may well be that his having formed part of the mother in the pre-natal state contributes to the infant's innate feeling that there exists outside him something that will give him all he needs and desires. The good breast is taken in and becomes part of the ego, and the infant who was first inside the mother now has the mother inside himself.

While the pre-natal state no doubt implies a feeling of unity and security, how far this state is undisturbed must depend on the psychological and physical condition of the mother, and possibly even on certain still unexplored factors in the unborn infant. We might, therefore, consider the universal longing for the pre-natal state also partly as an expression of the urge for idealization. If we investigate this longing in the light of idealization, we find that one of its sources is the strong persecutory anxiety stirred up by birth. We might speculate that this first form of anxiety possibly extends to the unborn infant's unpleasant experiences which, together with the feeling of security in the womb, foreshadow the double relation to the mother: the good and the bad breast.

External circumstances play a vital part in the initial relation to the breast. If birth has been difficult, and in particular if it results in complications such as lack of oxygen, a disturbance in the adaptation to the external world occurs and the relation to the breast starts at a great disadvantage. In such cases the baby's ability to experience new sources of gratification is impaired and in consequence he cannot sufficiently internalize a really good primal object. Furthermore, whether or not the child is adequately fed and mothered, whether the mother fully enjoys the care of the child or is anxious and has psychological difficulties over feeding – all these factors influence the infant's capacity to accept the milk with enjoyment and to internalize the good breast.

An element of frustration by the breast is bound to enter into the infant's earliest relation to it, because even a happy feeding situation cannot altogether replace the pre-natal unity with the mother. Also, the infant's longing for an inexhaustible and ever-present breast stems by no means only from a craving for food and from libidinal desires. For the urge even in the earliest stages to get constant evidence of the mother's love is fundamentally rooted in anxiety. The struggle between life and death instincts and the

> ensuing threat of annihilation of the self and of the object by destructive impulses are fundamental factors in the infant's initial relation to his mother. For his desires imply that the breast, and soon the mother, should do away with these destructive impulses and the pain of persecutory anxiety.
>
> Together with happy experiences, unavoidable grievances reinforce the innate conflict between love and hate, in fact, basically between life and death instincts, and result in the feeling that a good and a bad breast exist. As a consequence, early emotional life is characterized by a sense of losing and regaining the good object. In speaking of an innate conflict between love and hate, I am implying that the capacity both for love and for destructive impulses is, to some extent, constitutional, though varying individually in strength and interacting from the beginning with external conditions.
>
> (pp. 178–180)

Klein's investigation of the 'mind of the baby' takes her directly to the depiction of the interaction of the baby's own endowment (the innate factors), which she movingly describes as potentially contributing to the discovery of a loved external mother linking with his pre-natal experience of bodily unity with mother, and his mother's state of mind and body. She refers to the potentially catastrophic anxiety stirred up by a difficult birth, or by problems the mother experiences in relating to the new baby. She describes the baby's belief that all his painful experiences should be taken away by mother and the 'unavoidable grievances' arising in the baby from the disappointment of this illusion of the all-powerful ideal mother.

It is notable in these passages that Klein's ideas are very eloquently set out, and indeed 'Envy and gratitude' is a much easier book to read and understand than some of her dense earlier papers. There are sentences of great beauty which stay in the mind, such as this one: 'The good breast is taken in and becomes part of the ego, and the infant who was first inside the mother now has the mother inside himself.' A footnote introduces the memorable and much-quoted phrase 'memories in feelings', which relates the language of the unconscious to the work which can take place during the analytic process:

> All this is felt by the infant in much more primitive ways than language can express. When these pre-verbal emotions and phantasies are revived in the transference situation, they appear as 'memories in feelings', as I would call them, and are reconstructed and put into words with the help of the analyst. In the same way, words have to be used when we are reconstructing and describing other phenomena belonging to the early stages of development. In fact we cannot translate the language of the unconscious into consciousness without lending it words from our conscious realm.
>
> (p. 180)

Although included only as a footnote, this vitally important paragraph delineates Klein's understanding of the way in which early infantile experiences gain expression in the analytic relationship. We can see her attitude to the responsibility the analyst has to 'listen' for these communications and to search for words which can serve to describe phenomena which precede the infant's knowledge of language.

Klein's deep commitment to the verbalisation of infantile layers of experience is one of the most striking elements of her clinical technique. The phrase 'memories in feelings' has become a highly significant reference point in analytic discourse because of its brilliant condensation of recognisable clinical phenomena.

Envy, jealousy and greed

She continues with a discussion of the distinctions between envy, jealousy and greed, whose power is a consequence of the profound dependence of the infant on the mother's good qualities, her 'inexhaustible patience, generosity and creativeness'. What is at the heart of Klein's concern is the way that these emotions can interfere with the building up of a good internal object because the infant's frustration leads to his attributing his painful experiences to mother's gratification of herself or others, at his expense. His capacity for happiness is undermined when his hope and trust in a good object are lessened.

> A distinction should be drawn between envy, jealousy, and greed. Envy is the angry feeling that another person possesses and enjoys something desirable—the envious impulse being to take it away or to spoil it. Moreover, envy implies the subject's relation to one person only and goes back to the earliest exclusive relation with the mother. Jealousy is based on envy, but involves a relation to at least two people; it is mainly concerned with love that the subject feels is his due and has been taken away, or is in danger of being taken away, from him by his rival. In the everyday conception of jealousy, a man or a woman feels deprived of the loved person by somebody else.
>
> Greed is an impetuous and insatiable craving, exceeding what the subject needs and what the object is able and willing to give. At the unconscious level, greed aims primarily at completely scooping out, sucking dry, and devouring the breast: that is to say, its aim is destructive introjection; whereas envy not only seeks to rob in this way, but also to put badness, primarily bad excrements and bad parts of the self, into the mother, and first of all into her breast, in order to spoil and destroy her. In the deepest sense this means destroying her creativeness. This process, which derives from urethral- and anal-sadistic impulses, I have elsewhere defined as a destructive aspect of projective identification starting from the beginning of life. One essential difference between greed and envy, although no rigid dividing line can be drawn since they are so closely associated, would accordingly be that greed is mainly bound up with introjection and envy with projection.
>
> (p. 181)

She then pursues her contention that the mother's feeding breast is the first object of envy and that this infantile envy 'gives particular impetus' to the infant's phantasies of sadistic attacks on mother's body. She draws attention to the paradoxical impact of deprivation. She is here theorising her earlier description (in *The Psycho-Analysis of Children*, 1932) of sadistic phantasies of attacks on mother's body in a new way. The greed and destructive impulses are now presented and linked to a desire to spoil, rooted in envy. Quoting *Othello,* Klein reminds us of the everyday saying about biting the hand that feeds us.

> If we consider that deprivation increases greed and persecutory anxiety, and that there is in the infant's mind a phantasy of an inexhaustible breast which is his greatest desire, it becomes understandable how envy arises even if the baby is inadequately fed. The infant's feelings seem to be that when the breast deprives him, it becomes bad because it keeps the milk, love, and care associated with the good breast all to itself. He hates and envies what he feels to be the mean and grudging breast.
>
> (p. 183)

This insight has proved to be of immense value in understanding the way in which extreme deprivation in early childhood can damage the child's capacity to benefit from non-depriving relationships when they are open to him.

Envy in the transference

The clinical significance of this primitive form of envy and defences against it in the evolution of the transference relationship in analysis is then described:

> The envious patient grudges the analyst the success of his work; and if he feels that the analyst and the help he is giving have become spoilt and devalued by his envious criticism, he cannot introject him sufficiently as a good object nor accept his interpretations with real conviction and assimilate them. Real conviction, as we often see in less envious patients, implies gratitude for a gift received. The envious patient may also feel, because of guilt about devaluing the help given, that he is unworthy to benefit by analysis.
>
> Needless to say, our patients criticize us for a variety of reasons, sometimes with justification. But a patient's need to devalue the analytic work which he has experienced as helpful is the expression of envy. In the transference we discover the root of envy if we trace back the emotional situations we encounter in earlier stages down to the primary one. Destructive criticism is particularly evident in paranoid patients who indulge in the sadistic pleasure of disparaging the analyst's work, even though it has given them some relief. In these patients envious criticism is quite open; in others it may play an equally important rôle but remains unexpressed and even unconscious. In my experience, the slow progress we make in such cases is also connected with envy. We find that their doubts and uncertainties about the value of the analysis persist. What happens is that the patient has split off the envious and hostile part of his self and constantly presents to the analyst other aspects that he feels to be more acceptable. Yet the split-off parts essentially influence the course of the analysis, which ultimately can only be effective if it achieves integration and deals with the whole of the personality. Other patients try to avoid criticism by becoming confused. This confusion is not only a defence but also expresses the uncertainty as to whether the analyst is still a good figure, or whether he
>
> *(continued)*

(continued)

and the help he is giving have become bad because of the patient's hostile criticism. This uncertainty I would trace back to the feelings of confusion that are one of the consequences of the disturbed earliest relation to the mother's breast. The infant who, owing to the strength of paranoid and schizoid mechanisms and the impetus of envy, cannot divide and keep apart successfully love and hate, and therefore the good and bad object, is liable to feel confused between what is good and bad in other connections.

In these ways envy, and the defences against it, play an important part in the negative therapeutic reaction, in addition to the factors discovered by Freud and further developed by Joan Riviere.

For envy, and the attitudes it gives rise to, interfere with the gradual building up of a good object in the transference situation. If at the earliest stage the good food and the primal good object could not be accepted and assimilated, this is repeated in the transference and the course of the analysis is impaired.

(pp. 184–185)

Klein shows how the patient's feelings as a baby can be understood through analysing the transference in great detail: the milk (interpretation) came too quickly or too slowly or too late, or the feed was interrupted. These examples give a very vivid sense of her clinical technique, showing how her observation of the baby feelings stirred up by the analytic situation could enable her to talk to her patients about these hitherto unconscious aspects of their emotional lives.

Envy and gratitude in infancy

She goes on to describe how, alongside the desire for gratification at the breast, there is a profound longing for freedom from persecuting anxieties, and the demand that mother take away all such pain. Reflections on the effect of maternal anxiety on a baby's experience lead on to some thoughts about the damaging impact of both excessive frustration and indulgence, and a description of the importance of bearing some frustration in the development of a sense of reality and of creativity. Klein's strong emphasis on the importance of creative sublimation is a theme developed by later analysts, particularly Hanna Segal, in relation to the work of artistic creation, and by D.W. Winnicott in his emphasis on play.

In fact, a certain amount of frustration followed by gratification might give the infant the feeling that he has been able to cope with his anxiety. I have also found that the infant's unfulfilled desires – which are to some extent incapable of fulfilment – are an important contributory factor to his sublimations and creative activities. The absence of conflict in the infant, if such a hypothetical state could be imagined, would deprive him of enrichment of his personality and of an important factor in the strengthening of his ego. For conflict, and the need to overcome it, is a fundamental element in creativeness.

(p. 186)

Klein strongly emphasises the importance of the baby's enjoyment of the feeding relationship, and it is enjoyment which envy can so easily spoil. She links enjoyment to the growth of gratitude which can 'mitigate destructive impulses, envy and greed'. She goes on to contrast a tendency to anxious, greedy and indiscriminate identifications, based on doubts about the possession of a good object, with the position of a child who has been able to build up a good internal object:

> In contrast with the infant who, owing to his envy, has been unable to build up securely a good internal object, a child with a strong capacity for love and gratitude has a deep-rooted relation with a good object and can, without being fundamentally damaged, withstand temporary states of envy, hatred, and grievance, which arise even in children who are loved and well mothered. Thus, when these negative states are transient, the good object is regained time and time again. This is an essential factor in establishing it and in laying the foundations of stability and a strong ego. In the course of development, the relation to the mother's breast becomes the foundation for devotion to people, values, and causes . . .
>
> . . . Gratitude is rooted in the emotions and attitudes that arise in the earliest stage of infancy, when for the baby the mother is the one and only object . . .
>
> . . . The infant can only experience complete enjoyment if the capacity for love is sufficiently developed; and it is enjoyment that forms the basis for gratitude. Freud described the infant's bliss in being suckled as the prototype of sexual gratification. In my view these experiences constitute not only the basis of sexual gratification but of all later happiness, and make possible the feeling of unity with another person; such unity means being fully understood, which is essential for every happy love relation or friendship. At best, such an understanding needs no words to express it, which demonstrates its derivation from the earliest closeness with the mother in the preverbal stage. The capacity to enjoy fully the first relation to the breast forms the foundation for experiencing pleasure from various sources . . .
>
> . . . A full gratification at the breast means that the infant feels he has received from his loved object a unique gift which he wants to keep. This is the basis of gratitude. Gratitude is closely linked with the trust in good figures. This includes first of all the ability to accept and assimilate the loved primal object (not only as a source of food) without greed and envy interfering too much; for greedy internalization disturbs the relation to the object. The individual feels that he is controlling and exhausting, and therefore injuring it, whereas in a good relation to the internal and external object, the wish to preserve and spare it predominates.
>
> (pp. 187–188)

To this description Klein adds the role that feelings of gratitude play in the capacity to make reparation and in all sublimations, and expressions of generosity. This benign circle she contrasts with the especially problematic aspect of envy, namely that it 'spoils and harms the good object which is the source of life'. One could suggest that envy is in fact the reverse side of admiration, and that it is only when we can appreciate and admire that envy kicks in. She seems to agree with Chaucer, whom she quotes, that it is the greatest of the seven deadly sins because of its assault on anything that evokes esteem. 'It is certain that envy is the worst sin that is; for all other sins are sins only against one virtue, whereas envy is against all virtue and against all goodness' (*The Parson's Tale*).

The early formation of the ego

A review of her understanding of the early ego follows immediately in Klein's text:

> I believe that it exists from the beginning of post-natal life, though in a rudimentary form and largely lacking coherence. Already at the earliest stage it performs a number of important functions. It might well be that this early ego approximates to the unconscious part of the ego postulated by Freud. Though he did not assume that an ego exists from the beginning, he attributed to the organism a function which, as I see it, can only be performed by the ego. The threat of annihilation by the death instinct within is, in my view – which differs from Freud's on this point – the primordial anxiety, and it is the ego which, in the service of the life instinct – possibly even called into operation by the life instinct – deflects to some extent that threat outwards. This fundamental defence against the death instinct Freud attributed to the organism, whereas I regard this process as the prime activity of the ego.
>
> (pp. 190–191)

She then summarises her view of the struggle between the life and death instincts, the polarities of the processes of integration and of the necessary defensive splitting of self and object, and suggests that the damaging force of early envy lies in its interference with primal splitting and the building up of a strongly rooted good object around which the ego can cohere. She emphasises the difference between a good and an idealised object, idealisation indicating that destructive impulses and persecutory anxiety are being held at bay. Klein's picture of the vital link between the growth of the ego and the relationship to the primary object and to a degree of stability is particularly clear:

> A very deep split between the two aspects of the object indicates that it is not the good and bad object that are being kept apart but an idealized and an extremely bad one. So deep and sharp a division reveals that destructive impulses, envy, and persecutory anxiety are very strong and that idealization serves mainly as a defence against these emotions.
>
> If the good object is deeply rooted, the split is fundamentally of a different nature and allows the all-important process of ego integration and object synthesis to operate. Thus a mitigation of hatred by love can come about in some measure and the depressive position can be worked through. As a result, the identification with a good and whole object is the more securely established; and this also lends strength to the ego and enables it to preserve its identity as well as a feeling of possessing goodness of its own. It becomes less liable to identify indiscriminately with a variety of objects, a process that

> is characteristic of a weak ego. Furthermore, full identification with a good object goes with a feeling of the self possessing goodness of its own. When things go wrong, excessive projective identification, by which split-off parts of the self are projected into the object, leads to a strong confusion between the self and the object, which also comes to stand for the self. Bound up with this is a weakening of the ego and a grave disturbance in object relations.
>
> (p. 192)

Later she continues:

> While people who have been able to establish the primal good object with relative security are capable of retaining their love for it in spite of its shortcomings, with others idealization is a characteristic of their love relations and friendships. This tends to break down and then one loved object may frequently have to be exchanged for another; for none can come fully up to expectations. The former idealized person is often felt as a persecutor (which shows the origin of idealization as a counterpart to persecution), and into him is projected the subject's envious and critical attitude. It is of great importance that similar processes operate in the internal world which in this way comes to contain particularly dangerous objects. All this leads to instability in relationships. This is another aspect of the weakness of the ego, to which I referred earlier in connection with indiscriminate identifications.
>
> (p. 193)

The effect of early envy and guilt on sexual development

Early persecutory forms of guilt are a consequence of strong feelings of envy. Klein revisits here her theory of the depressive position and provides an example of her reflection over time on her overall understanding of the earliest mental processes. Recalling her initial observations of guilt and persecution in very young children, she suggests that too schematic a distinction between paranoid and depressive states leaves out this difficult early awakening of guilt with which the baby cannot cope. Here Klein is specifically investigating the consequences of unconscious envy of the feeding mother (breast), but we might also note the importance of this description for understanding the states of mind of infants exposed to very depressed mothers or to severe deprivation or abuse. Without the experience of a good external object, neither the coherence nor the belief in the goodness of the self can grow. Klein suggests that this situation stimulates premature genital excitement and confusion between oral and genital impulses. This idea has proved to be of great importance in understanding the sexualised states of the many children now seen in clinical practice who have had very adverse early experiences.

The connection between emotional deprivation (relating broadly to feeding, nurture and orality) and premature sexualisation gives theoretical depth to the sometimes more superficial connections made between deprivation and acting out. Premature sexualisation is a significant problem, for example, among some children who have been adopted or fostered following the breakdown of care in their birth family (Boston and Szur, 1983; Rustin *et al.*, 1997).

Excessive envy interferes with adequate oral gratification and so acts as a stimulus towards the intensification of genital desires and trends. This implies that the infant turns too early towards genital gratification, with the consequence that the oral relation becomes genitalized and the genital trends become too much coloured by oral grievances and anxieties. I have often contended that genital sensations and desires are possibly operative from birth onwards; for instance, it is well known that infant boys have erections at a very early stage. But in speaking of these sensations arising prematurely I mean that genital trends interfere with oral ones at a stage when normally the oral desires are uppermost. Here again we have to consider the effects of early confusion, which expresses itself in a blurring of the oral, anal, and genital impulses and phantasies. An overlapping between these various sources both of libido and of aggressiveness is normal. But when the overlapping amounts to an incapacity to experience sufficiently the predominance of either of these trends at their proper stage of development, then both later sexual life and sublimations are adversely affected. Genitality based on a flight from orality is insecure because into it are carried over the suspicions and disappointments attaching to the impaired oral enjoyment. The interference with oral primacy by genital trends undermines the gratification in the genital sphere and often is the cause of obsessional masturbation and of promiscuity. For the lack of the primary enjoyment introduces into the genital desires compulsive elements and, as I have seen with some patients, may therefore lead to sexual sensations entering into all activities, thought processes, and interests. With some infants, the flight into genitality is also a defence against hating and injuring the first object towards which ambivalent feelings operate. I have found that the premature onset of genitality may be bound up with the early occurrence of guilt and is characteristic of paranoid and schizoid cases.

('Envy and gratitude', 1957; pp. 195–196)

In this paragraph Klein is following Freud's original model of the stages in infantile development in which oral precedes genital primacy, and making a most important point about how damaging it can be when this ordinary sequencing is disrupted. Klein links Freud's delineation of the normal stages of psychic development with her understanding of the great importance of satisfactory early splitting and the severe problems arising when this is not achieved, and in consequence when confusion reigns. Confusion between good and bad and confusion between oral and genital impulses both give rise to difficulties in establishing stable object relations and may of course both operate.

She goes on to integrate these elements with her theory of paranoid and depressive positions, in particular contrasting these early forms of persecutory guilt with the encounter with guilt in the context of anxieties about damage to the good object. This later form of guilt is more open to mitigation by hope. Here she is elaborating the links between her new understanding of destructive envy and her earlier distinction between paranoid and depressive anxieties. The form of envy primarily discussed in 'Envy and gratitude' is the very early unconscious envy of the primary object, and understanding this phenomenon adds an important dimension to the landscape of paranoid-schizoid states of mind. The depressive position, involving concern for the object, is based on the development of increased trust in the good object and in the good aspects of the self, and involves a different form of guilt.

> This hope is based on the growing unconscious knowledge that the internal and external object is not as bad as it was felt to be in its split-off aspects. Through mitigation of hatred by love the object improves in the infant's mind. It is no longer so strongly felt to have been destroyed in the past and the danger of its being destroyed in the future is lessened; not being injured, it is also felt to be less vulnerable in the present and future. The internal object acquires a restraining and self-preservative attitude and its greater strength is an important aspect of its super-ego function.
>
> In describing the overcoming of the depressive position, bound up with the greater trust in the good internal object, I do not intend to convey that such results cannot be temporarily undone. Strain of an internal or external nature is liable to stir up depression and distrust in the self as well as in the object. However, the capacity to emerge from such depressive states, and to regain one's feeling of inner security, is in my view the criterion of a well-developed personality. By contrast, the frequent way of dealing with depression by hardening one's feelings and denying depression is a regression to the manic defences used during the infantile depressive position.
>
> (p. 196)

This last paragraph reminds us that Klein's conception of the depressive position was not that it involved an on-going depressed state, but that it represented an internal relationship to objects which made possible a development beyond the oscillation between depression and mania. But she also delineates here a sense of the life of any individual, including continuing fluctuations in inner states.

Oedipal issues in infancy

Following this discussion of the impact of envy on the initial two-person relationship between baby and mother, Klein turns to the Oedipal dimension and the links between envy and jealousy. She picks up again the problem of the baby's readiness or lack of it for facing triangular relations, which she believes is bound up with an early good experience of the 'exclusive' relationship to mother which has not been too much disturbed by envy or other factors. She presents the Oedipal three-person drama as one which in ordinary circumstances follows and can build on what the mother–baby couple have established and what has been internalised in the baby.

> The development of the Oedipus complex is strongly influenced by the vicissitudes of the first exclusive relation with the mother, and when this relation is disturbed too soon, the rivalry with the father enters prematurely. Phantasies of the penis inside the mother, or inside her breast, turn the father into a hostile intruder. This phantasy is particularly strong when the infant has not had the full enjoyment and happiness that the early relation to the mother can afford him and has not taken in the first good object with some security. Such failure partly depends on the strength of envy.
>
> *(continued)*

(continued)

When in earlier writings I described the depressive position, I showed that at that stage the infant progressively integrates his feelings of love and hatred, synthesizes the good and bad aspects of the mother, and goes through states of mourning bound up with feelings of guilt. He also begins to understand more of the external world and realizes that he cannot keep his mother to himself as his exclusive possession. Whether or not the infant can find help against that grief in the relation to the second object, the father, or to other people in his surroundings, largely depends on the emotions which he experiences towards his lost unique object. If that relation was well founded, the fear of losing the mother is less strong and the capacity to share her is greater. Then he can also experience more love towards his rivals. All this implies that he has been able to work through the depressive position satisfactorily, which in turn depends on envy towards the primal object not being excessive.

Jealousy is, as we know, inherent in the Oedipus situation and is accompanied by hate and death wishes. Normally, however, the gain of new objects who can be loved – the father and siblings – and other compensations which the developing ego derives from the external world, mitigate to some extent jealousy and grievance. If paranoid and schizoid mechanisms are strong, jealousy – and ultimately envy – remain unmitigated. The development of the Oedipus complex is essentially influenced by all these factors.

Among the features of the earliest stage of the Oedipus complex are the phantasies of the mother's breast and the mother containing the penis of the father, or the father containing the mother. This is the basis of the combined parent figure, and I have elaborated the importance of this phantasy in earlier writings. The influence of the combined parent figure on the infant's ability to differentiate between the parents, and to establish good relations with each of them, is affected by the strength of envy and the intensity of his Oedipus jealousy. For the suspicion that the parents are always getting sexual gratification from one another reinforces the phantasy – derived from various sources – that they are always combined. If these anxieties are strongly operative, and therefore unduly prolonged, the consequence may be a lasting disturbance in the relation to both parents. In very ill individuals, the inability to disentangle the relation to the father from the one to the mother, because of their being inextricably interlinked in the patient's mind, plays an important rôle in severe states of confusion.

If envy is not excessive, jealousy in the Oedipus situation becomes a means of working it through.

(pp. 197–198)

This last sentence is particularly interesting because it highlights the enrichment of the infant's world of the widening group of family relationships. Klein sees jealousy of father and siblings as providing a context for hostility to be 'distributed'. Mother does not have to be the only repository of hatred! Similarly, relationships offer new opportunities for love and the experience of being loved. The enlarged world of the infant provides a fresh context for 'working through' as long as some experience of such a process has already been achieved, in Klein's view. This, however, depends on the security arising from a good early relationship to the mother having been achieved. Where there has been early deprivation or disruption of the mother–infant bond, the child will be even more vulnerable to Oedipal difficulties, particularly when premature genital excitement and phantasy have replaced the compromised oral gratification.

There is an obvious connection between the illness Klein described as rooted in a disturbed confusion between mother and father (a combined parental figure which cannot be separated into its component parts) and her earlier point about premature genital primacy interfering with early object relations. She is here explaining how the failure to establish a good object which can serve as the stable core of the ego leads to further problems as the baby confronts further awareness of the father and siblings. The whole Oedipal situation is distorted and cannot be worked through.

It is interesting to follow some of the later debates about Klein's view of envy as dyadic. Her own description of the 'premature' rivalry with father seems to join up envy and jealousy very closely, perhaps leaving us with a theory of envy as dyadic but a clinical description which is more complicated. In explaining this complexity, Sodré (2008) suggests that envy appears once separateness is felt, and that the feeding breast (Klein's object of envy) is not equated with goodness but experienced as possessing goodness, which implies a three-part relation. In somewhat similar vein, Meltzer (1973) developed further the idea of nipple and breast as representing the paternal and maternal aspects of the combined parental object (the nipple being evidence of the penis within mother), which also reframes the first relationship to mother's breast as one in which mother's relationship to father is unconsciously recognised.

The overall picture of development we are introduced to in Klein's discussion of early infancy is very rich and wide ranging. Her imaginative freedom is evident in the way she moves between descriptions of infantile states and the clinical experiences which have fertilised her conceptualisations, which range from observations about ambition to penis envy, frigidity, some elements of homosexuality, and the differential male and female experience of parenthood.

She then returns to her emphasis on the importance of creativity in human life, and the interaction between envious impulses and creative potential.

Envy, creativity and the power of gratitude

> The capacity to give and to preserve life is felt as the greatest gift and therefore creativeness becomes the deepest cause for envy. The spoiling of creativity implied in envy is illustrated in Milton's *Paradise Lost* where Satan, envious of God, decides to become the usurper of Heaven. He makes war on God in his attempt to spoil the heavenly life and falls out of Heaven. Fallen, he and his other fallen angels build Hell as a rival to Heaven, and become the destructive force which attempts to destroy what God creates. This theological idea seems to come down from St Augustine, who describes Life as a creative force opposed to Envy, a destructive force. In this connection, the First Letter to the Corinthians reads, 'Love envieth not'.
>
> My psycho-analytic experience has shown me that envy of creativeness is a fundamental element in the disturbance of the creative process. To spoil and destroy the initial source of goodness soon leads to destroying and attacking the babies that the mother contains and results in the good object being turned into a hostile, critical, and envious one. The super-ego figure on which strong envy has been projected becomes particularly persecutory and interferes with thought processes and with every productive activity, ultimately with creativeness.
>
> (p. 202)

The link between the capacity for gratitude and creativity has been developed by a number of later writers. Bion, Meltzer and Caper, for example, have all explored the idea that the establishment of an internal parental couple felt to be creatively linked, and also represented by the analyst–patient couple working together towards containment of envy, was both the bulwark against destructive envy and its main object of attack. It is interesting that, in writing about envy, Klein makes so much use of literature: the Old and New Testaments, Shakespeare, Chaucer, Milton, Spenser and Goethe all contribute to the richness of her text. This turn towards literature and myth is evident also in many later writers on envy who draw on Shakespeare and others to elaborate the subtle workings of the envious disposition. Klein also describes movingly how inter-generational relationships can express gratitude and relative freedom from envy:

> Whereas envy is a source of great unhappiness, a relative freedom from it is felt to underlie contented and peaceful states of mind – ultimately sanity. This is also in fact the basis of inner resources and resilience which can be observed in people who, even after great adversity and mental pain, regain their peace of mind. Such an attitude, which includes gratitude for pleasures of the past and enjoyment of what the present can give, expresses itself in serenity. In old people, it makes possible the adaptation to the knowledge that youth cannot be regained and enables them to take pleasure and interest in the lives of young people. The well-known fact that parents relive in their children and grand-children their own lives – if this is not an expression of excessive possessiveness and deflected ambition – illustrates what I am trying to convey. Those who feel that they have had a share in the experience and pleasures of life are much more able to believe in the continuity of life.
>
> (p. 203)

The role of analytic work in enabling envy to be mitigated

The extensive clinical examples which follow in Klein's text underline her conviction of the importance of analysing the transference, and her understanding of the pain occasioned by insight when it is closely linked to emotional experience. The clinical examples, which include examples of how dream analysis contributes to the analytic process, demonstrate how Klein's tolerant and exploratory attitude enabled her patients to feel relief: envy could be contained and rendered knowable and in consequence become a less dangerous emotion, mitigated by feelings of gratitude for pain that had been understood. The range of patients referred to also serves to demonstrate the continuity between more disturbed and more 'normal' states, and the corrosive operation of envy at all these different levels of development. Klein's conception of psychoanalysis as a developmental process shines through. Her hope for her patients is the re-integration of split-off, often destructive aspects of the self, the awareness of which initially causes shock, depression and anxiety but which, if held on to, can expand and strengthen the personality.

> I shall now illustrate some of my conclusions by clinical material. My first instance is taken from the analysis of a woman patient. She had been breast-fed, but circumstances had otherwise not been favourable and she was convinced that her babyhood and feeding

had been wholly unsatisfactory. Her grievance about the past linked with hopelessness about the present and future. Envy of the feeding breast, and the ensuing difficulties in object relations, had already been extensively analysed prior to the material to which I am going to refer.

The patient telephoned and said that she could not come for treatment because of a pain in her shoulder. On the next day she rang me to say that she was still not well but expected to see me on the following day. When, on the third day, she actually came, she was full of complaints. She had been looked after by her maid, but nobody else had taken an interest in her. She described to me that at one moment her pain had suddenly increased, together with a sense of extreme coldness. She had felt an impetuous need for somebody to come at once and cover up her shoulder, so that it should get warm, and to go away again as soon as that was done. At that instant it occurred to her that this must be how she had felt as a baby when she wanted to be looked after and nobody came.

It was characteristic of the patient's attitude to people, and threw light on her earliest relation to the breast, that she desired to be looked after but at the same time repelled the very object which was to gratify her. The suspicion of the gift received, together with her impetuous need to be cared for, which ultimately meant a desire to be fed, expressed her ambivalent attitude towards the breast. I have referred to infants whose response to frustration is to make insufficient use of the gratification that the feed, even if delayed, could give them. I would surmise that though they do not give up their desires for a gratifying breast, they cannot enjoy it and therefore repel it. The case under discussion illustrates some of the reasons for this attitude: suspicion of the gift she wished to receive because the object was already spoilt by envy and hatred, and at the same time deep resentment about every frustration. We also have to remember – and this applies to other adults in whom envy is marked – that many disappointing experiences, no doubt partly due to her own attitude, had contributed to her feeling that the desired care would not be satisfactory.

In the course of this session the patient reported a dream: she was in a restaurant, seated at a table; however nobody came to serve her. She decided to join a queue and fetch herself something to eat. In front of her was a woman who took two or three little cakes and went away with them. The patient also took two or three little cakes. From her associations I am selecting the following: the woman seemed very determined, and her figure was reminiscent of mine. There was a sudden doubt about the name of the cakes (actually *petits fours*) which she first thought were 'petit fru', which reminded her of 'petit frau' and thus of 'Frau Klein'. The gist of my interpretations was that her grievance about the missed analytic sessions related to the unsatisfactory feeds and unhappiness in babyhood. The two cakes out of the 'two or three' stood for the breast which she felt she had been twice deprived of by missing analytic sessions. There were 'two or three' because she was not sure whether she would be able to come on the third day. The fact that the woman was 'determined' and that the patient followed her example in taking the cakes pointed both at her identification with the analyst and at projection

(continued)

(continued)

of her own greed on to her. In the present context, one aspect of the dream is most relevant. The analyst who went away with the two or three *petits fours* stood not only for the breast which was withheld, but also for the breast which was going to *feed itself*. (Taken together with other material, the 'determined' analyst represented not only a breast but a person with whose qualities, good and bad, the patient identified herself.)

To frustration had thus been added envy of the breast. This envy had given rise to bitter resentment, for the mother had been felt to be selfish and mean, feeding and loving herself rather than her baby. In the analytic situation I was suspected of having enjoyed myself during the time when she was absent, or of having given the time to other patients whom I preferred. The queue which the patient had decided to join referred to other more favoured rivals.

The response to the analysis of the dream was a striking change in the emotional situation. The patient now experienced a feeling of happiness and gratitude more vividly than in previous analytic sessions. She had tears in her eyes, which was unusual, and said that she felt as if she now had had an entirely satisfactory feed. It also occurred to her that her breast-feeding and her infancy might have been happier than she had assumed. Also, she felt more hopeful about the future and the result of her analysis. The patient had more fully realized one part of herself, which was by no means unknown to her in other connections. She was aware that she was envious and jealous of various people but had not been able to recognize it sufficiently in the relation to the analyst because it was too painful to experience that she was envying and spoiling the analyst as well as the success of the analysis. In this session, after the interpretations referred to, her envy had lessened; the capacity for enjoyment and gratitude had come to the fore, and she was able to experience the analytic session as a happy feed. This emotional situation had to be worked through over and over again, both in the positive and negative transference, until a more stable result was achieved.

It was by enabling her gradually to bring the split-off parts of her self together in relation to the analyst, and by her recognizing how envious and therefore suspicious she was of me, and in the first place of her mother, that the experience of that happy feed came about. This was bound up with feelings of gratitude. In the course of the analysis envy was diminished and feelings of gratitude became much more frequent and lasting.
(pp. 204–206)

In characteristic fashion, after the discussion of anxieties associated with unconscious envy Klein tackles the description of defences, making clear her appreciation of the ego's task to defend the individual from levels of anxiety which would be overwhelming. She highlights the defensive use of idealisation ('strongly exalting the object and its gifts is an attempt to diminish envy'), confusion (between good and bad) which disturbs the capacity for clear thinking, flight from the close relationship to mother to a focus on others (often father in the first instance) in order to preserve mother from hostile envy, dispersal of intense feelings (a basis for promiscuity), devaluation of the object (which involves ingratitude) and of the self (the incapacity to enjoy one's own gifts). The link between envy and greed can be detected when internalising processes (like a 'greedy' baby at the breast) are so greedy in quality that the object is felt to be entirely possessed and controlled, and all its goodness becomes one's own.

The painfulness of feeling envious (the 'pangs' of envy of common speech) can be avoided by stirring up envy in others and thus reversing the situation and pain can also be evaded by the 'stifling of feelings of love and corresponding intensifying of hate' or indifference, because this obscures the guilt associated with envy and hatred of the loved object.

Despite the evocativeness of these descriptions of defences against envy, Klein does not herself provide clinical examples which delineate these. It may be useful to offer a brief clinical vignette from work with a child which picks up on some of the elements she pinpoints. Klein's own examples are all from adult analyses, although she emphasises the importance of her experience as a child analyst in understanding these aspects of the mind.

Clinical vignette

The patient, Bella, is a somewhat immature nine-year-old girl whose severe difficulties had earlier led to a period of inpatient treatment. At this point she is attending three times weekly psychotherapy in an outpatient clinic.

She is restricted in all areas of her life, having problems in making friends, in learning, and in enjoying family relationships.

She has always been extremely preoccupied with her therapist's clothes, and especially shoes. One day she drew her therapist's attention to her T-shirt which read, 'I'm feeling sweet', but following this she asked, 'Why aren't you wearing your silver shoes? Why do you always wear heels?' She went on to construct a plasticine scene in which a 'colourful caterpillar' and a 'cat with a long tail' teased a lonely spider who was tormented and excluded by the caterpillar–cat couple. The therapist's efforts to sympathise with the jealous spider led to Bella complaining that she did not like sitting on a chair smaller than the therapist's, and moving to one identical to hers. Later there were references to repair work she had observed in the clinic building which had sparked curiosity and anxiety. As the end of the session approached, Bella started to hit her therapist's feet. The therapist commented that she did not like to see the shoes which made her feel different. Bella asked, pointing to a crease in the shoe leather, 'who scratched it?' Then she went to sit in the largest chair in the room. Her therapist said, 'When you feel different and small it makes you feel upset. You would like to feel big just now. You do not like my feet which take me away from you when the session ends and you feel like scratching and messing up my shoes.'

Here we have an example in which a little girl's wish to feel sweet and beautiful stirs up furious envy of her therapist who is felt to have all the good things – silver shoes, heels (the evidence of growing status), the big chair, a partner, knowledge of what is going on in the clinic building. The caterpillar–cat couple suggest a smug pair, cruelly enjoying the exclusion of the miserable spider, a picture of a sexual couple completely unable to feel for the jealous and envious child. 'The spider has to be alone,' said Bella with a nasty smile. There is a glimpse here of the idealisation (the 'silver shoes') Klein refers to, and of the devaluation (the scratching spoiling of the admired and envied shoes) and confusion (the nice and nasty therapist is conflated in Bella's mind). Bella's state delineates Klein's point that defences against envy do not really work and that they simultaneously further deplete the individual's capacity to benefit from relationships.

Klein goes on to note work by colleagues (Rosenfeld and others) on the role of envy in extreme states of disturbance, in just the way that we can see arises in Bella's relationship with her therapist:

> When schizoid and paranoid features are in the ascendant, defences against envy cannot be successful, for the attacks on the subject lead to an increased feeling of persecution that can only be dealt with by renewed attacks, that is to say, by reinforcing the destructive impulses. In this way is set up a vicious circle that impairs the ability to counteract envy. This applies particularly to schizophrenic cases and explains to some extent the difficulties in the way of curing them.
>
> (p. 219)

In summary, she groups these defences as among those which combine to form the basis for a negative therapeutic reaction during analysis. This leads on to a discussion of difficulties which can impede analytic progress, and the need to be prepared for 'fluctuations between improvements and setbacks', an insight further developed in Britton's conceptualisation, following Bion, of the necessary oscillations between paranoid-schizoid and depressive configurations (Britton, 1998a).

Impediments to gratitude

Klein links this to the problem of gratitude:

> The incapacity of the patient to accept with gratitude an interpretation which in some parts of his mind he recognizes as helpful is one aspect of the negative therapeutic reaction. Under the same heading there are many other difficulties, a few of which I shall now mention. We must be prepared to find that whenever the patient makes progress in integration, that is to say, when the envious, hating and hated part of the personality has come closer together with other parts of the self, intense anxieties might come to the fore, and increase the patient's distrust in his loving impulses. The stifling of love, which I have described as a manic defence during the depressive position, is rooted in the danger threatening from destructive impulses and persecutory anxiety. In an adult, dependence on a loved person revives the helplessness of the infant and is felt to be humiliating. But there is more to it than infantile helplessness: the child can be excessively dependent on the mother, if his anxiety lest his destructive impulses change her into a persecutory or damaged object is too great; and this over-dependence can be revived in the transference situation. The anxiety lest, if one gives way to love, greed should destroy the object, is another cause for stifling loving impulses. There is also the fear that love will lead to too much responsibility and that the object will make too many demands. The unconscious knowledge that hate and destructive impulses are operative may make the patient feel more sincere in not admitting love either to himself or others.
>
> ('Envy and gratitude', 1957; pp. 222–223)

She also notes the inevitable defensive role of splitting, repression, the clinging to a strong positive transference, and increase in omnipotent and megalomaniac phantasies, but concludes thus:

> I [have] stressed the difficulties arising at certain points in the analysis of patients whose envy is constitutionally strong. However, the analysis of those deep and severe disturbances is in many cases a safeguard against potential danger of psychosis resulting from excessively envious and omnipotent attitudes. But it is essential not to attempt to hurry these steps in integration. For if the realization of the division in his personality were to come suddenly, the patient would have great difficulties in coping with it. The more strongly had the envious and destructive impulses been split off, the more dangerous the patient feels them to be when he becomes conscious of them. In analysis we should make our way slowly and gradually towards the painful insight into the divisions in the patient's self. This means that the destructive sides are again and again split off and regained, until greater integration comes about. As a result, the feeling of responsibility becomes stronger, and guilt and depression are more fully experienced. When this happens, the ego is strengthened, omnipotence of destructive impulses is diminished, together with envy, and the capacity for love and gratitude, stifled in the course of splitting processes, is released. Therefore the split-off aspects gradually become more acceptable and the patient is increasingly able to repress destructive impulses towards loved objects instead of splitting the self. This implies that the projection on the analyst, which turns him into a dangerous and retaliating figure, also diminishes, and that the analyst in turn finds it easier to help the patient towards further integration. That is to say, the negative therapeutic reaction is losing in strength.
>
> (pp. 224–225)

Klein contrasts her technique with an approach which reinforces the positive transference and avoids the negative, and attempts to take the role of the good object. She argues, as so often elsewhere, that techniques based on reassurance do not produce lasting results. But she also emphasises the degree of pain evoked by a dawning awareness of destructive envy, and the repeated efforts to avoid this which take place. This links to later work on pathological organisations by O'Shaughnessy (1981a, 1992) and Steiner (1993), and on destructive narcissism by Rosenfeld (1964, 1971, 1987), which amplify understanding of analytic impasses.

Constitutional and environmental factors

Before summarising her conclusions, Klein reiterates her view (which she bolsters with reference to Freud and Abraham) of the importance of constitutional factors in the individual variations in development, but she balances this with attention to the variety of external experiences:

> I have previously suggested that greed, hate, and persecutory anxieties in relation to the primal object, the mother's breast, have an innate basis. In this discussion, I have added that envy too, as a powerful expression of oral- and anal-sadistic impulses, is
>
> *(continued)*

(continued)

constitutional. The variations in the intensity of these constitutional factors are in my view linked with the preponderance of the one or other instinct in the fusion of the life and death instincts postulated by Freud. I believe there is a connection between the preponderance of the one or other instinct and the strength or weakness of the ego. I have often referred to the strength of the ego in relation to the anxieties it has to cope with as a constitutional factor. Difficulties in bearing anxiety, tension, and frustration are an expression of an ego which, from the beginning of post-natal life, is weak in proportion to the intense destructive impulses and persecutory feelings it experiences. These strong anxieties imposed on a weak ego lead to an excessive use of defences such as denial, splitting, and omnipotence, which to some extent are always characteristic of earliest development. In keeping with my thesis, I would add that a constitutionally strong ego does not easily become a prey to envy and is more capable of effecting the splitting between good and bad which I assume to be a precondition for establishing the good object. The ego is then less liable to those splitting processes which lead to fragmentation and are part of marked paranoid-schizoid features.

Another factor that influences development from the beginning is the variety of external experiences through which the infant goes. This in some measure explains the development of his early anxieties, which would be particularly great in a baby who had a difficult birth and unsatisfactory feeding. My accumulated observations, however, have convinced me that the impact of these external experiences is in proportion to the constitutional strength of the innate destructive impulses and the ensuing paranoid anxieties. Many infants have not had very unfavourable experiences and yet suffer from serious difficulties in feeding and sleeping, and we can see in them every sign of great anxiety for which external circumstances do not account sufficiently.

It is also well known that some infants are exposed to great deprivations and unfavourable circumstances, and yet do not develop excessive anxieties, which would suggest that their paranoid and envious traits are not predominant; this is often confirmed by their later history.

I have had many opportunities in my analytic work to trace the origin of character formation to variations in innate factors. There is much more to be learnt about prenatal influences; but even greater knowledge about them would not detract from the importance of inborn elements in determining the strength of the ego and of instinctual drives.

The existence of the innate factors referred to above points to the limitations of psycho-analytic therapy. While I fully realize this, my experience has taught me that nevertheless we are able in a number of cases to produce fundamental and positive changes, even where the constitutional basis was unfavourable.

('Envy and gratitude', 1957; pp. 229–230)

These paragraphs present Klein's characteristic balance in firmly arguing for the importance of innate factors in psychic development, at the same time referring to the impact of early experience. While this balance has by no means been fully recognised in many of the responses to Klein's work, it is none the less quite evident. Clinical work during the decades since her death has continued to investigate the differential contribution of 'constitutional' and 'environmental' factors (Rosenfeld, 1987; Roth and Lemma, 2008) through scrutinising transference and countertransference phenomena in fine detail.

Klein's careful discussion in this passage of the contribution of innate and environmental factors in bringing about severe difficulties in psychic development and character formation has been of special importance in subsequent analytic work with children and adolescents. The expansion of psychoanalytic psychotherapy for children in publicly funded clinics meant that some who had suffered from severe deprivation and/or maltreatment in their early years was offered therapy, and in hospital departments children with a variety of complex illnesses and disabilities were also considered for treatment. These developments opened up a wide field of study in exploring the relative weight and interaction of innate and environmental features of the clinical picture. It also meant that assessment of the child's potential to make use of treatment was required in the light of limited resources. Klein's psychoanalytic attitude, which embraced an awareness of the potential limitations of therapeutic outcome while demonstrating that fundamental change could be achieved even when environment and constitution were negative factors, has proved inspirational in supporting this extension of psychoanalytic approaches to childhood disturbance.

Her concluding remarks highlight what she sees as her fresh contribution to theory in this book:

- the spoiling and destructive quality of envy
- the importance of the relation to the analyst as an internal object
- the 'envious superego' which can destroy reparation and creative activity
- the importance of primary envy, and early splitting and integrative processes in laying the foundations of the ego's capacity for repression in the second year of life
- a persevering technique which gives adequate space for 'working through'.

As we can see, most of these points focus on envy, and imply some imbalance in the exploration of the polarities of envy and gratitude. What should surely be added to Klein's list is her exploration of the place of gratitude not only in mitigating envy but in strengthening the inner relationship to good objects and in supporting creative sublimation. Perhaps some imbalance is unavoidable, since clinical material is inevitably more attuned to the difficulties that patients bring for which they are seeking help. On the whole, analytic writers are very modest in their description of patients' recovery and the development of their personalities and good qualities, being wary of idealisation by the patient or indeed of their own work. The clinical basis of psychoanalytic theory is always somewhat liable to the criticism that it foregrounds the pathological rather than the developmental or 'healthier' attributes of analysands. Klein's reputation as the analyst who emphasised the role of envy is a particular instance of this tendency. At the same time, the weightiness of what she is describing is indeed a demand on her readers to take a very dispassionate – indeed, a psychoanalytic – attitude to such disturbing clinical observations.

Her own final reflections include a discussion of the possibility that a patient's severe depressive pains and anxiety may outweigh the desire for truth and thus limit what analysis can achieve. The split-off part of the self can be feared as totally inimical to both self and object and be felt to be too dangerous to admit to consciousness. The humanity and wisdom with which she writes of the intense suffering of such individuals are also present in her more hopeful assessment of less disturbed individuals, but she also warns:

> Complete and permanent integration is in my view never possible. For under strain from external or internal sources, even well-integrated people may be driven to stronger splitting processes, even though this may be a passing phase.
>
> (p. 233)

The value of psychoanalysis

Her approach to her work as an analyst is beautifully conveyed in the penultimate paragraph:

> In taking the analysis back to earliest infancy, we enable the patient to revive fundamental situations – a revival which I have often spoken of as 'memories in feeling'. In the course of this revival, it becomes possible for the patient to develop a different attitude to his early frustrations. There is no doubt that if the infant was actually exposed to very unfavourable conditions, the retrospective establishing of a good object cannot undo bad early experiences. However, the introjection of the analyst as a good object, if not based on idealization has, to some extent, the effect of providing an internal good object where it has been largely lacking. Also, the weakening of projections, and therefore the achieving of greater tolerance, bound up with less resentment, make it possible for the patient to find some features and to revive pleasant memories of the past, even when the early situation was very unfavourable. The means by which this is achieved is the analysis of the negative and positive transference which takes us back to earliest object relations. All this becomes possible because the integration resulting from the analysis has strengthened the ego, which was weak at the beginning of life. It is on these lines that the psycho-analysis of psychotics may also succeed.
>
> (pp. 234–235)

This eloquent summary of the potential of psychoanalytic therapy reminds us that Klein's assumption was that the analyst had to bear fully the patient's painful negative feelings in the transference relationship. This can be a very prolonged and difficult experience, evoking feelings of despair in the analyst where there seems little evidence in the patient of a capacity for love. However, this is precisely what enables the analyst to understand the hopelessness and depression of the patient when cut off from good aspects of self and objects.

Part 2

Chapter 9

Introduction to Part 2

Ethics, aesthetics, society and the work of Melanie Klein

Klein's writing was almost entirely focused on the clinical practice and theory of psychoanalysis, and was based largely on her experiences in the consulting room and on her engagement with the work of other psychoanalysts, whether as analysts, teachers or colleagues. Freud had sought to demonstrate the relevance of psychoanalytic conceptions and methods to almost the whole field of human civilisation and culture, although clinical practice with individual analysands remained for him at the centre of psychoanalysis. Over subsequent years, psychoanalysis became professionalised through the development of structured and regulated trainings, in which personal analysis, the transmission of theoretical principles and clinical supervision remained its central activities. None of Freud's contemporaries and followers equalled him in his capacity and zeal to extend the field of application of psychoanalysis so widely, without straying from a primary commitment to psychoanalytic practice itself.

While therefore Freud published widely, for many audiences and on many subjects, Klein by contrast wrote largely for psychoanalysts and those professionally committed to the psychoanalytic field. Freud became a world-famous public figure, from early in his psychoanalytic career, but Klein did not seek wider attention, and became publicly well known only later in her career, as her ideas were taken up and developed by followers and colleagues and as her papers were collected and published in books. She did address a small number of papers to lay audiences, in a direct and expressive way, and she wrote occasionally on non-clinical subjects, but these writings were a small proportion of her published work. It has however become apparent in recent years that the psychoanalytic ideas of 'the Kleinian tradition' have no less relevance and application to various spheres of culture and society than those of Freud. Indeed, 'the Kleinian development' of Freud's ideas can be found to have relevance to most of the extra-clinical domains about which Freud himself wrote – for example, to questions of ethics, the arts and aesthetics, and to society and politics. Yet since Klein's own writings in only a small number of instances extended beyond the clinical domain, making these wider connections is work that has been left to the many colleagues and followers inspired and influenced by her ideas.

In the second part of this book, we will show how key ideas from Klein's own writing became the basis for their development in the spheres of aesthetics, ethics and social science. The volume of papers, *New Directions in Psycho-Analysis*, edited by Melanie Klein, Paula Heimann and Roger Money-Kyrle (1955), and thus a part of Klein's own output of published work, will be one of our starting points for each of these areas of application of her ideas.

Chapter 10

Kleinian ethics

The morality of love and hate

The link between Klein's writing and the concerns of moral philosophy and ethics is a paradoxical one. She scarcely addressed herself explicitly to writings on this subject, other than those occurring within the field of psychoanalysis itself. Unlike Freud, she only rarely referred to or engaged with recognised works or classics of philosophy, literature or other fields of scholarship in her reflections on human nature and its moral propensities. Yet on the other hand, her work is saturated with investigations of human dispositions and states of mind which have a deeply ethical significance. She writes, for example, about greed, jealousy, envy, gratitude, guilt, love, hate and reparation, as central themes of her work – all of these are concepts of obvious moral significance, since they refer to normatively framed ways in which human beings relate to one another, in their thoughts, emotions and actions. The psyche in Klein's account is organised through its relations to what it experiences as good and bad. Her account of the psychological development of human beings from infancy gives a large significance to the emergence of a moral sense, although she describes this in terms of emotions, dispositions and orientations towards others, and not in the language of philosophical ethics. Klein believed that a capacity for love and concern for others was innate in human beings, although it always co-existed with opposed dispositions to hate and to injure. Her account of the form taken in the earliest stages of life of the impulses to love and hate – their oral and anal dimensions, their passion and infantile ferocity – shocked many readers, as it challenged (as Freud had done) commonly held notions of the essential innocence of infants. The starkness of her descriptions may have contributed to the misleading view of Klein as giving excessive emphasis to the destructive dimensions of human nature, when this is far from the central perspective of her work. Her theory of the paranoid-schizoid and depressive positions challenges Freud's account of the origins and nature of the moral sense. The idea of morality as embodied in the functions of the superego, as a form of internalised coercion or repression, is radically supplemented in Klein's account by the idea of the normal emergence, in the development of the 'depressive position', of concern for the well-being of the object and of desire to make reparation for harms inflicted (in phantasy and reality) upon it. In essence, in Klein's view, the moral sense arises both from a primitively internalised fear of punishment and retribution, and, in healthy development, from the emergence of a concern for the well-being of others motivated by love, which Klein thought of as the 'normal' superego (O'Shaughnessy, 1999).

We shall try to demonstrate in this chapter the relevance of Klein's psychoanalytical account of human nature and its development, to the broader understanding of ethical issues, especially as these have been formulated by moral philosophers.

Moral philosophies customarily set out views of the principles of conduct which human beings ought to follow, and/or of the goods or virtues to which they should aspire. But such statements of the desirable, the ideal or the obligatory need to pay regard to the facts or realities of human nature as they are understood to be, or they become mere ungrounded prescriptions. It is these realities of human nature which Klein's work addressed.[1]

We will first set out several dimensions of Klein's thinking which have relevance to questions of morality and goodness:

1 her insistence that human beings are essentially social in their nature, psychologically connected to others and 'object-related', from the very beginning of their lives;
2 her idea that the personality is formed, as development takes place, through processes of projective and introjective identification with those persons – especially a child's parents or parent-substitutes – in close relationships with it (these are referred to as 'objects' in psychoanalytic theory, but they are primarily human beings or aspects of them);
3 her view that the principal determinant of the orientation of individuals towards others is the balance of love and hate in their personalities. The balance between these dispositions is shaped by experiences of nurturance and care, as well as by innate aspects of the personality;
4 her contention that the superego, described by Freud as emerging as a response to the Oedipal situation in the third year of life, as the embodiment of the moral sense, in fact emerges earlier than this, in a more primitive form which can undermine rather than support the human capacity for moral relatedness;
5 her account of the paranoid-schizoid and depressive positions, and the idea that central to the depressive position is an extended conception of moral capability, based on the wish to make reparation to the other or 'object' for the harm imagined or believed to have been inflicted by the self. Ethical impulses – the desire to do good to others (and also to care for the self) – are thus for Klein based not only on rules imposed by the conscience or primitive superego, but also on dispositions to love and restore;
6 finally, the perspective she shared with Freud that behaviour towards others, and towards the self, is substantially shaped by unconscious or 'internal' states of mind. It followed from Klein's view not only that individuals could be made less subject to anxieties and compulsions in their lives through the understanding of unconscious states of mind, but also that such understanding might enhance their dispositions to take account of the needs of others, and behave with greater care and responsibility towards them.

These ideas, developed by Klein throughout her work, are, taken together, a significant contribution to the understanding of moral capabilities. They should be understood as a major contribution to moral philosophy, although only a small number of philosophers have recognised them as such.[2] We suggest that they are as important as any ideas bearing on ethical issues that were produced in the human sciences during her lifetime.

1 The psychoanalyst close to Klein who explored implications of her ideas for ethics and politics was Roger Money-Kyrle. In his essay 'Psycho-analysis and ethics' in the *New Directions in Psycho-Analysis* volume (1955), in his book *Psychoanalysis and Politics* (1951) and in later essays published in his *Collected Papers* (Meltzer, 1978), Money-Kyrle sought to show that the psychoanalytic understanding of unconscious motivations, and in particular of the paranoid-schizoid and depressive aspects of the superego, provides moral insights which can contribute to a morally and socially responsible way of life.

2 These philosophers include Richard Wollheim, Sebastian Gardner, Jim Hopkins and Jonathan Lear.

We shall follow the practice of previous chapters in presenting passages from some key texts in which Klein's ideas were set out, before describing their significance.

Relatedness as the essence of human nature

> The analysis of very young children has taught me that there is no instinctual urge, no anxiety situation, no mental process, which does not involve objects, external or internal; in other words, object-relations are at the *centre* of emotional life. Furthermore, love and hatred, phantasies, anxieties, and defences are also operative from the beginning and are *ab initio* indivisibly linked with object-relations. This insight showed me many phenomena in a new light.
>
> ('The origins of transference', 1952; p. 53)

This idea is the foundation stone not only of Kleinian psychoanalysis, but of psychoanalytic object-relations theory more broadly. Other object-relations theorists like Winnicott accepted this idea of Klein's (and similar ideas developed contemporaneously by other writers such as Fairbairn, to a degree anticipating her work) but rejected other of her theoretical commitments, notably the idea of primary destructiveness and envy. Although her idea challenged Freud's original view of the infant's development, it was consistent with, and indeed developed from, what Freud said in his later work. It was Freud's discussions in 'Mourning and melancholia' (1917) and 'Group psychology and the analysis of the ego' (1921) which began to set out a more complex and meaning-centred idea of the psyche, in contrast to Freud's earlier, more biological instinct-driven model. In 'Mourning and melancholia', the concept of identification with a loved person became central, and this developed into object-relations theory, and into the belief that relatedness was the precondition of psychic well-being. The development of Freud's own ideas during his lifetime, and the writing of some of his colleagues such as Ferenczi and Abraham, was a precondition of the development of Kleinian ideas. Nevertheless, around the theory of primary narcissism, and the early development of the infant's mind, the difference between Freud's and Klein's view is significant.

What is challenged in Klein's assertion, and in the psychoanalytic research programme which followed from it, is the presupposition of a relationship to the world dominated by needs and desires for instinctual gratification which had underpinned Freud's early theory.[3] The counterpoint to this view of the self as fundamentally driven by desires of both libidinal and destructive kinds was Freud's concept of the superego, and its function in inhibiting the recognition and expression of these desires. This idea, that human beings are born as self-gratifying individuals, requiring to be 'socialised' and inducted into relationships as they

3 This is connected to the biological and neurological basis of Freud's earlier theories, in which 'quantitative' explanations in terms of flows of energy and discharges of tension are proposed as explanations of motivation. There seems to be a connection between this psychic model and the materialist presuppositions of the philosophical empiricism of Hobbes, whose goal had been to explain human motivation by developing an equivalent of the 'laws of motion' which Galileo had deployed in relation to physical nature, and Newton was later to develop, in a further relation to human nature. Hobbes's version of this was his theory of appetites and aversions, and the primary human motivation to seek pleasure and avoid pain, which become the foundations of utilitarian moral theory. The shadow of these ideas can surely still be seen in Freud's instinct theory.

develop, is challenged in the Kleinian view, which instead describes a condition of passionate emotional interdependency from the beginning of life.

This realignment in psychoanalytic theory after Freud without doubt has a significantly gendered aspect. The idea that humans begin their lives in a state of primary interdependency and relatedness (although one which is full of conflict and tension) is made especially meaningful by the experience of giving birth and holding a newborn baby at the breast, which Klein of course had herself known. Mothers' as well as babies' mental states become topics of interest to Klein and her successors in the light of this primary experience; for example, the conceptions of the states of 'reverie' and 'primary maternal preoccupation' which Bion and Winnicott respectively described. Klein's imaginative insight enabled her to extrapolate from her understanding of the core experience of mothers and infants theoretical conjectures which were radically to change the understanding of human nature.

The exceptional quality of Klein's insights has been confirmed by subsequent developments not only in psychoanalysis, but in empirical studies of infant development. The first few months of life, once thought of as a blank period so far as mental life is concerned, have been shown to have a remarkable complexity. Infants once thought to be indifferent to the particular identity of the adults who looked after them, with basic needs once believed to be largely for physical care, are now known to be able to recognise their mothers by sound and smell minutes after birth. The organic development of the infant's brain and its neural system, which continues for two years or so after birth, appears to be responsive to the baby's emotional well-being, measured by indicators of stress and anxiety. Ethologists have demonstrated many parallels between mammalian and human attachment patterns. Evolutionary biologists have been able to show that a variety of patterns of attachment behaviour in infants – the repertoire of characteristics and behaviours which makes them attractive to their mothers in particular, and to adults in general, their innate suspicion of strangers, their innate rivalry with siblings – was functional for survival in the hunter-gatherer societies in which the human genetic endowment became more or less fixed, and remain as templates of mental life today. Sarah Hrdy's remarkable book on this topic (Hrdy, 1999) convincingly suggests that mother and baby – even mother and placenta – are in certain circumstances competitors for scarce 'survival resources', notably food. Jim Hopkins (2003) has suggested that her account of the early evolution of human dispositions, in the hunter-gatherer conditions within which human beings were formed genetically, explains the conflictful and ambivalent nature of mother–infant mental life which Klein formulated psychoanalytically.[4] Many of Klein's conjectures about infant mental life, made in some cases in the 1920s, have been supported by empirical researches conducted many decades later.[5] A fully relational theory of human development, which connects neurological conditions, states of mind and social interactions, is in process of emerging, as a rival to a variety of one-dimensional theories of atomistic individualism, whether these be based on materialist, organicist, information-

4 This argument is part of Hopkins's broader thesis (Hopkins, 2014) that a number of developments in the empirical human sciences, in particular in neuroscience, are now demonstrating substantial convergences with psychoanalytic theories which have hitherto been based mainly on the reconstructive evidence and inferences of psychoanalytic clinical practice.

5 Peter Fonagy and Mary Target (2003, Chapter 6) review the recent empirical research bearing on Klein's theoretical conjectures. They conclude: 'it has to be said that some of Melanie Klein's ideas no longer seem as far-fetched as they did at first. None of this is proof of her ideas . . . but [they] . . . cannot be dismissed as implausible given the direction in which developmental science is progressing' (p. 134).

processing, or hedonistic building blocks.[6] Although Melanie Klein's is only one significant contribution to this evolving multi-disciplinary paradigm shift, her's was one of the first and most significant. How striking it is that this revolution in the understanding of human nature and its relational basis should have depended on a gendered, female perspective, in a world of science and ideas previously almost wholly dominated by men.

Projective and introjective identification

In the following passage, Klein describes how the personality develops through processes of identification, beginning early in life within the constellation of intimate family relationships.

> I have already mentioned that the mother is introjected, and that this is a fundamental factor in development. As I see it, object relations start almost at birth. The mother in her good aspects – loving, helping, and feeding the child – is the first good object that the infant makes part of his inner world. His capacity to do so is, I would suggest, up to a point innate. Whether the good object becomes sufficiently part of the self depends to some extent on persecutory anxiety – and accordingly resentment – not being too strong; at the same time a loving attitude on the part of the mother contributes much to the success of this process. If the mother is taken into the child's inner world as a good and dependable object, an element of strength is added to the ego. For I assume that the ego develops largely round this good object, and the identification with the good characteristics of the mother becomes the basis for further helpful identifications. The identification with the good object shows externally in the young child's copying the mother's activities and attitudes; this can be seen in his play and often also in his behaviour towards younger children. A strong identification with the good mother makes it easier for the child to identify also with a good father and later on with other friendly figures. As a result, his inner world comes to contain predominantly good objects and feelings, and these good objects are felt to respond to the infant's love. All this contributes to a stable personality and makes it possible to extend sympathy and friendly feelings to other people. It is clear that a good relation of the parents to each other and to the child, and a happy home atmosphere, play a vital role in the success of this process.
> ('Our adult world and its roots in infancy', 1959; pp. 251–252)

Klein here sets out her idea that the personality is formed from the beginning of life through its identifications with others. In favourable circumstances, identification is with a 'good object', experienced as kind and loving. Klein's view is that the formation, development and conception of the self as capable of loving depend on this early identification. She believes that the infant innately anticipates the presence of an object of this kind available to it. It follows that infants may be able to hold on to whatever their environment offers them of this kind, even in unfavourable circumstances. Her theory of identification does not imply that infants passively mirror the caring environment around them.

According to Klein's view, individuals first come to know and recognise their own states of mind and feeling through the ways in which these are responded to by those who care for

6 Alan Shuttleworth (2002) has referred to this as 'a bio-psycho-social model'.

them.[7] The development of character, in all its forms – everyone knows about the similarities of gesture and expression that one sometimes sees between parents and children – thus parallels the learning of language itself, as an essentially social and interactive process.

Love and hate

Klein goes on to discuss other aspects of this process of identification. First are the feelings of aggression and hate, which remain an element of its identifications, 'however good are the child's feelings towards both parents'. Klein ascribes these feelings, following Freud, to the Oedipal rivalries of male and female children with their same-sex parent. Identification will thus have its negative as well as positive aspects – the self will not be formed in an entirely benign and positive way through these processes.

> Yet, however good are the child's feelings towards both parents, aggressiveness and hate also remain operative. One expression of this is the rivalry with the father which results from the boy's desires towards the mother and all the phantasies linked with them. Such rivalry finds expression in the Oedipus complex, which can be clearly observed in children of three, four, or five years of age. This complex exists, however, very much earlier and is rooted in the baby's first suspicions of the father taking the mother's love and attention away from him.
>
> ('Our adult world and its roots in infancy', 1959; p. 252)

Identification, Klein goes on to argue, comes about through processes of projection as well as introjection. Through projecting part of ourselves into the other person, we come to understand that person as similar to ourselves, although if projection is excessive, it can lead to confusion of the self with its object. We see this in extreme states of mind, for example, when an infant projects its rage into its parent, and then feels terrified of its parent as a consequence. Conversely, excessive introjection can lead to the self becoming dominated by its object. Introjection of a 'bad object' – for example, an actively abusive or violent parent – can lead to the formation of a personality dominated by identification with the abuser.

> We turn now again to projection. By projecting oneself or part of one's impulses and feelings into another person, an identification with that person is achieved, though it will differ from the identification arising from introjection. For if an object is taken into the self (introjected), the emphasis lies on acquiring some of the characteristics of this object and on being influenced by them. On the other hand, in putting part of oneself into the other person (projecting), the identification is based
>
> *(continued)*

7 Meira Likierman (2001; p. 160) put it thus: 'Klein offers a very unusual angle on the development of identity. She shows that it is not a question of simple and increasing self-awareness. The most intense and disturbing parts of the self are only accommodated after they have journeyed through the minds of others, and after the infant has thus externalized his ego's relationship with its most disturbing aspects.'

(continued)

repercussions. We are inclined to attribute to other people – in a sense, to put into them – some of our own emotions and thoughts; and it is obvious that it will depend on how balanced or persecuted we are whether this projection is of a friendly or a hostile nature. By attributing part of our feelings to the other person, we understand their feelings, needs, and satisfactions; in other words, we are putting ourselves into the other person's shoes. There are people who go so far in this direction that they lose themselves entirely in others and become incapable of objective judgement. At the same time excessive introjection endangers the strength of the ego because it becomes completely dominated by the introjected object. If projection is predominantly hostile, real empathy and understanding of others is impaired. The character of projection is, therefore, of great importance in our relations to other people. If the interplay between introjection and projection is not dominated by hostility or overdependence, and is well balanced, the inner world is enriched and the relations with the external world are improved.

('Our adult world and its roots in infancy', 1959; pp. 252–253)

Splitting is an unavoidable aspect of the process of early personality formation, but also an absolutely vital early mental achievement. In order to protect its belief in a good object and in its capacity to love it, the infant splits off its hostile feelings, so that the good and bad aspects of its immediate environment (primarily its mother, often referred to by Klein as the breast) are kept apart from one another. Splitting is therefore a means of protecting the self from its destructive states of mind, and is likely to be resorted to as a defence at moments throughout life, especially when the personality is assailed by anxiety and when negative emotions of fear or hatred threaten to overwhelm the self.

I referred earlier to the tendency of the infantile ego to split impulses and objects, and I regard this as another of the primal activities of the ego. This tendency to split results in part from the fact that the early ego largely lacks coherence. But – here again I have to refer to my own concepts – persecutory anxiety reinforces the need to keep separate the loved object from the dangerous one, and therefore to split love from hate. For the young infant's self-preservation depends on his trust in a good mother. By splitting the two aspects and clinging to the good one he preserves his belief in a good object and his capacity to love it; and this is an essential condition for keeping alive.

('Our adult world and its roots in infancy', 1959; p. 253)

The outcome of these processes of identification depended, in Klein's view, on a combination of the balance of love and hate (or indifference) in the caring environment, and to a degree on the innate dispositions – the emotional resilience – of the infant. Both the 'external' and 'internal' dimensions of experience were crucial to development, in her view, contrary to the view which is sometimes imputed to her.

According to Klein's view, human individuals develop from the beginning in relationship to others:

> I said before that feelings of love and gratitude arise directly and spontaneously in the baby in response to the love and care of his mother. The power of love – which is the manifestation of the forces which tend to preserve life – is there in the baby as well as the destructive impulses, and finds its first fundamental expression in the baby's attachment to his mother's breast, which develops into love for her as a person. My psycho-analytic work has convinced me that when in the baby's mind the conflicts between love and hate arise, and the fears of losing the loved one become active, a very important step is made in development. These feelings of guilt and distress now enter as a new element into the emotion of love. They become an inherent part of love, and influence it profoundly both in quality and quantity.
>
> ('Love, guilt and reparation', 1937; p. 311)

She goes on to discuss identification and making reparation:

> To be genuinely considerate implies that we can put ourselves in the place of other people: we 'identify' ourselves with them. Now this capacity for identification with another person is a most important element in human relationships in general, and is also a condition for real and strong feelings of love. We are only able to disregard or to some extent sacrifice our own feelings and desires, and thus for a time to put the other person's interests and emotions first, if we have the capacity to identify ourselves with the loved person.
>
> ('Love, guilt and reparation', 1937; p. 311)

We can see in these passages the fully 'social view' of human nature that Klein's psychoanalytic thinking implied, and the close connection in her theory between the moral sense and the desire to make reparation. It is striking that this psychoanalyst, so misleadingly thought of as preoccupied with negative emotions and states of mind, in reality had such a passionate commitment to the power of love.

Klein's thinking extrapolates Winnicott's memorable aphorism, 'There is no such thing as a baby . . . one sees a nursing couple' (Winnicott, 1952, p. 99), as a lifelong condition, such that there can be no such thing as an isolated individual, but only an individual located in a matrix of relationships, both internal and external.

Or as John Donne put it:

> No man is an island,
> Entire unto itself;
> Every man is a piece of the continent
> A part of the main.[8]

The implications of these assertions for moral thinking will be examined further below.

8 Psychoanalytic understandings have been more commonly anticipated, matched and exceeded in the symbolic forms of literature and art, than in the human sciences.

The superego and its functions

A connection that is often made between moral philosophy and psychoanalysis is through the idea of the superego. Freud had located the idea of the conscience or the moral will, which are central to Kant's moral philosophy and developed in his writing as a secularised version of biblical moral thinking, in a distinct element or structure of the unconscious mind. Freud's view explained the origins of the moral sense largely as the internalisation of parental authority, in particular as the unconscious internalisation of the prohibitions and inhibitions of infantile Oedipal desires. This theory explains the unconscious power of guilt as a moral regulator. There is a connection between this moral tradition and the particular indifference or antipathy of the Christian moral tradition to sensual pleasures.

Klein deepens Freud's investigations into the functions of the superego, and as with other aspects of her revision of Freud's theory, she sees its functions beginning even earlier in the infant's life than Freud had proposed. While sharing Freud's understanding of the superego as the regulator of amoral or anti-social desires, she laid greater emphasis on its persecutory and destructive functions than Freud, but also on the more benign moral sense linked to the possibilities of reparation. Just as Freud had done, but more forcefully, she saw an excessively punitive superego, liable to be dominated by feelings of hatred, as potentially harmful to human flourishing, and even as a cause of, rather than as the remedy for, anti-social and criminal behaviour.

The paranoid-schizoid and depressive positions and moral capabilities

Klein's psychoanalytic theory places the moral sense – the capacity and disposition to be concerned for the well-being of others – at the centre of her view of the development of the individual. She sees this not in terms primarily of an internalised prohibition – the feeling of 'thou shalt not' – as Freud was inclined to do. Rather Klein saw this prohibitive, punishing morality as merely the early and primitive form of moral awareness, which in favourable developmental circumstances becomes to a degree transcended by a concern for the other as of intrinsic value, as an object of love. This is the significance for moral theory of Klein's crucial distinction between the paranoid-schizoid and depressive positions, which she describes in the following passage:

> In my paper 'A Contribution to the Psychogenesis of Manic-Depressive States', I introduced the conception of the *infantile depressive position* and . . . I said there that the baby experiences depressive feelings which reach a climax just before, during and after weaning. This is the state of mind in the baby which I termed the 'depressive position', and I suggested that it is a melancholia *in statu nascendi*. The object which is being mourned is the mother's breast and all that the breast and the milk have come to stand for in the infant's mind: namely, love, goodness and security. All these are felt by the baby to be lost, and lost as a result of his own uncontrollable greedy and destructive phantasies and impulses against his mother's breasts. Further distress about impending loss (this time of both parents) arises out of the Oedipus situation, which sets in so early and in such close connection with breast frustrations that in its beginnings it is

dominated by oral impulses and fears. The circle of loved objects who are attacked in phantasy, and whose loss is therefore feared, widens owing to the child's ambivalent relations to his brothers and sisters. The aggression against phantasied brothers and sisters, who are attacked inside the mother's body, also gives rise to feelings of guilt and loss. The sorrow and concern about the feared loss of the 'good' objects, that is to say, the depressive position, is, in my experience, the deepest source of the painful conflicts in the Oedipus situation, as well as in the child's relations to people in general. In normal development these feelings of grief and fears are overcome by various methods . . .

. . . In the process of acquiring knowledge, every new piece of experience has to be fitted into the patterns provided by the psychic reality which prevails at the time; whilst the psychic reality of the child is gradually influenced by every step in his progressive knowledge of external reality. Every such step goes along with his more and more firmly establishing his inner 'good' objects, and is used by the ego as a means of overcoming the depressive position.

('Mourning and its relation to manic-depressive states', 1940; pp. 344–347)

The starting point of this paper in the experience of mourning indicates the debt that Klein's theory concept of identification owes to Freud's 'Mourning and melancholia' (1917), in which he developed his understanding of the way in which the self depended for its sense of well-being on its internalisation of loved objects. Thus arises the partial death which the self has to endure when a loved person dies or is otherwise lost to it.

Klein goes on to describe the complex relationships between internal and external reality which are involved in the development of the personality. Its development involves a continuing interplay between 'internal psychic reality' – the infant's internal world – and external reality – the actual qualities of its parents and others. Klein's view is that where the child's primary experiences are pleasurable ones, and its objects in the external world are mainly loving ones, its destructive impulses are likely to be contained, and its tendency to take flight from reality through splitting will be lessened. She puts forward a conception of the development of the mind as potentially capable of integrating the good and bad, the loved and hated aspects of its object, as dual aspects of its reality. As depressive anxiety – about the damage being done in phantasy to its objects – and manic flight from the depressive position[9] diminish, the capacity for recognition of the real qualities of its objects (emotionally significant persons) and for appreciative and reparative feelings towards them increases.

It becomes clear in this paper how important the idea of self-understanding, and thus of psychological integration, is to Klein's view of the personality. Emotional and moral development, in her view, depends on the understanding by the self of its different and conflicting desires and beliefs, and on its capacity to reflect on these. We have shown in Chapter 3 how

9 It is important to note that the 'depressive position' in Klein is an internal state full of anxiety about the hatred felt towards objects. This 'position', dominated by unconscious phantasy, can easily be confused with its resolution into a state of mind where 'depressive anxiety' mutates into actual concern for others, and the capacity to give real reparative expression to this. 'The depressive position' in Klein's theory is a step in the direction of emotional and psychological integration – it has to be 'worked through' – it is not a state of perfect integration. Klein describes in 'Notes on some schizoid mechanisms' (1946) the fluctuations between the depressive and the paranoid-schizoid positions which are a normal part of development.

the impulse to understand is seen by Klein as an 'epistemophilic instinct', which was later developed more fully in Bion's writing.

Here is how Klein further elaborates the significance of the depressive position:

> When I first introduced my concept of the depressive position . . . I suggested that depressive anxiety and guilt arise with the introjection of the object as a whole. My further work on the paranoid-schizoid position, which precedes the depressive position, has led me to the conclusion that though in the first stage destructive impulses and persecutory anxiety predominate, depressive anxiety and guilt already play some part in the infant's earliest object-relation, i.e. in his relation to his mother's breast.
>
> During the paranoid-schizoid position, that is, during the first three to four months of life, splitting processes, involving the splitting of the first object (the breast) as well as of the feelings towards it, are at their height. Hatred and persecutory anxiety become attached to the frustrating (bad) breast, and love and reassurance to the gratifying (good) breast. However, even at this stage such splitting processes are never fully effective; for from the beginning of life the ego tends towards integrating itself and towards synthesizing the different aspects of the object. (This tendency can be regarded as an expression of the life instinct.) There appear to be transitory states of integration even in very young infants – becoming more frequent and lasting as development goes on – in which the cleavage between the good and bad breast is less marked.
>
> In such states of integration, a measure of synthesis between love and hatred in relation to part-objects comes about, which according to my present view gives rise to depressive anxiety, guilt and the desire to make reparation to the injured loved object – first of all to the good breast. That is to say that I now link the onset of depressive anxiety with the relation to part-objects. This modification is the result of further work on the earliest stages of the ego and of a fuller recognition of the gradual nature of the infant's emotional development. There is no change in my view that the basis of depressive anxiety is the synthesis between destructive impulses and feelings of love towards *one* object . . .
>
> . . . [As] splitting processes diminish in strength . . . the contrasting aspects of the objects and the conflicting feelings, impulses and phantasies towards it, come closer together in the infant's mind. Persecutory anxiety persists and plays its part in the depressive position, but it lessens in quantity and depressive anxiety gains the ascendancy over persecutory anxiety. Since it is a loved person (internalized and external) who is felt to be injured by aggressive impulses, the infant suffers from intensified depressive feelings, more lasting than the fleeting experiences of depressive anxiety and guilt in the earlier stage. The more integrated ego is now increasingly confronted with a very painful psychic reality – the complaints and reproaches emanating from the internalized injured mother and father who are now complete objects, persons – and feels compelled under the stress of greater suffering to deal with the painful psychic reality. This leads to an over-riding urge to preserve, repair or revive the loved objects: the tendency to make reparation. As an alternative method, very likely a simultaneous one, of dealing with these anxieties, the ego resorts strongly to the manic defence.
>
> ('On the theory of anxiety and guilt', 1948; pp. 34–36)

To be noted here is the clarification of Klein's view that concern for the well-being of loved objects becomes, with maturation, an aspect of the self. Klein attributes both destructive and reparative attitudes to others primarily to emotions, the conflicting drives of hate and love towards the self's objects. What we might think of as a morally desirable state of affairs arises as a consequence of the predominance of feelings of love over those of hate, in relation to others. This state of affairs is facilitated by ensuring benign conditions of nurture (most of her theory of the paranoid-schizoid and depressive positions is based on her understanding of infancy), and also, when it comes to questions of remedy and repair, through psychoanalytically informed understanding. She primarily considered such understanding as occurring in the psychoanalytic consulting room, but we can also think of its extensions to many other social settings, including, in more enlightened circumstances, even those of the criminal justice system, which we consider in a later chapter.

Psychoanalytic practice and moral capabilities

Klein believed that dispositions to behave or to live well or badly were greatly influenced by unconscious states of mind, and therefore that understanding of these achieved through the psychoanalytic process was likely to be the most effective means of bringing about those changes in personality organisation that might influence behaviour for the better.

The relevance of Kleinian, and indeed other psychoanalytic, perspectives to moral capabilities lies not only in the developmental and theoretical understanding which they bring to these issues, but also to what they can accomplish in the practice of therapy. The process of understanding and discriminating between feelings and states of mind in psychotherapy inherently involves making discriminations of an ethically relevant kind. To come to recognise a desire as, for example, greedy, destructive or envious, or on the other hand as forgiving or reparative, is to have an understanding of their moral significance. Ethical meanings and criteria are embodied in the language of everyday life, or they would have little practical significance.

To illustrate this, we are going to provide an example from relatively recent child psychotherapy practice of the way in which a moral dimension emerges in a young child's mind.

First, a brief outline of the circumstances of the family circumstances of the patient:

> Jenny was adopted at about the age of one, and had suffered serious neglect from her drug-abusing young mother during her first year. Her father was serving a prison sentence. Her well-intentioned adoptive parents had found themselves horrified by her violent rejection of them, especially of mother, and her absolute unresponsiveness to ordinary discipline.

And here is a segment of material from a particular clinical session:

> Jenny has asked her therapist for new scissors as the old ones don't work well, and she finds the new ones as she opens her box of toys. The therapist has to explain that next week the session has to be at a different time which is being discussed just now with her parents. Jenny's project is to make a pair of glasses for herself, and although the
>
> *(continued)*

(continued)

new scissors cut paper well, they do not work on the transparent paper for the lenses. She makes various attempts and gradually becomes frustrated, but is making an effort not to lose her temper. She says, 'you are so stupid, what is your problem? I need *adult* scissors so I can do this.' The therapist replies that Jenny is angry and feels that she has not given her good enough stuff, so it is her fault. She is responsible for Jenny's being angry, she is the stupid one and Jenny is the smart one. 'But perhaps,' she adds, 'you may be afraid I am so stupid I cannot help you.' Jenny bangs the table, angrily. The therapist smiles, and Jenny smiles back. Jenny tries again with the scissors, knocking a pencil on to the floor. She orders her therapist to pick it up and the therapist comments that Jenny feels she is owed something and that the therapist should do whatever she says. Jenny then asks for help with the scissors – 'you cut it straight for me. If you cannot make it straight you will die.' The therapist tries to help, saying, 'You are very frustrated and you cannot give me the space to make a mistake. There is only one thing allowed.' The two then struggle together with the scissors, but fail nonetheless.

Suddenly Jenny says, 'I know what to make', and takes out some fresh paper, drawing attention to the things in her box from long ago. She says, 'I want to make a sword, or perhaps an electric mosquito zapper.' The therapist remarks 'both good for attacking things'. Folding the paper as she wishes also proves difficult, and there is another episode of her becoming frustrated. The therapist speaks of her not knowing yet what will happen next week, and that having to leave this to the grown-ups to sort out makes her feel small, and angry. Jenny then again asks for help and they are able to co-operate on making the sword. Jenny asks, 'how much time is left?' and the therapist says that she is now worried that there will not be enough time for her to finish her sword. Jenny becomes bossily demanding, issuing more orders, but she does not explode when the therapist points out what she can do for herself, and the sword is satisfactorily completed. When it is time to stop Jenny herself puts away the toys and asks her therapist to put the lid on the box.

Here we can see how an angry child projects her frustration, her bad feelings, into her therapist who becomes the stupid one. When these feelings are tolerated and made sense of, she recovers a sense that there is someone helpful around, and that she herself can seek help, that there can be two people working well together. She shows how touchingly aware she is of the different state of mind she is in now from the violent hate-filled start of her therapy when she looks back at the old things in the box, and when, in smiling at the therapist, she acknowledges that her angry banging of the table is only one part of her feelings. The adult scissors she wants also refer to her sense of a growing-up aspect of herself, able to use scissors to cut paper and make things, not as a weapon to hurl at her therapist. Later, the sword-making echoes this. Her aggression can be mobilised constructively for symbolic play, and is no longer something she is taken over by. Alongside this containment of violent impulses is her expanding use of her mind to think with potent thought replacing impotent rage.

We can see this process as the emergence of a moral sensibility in Jenny, as she finds that she does not only feel self-righteous blame towards her therapist, but can now begin to recognise her as someone who both wants to help her and whom she can help too, for example in the clearing up at the end of the session. This happens because she has found herself in a relationship in which she can begin to express herself positively as well as negatively. The new scissors were a failure, but they also signalled for Jenny her therapist's attempt to provide what she needed. This good intention could then be separated from the disappointment in the practical outcome. The threat Jenny utters more than once ('if you cannot make it straight you will die') describes the world she lived in for a long time. She, the infant, could not make her mother better. Her adoptive mother was not the longed-for idealised lost mother, and was therefore all wrong, from Jenny's point of view. This had been a catastrophic pairing of bad baby and bad mother. Jenny's therapist has had to live for a long time too in that sort of world, as Jenny's internal reality was re-lived in the therapy. But she had resources that Jenny lacked. Her capacity to think about what was happening enabled her to bear Jenny's anger, and thus enable her patient to see a potential for understanding and care beyond this. We can see here a recognition of differences between good and bad states of mind, of an incipient sense of moral responsibility, coming about through the psychotherapeutic process.

We suggest that this is the implicitly ethical dimension which is commonly present in Kleinian psychoanalytic practice. This is because the changes which it is hoped will accompany a successful psychoanalytic psychotherapy – the lessening of paranoid-schizoid splitting and of persecution by the superego, the strengthening of depressive concerns and identification with an object capable of both care and of thinking – are all elements of an ethical sensibility.

Kleinian ethics and moral philosophy

We will now consider the links between Klein's ideas on the origins and nature of the moral sense and the broader context of British moral philosophy.

Philosophy is a normative discipline. Philosophical reasoning sets out to determine what is necessary and unquestionable, regardless of whether this 'necessity' lies in the sphere of what is true, what is good or what is aesthetically valuable. Its method is a self-reflective one, and aims to make explicit the assumptions and implications of the ways in which understandings are represented in language. This philosophical focus is different from the contingent and empirical concerns of the sciences. In the context of the natural science of Newton and his contemporaries, John Locke referred to the role of philosophy as an 'under-labourer', that is to say, acknowledging that the primary source of scientific knowledge must be empirical, and that philosophy's contribution was mainly to clarify the assumptions and sharpen the conceptual tools on which investigation depended.

The particular focus of moral philosophy, as with much religious discourse within a theological basis of thinking, is with what is right or good. But even though its inquiries are concerned with ideals or norms of conduct or life, moral philosophy nevertheless can hardly refuse to take account of the realities of human nature as it is. Different moral philosophies in the Anglo-Saxon tradition have been configured according to differing 'empirical' definitions of this kind. Hobbes proposed a view of human nature as primarily organised around anxieties about survival, and about the need to make prudential adaptations to power to secure this. Hume and Adam Smith argued that human beings possessed an innate disposition to feel sympathy for the pains and pleasures of others, even though they remained primarily self-regarding. Later utilitarian moral philosophies such as that of Bentham and James Mill, following Hobbes, presupposed human beings who are essentially pleasure-seeking and pain-avoiding creatures. John Stuart Mill developed this conception by recognising that pleasures were subject to definition and choice, and that discriminations between their qualities and kinds were central to the ethical life. Kant asserted that the rational will, taking account of the equal worth of all persons considered as ends in themselves, was the essence of morality, holding that emotions and the motivations they gave rise to were irrelevant to questions of ethical value. Wittgenstein gave primary attention to the highly particular location of ethical and other forms of understanding in what we might think of as cultures or moral communities, which he investigated through the complex forms of ordinary language. He was suspicious of abstract, generalising laws or principles, believing them to be sources of confusion.

There are latent connections between Klein's psychoanalytic understanding of the moral sense, and each of these orientations in British moral philosophy. Klein's ideas add descriptive and explanatory depth to the psychological assumptions which are implicit in accepted philosophical formulations, and sometimes challenge them, just as Freud's theory of unconscious desires, motivations and compulsions have done.[10] Her theory of identification deepens the theory of sympathies, providing an account of their development and conflictful nature. Psychoanalytic understanding, from Freud's reflections on 'Group psychology and the analysis of the ego' (1921) and 'Civilization and its discontents' (1930) onwards, in its essence draws attention to the precariousness of the 'moral sentiments' which Hume and Adam Smith had described as facts of human nature, and to the propensity to destructiveness and delusion to which human societies were subject. But whereas Hume lived in a society which had recently passed from a period of violent religious turmoil into a state of greater peace and security, the psychoanalysts from Freud onwards were writing in the midst of the social catastrophes of the twentieth century.

Klein's account rejects the simplistic pleasure-seeking/pain-averse model of human nature advanced by the utilitarians. That is to say, it renders each of its aspects more complex. The experience of pleasures and pains, though bodily in origin, is far too varied to be understood through reduction to a rational calculus of quantity, intensity and duration, as Bentham attempted to do. Klein believed that pleasures and pains are not discrete phenomena, experienced by merely self-seeking individuals, but are embedded in complex relational and intentional states. Human beings understand pleasures and pains as being brought about by human agents, and what dominates and shapes the psyche are not merely pleasures and pains in themselves, but the meaning which these have in the context of relationships between the self and others. What is primary in Klein's view is the relationship between the self and its objects, both internal and external, and this is a matter of qualities, not quantities, of satisfaction. John Stuart Mill's elaboration of utilitarian doctrine – his idea that there were different forms and qualities of pleasure – that Bentham was wrong in his assertion that all pleasures and pains were morally equivalent – 'push-pin is as good as poetry' – went some way to redressing its limitations, as Richard Wollheim (1993b) has demonstrated. Before 'utilities' can be calculated, and questions of their just distribution can be decided, people have to work out what their 'utility' – what is meaningful and desirable for them – actually is. Wollheim has described this as Mill's commitment to a 'preliminary utilitarianism', and explained what some see as contradictions in Mill's moral philosophy (for example, his commitment to freedom of thought and expression as overruling the harm or displeasure that might be its consequence) as rather representing his recognition that 'utility' is an empty concept if there is no space to explore its meanings.

10 The insistence in the Kleinian tradition on clinical evidence as the primary basis of understanding seems to have been an adaptation by the Kleinians to the empiricist tendencies of British culture. It was through reference to clinical facts that Klein and her colleagues sought to defend their theoretical challenges to Freudian orthodoxy in the 'Controversial Discussions' of the 1940s (Rustin, 2007).

Klein's idea that it is the balance between the emotions of love and hate which is crucial in shaping dispositions and relations between persons gives an emphasis to moral issues which is also distinct from that of Kant's ascetic rationalism, which holds that sentiments should have no role in the ethical evaluation of actions. Klein's belief was that a fulfilled person – we might say also a morally responsible person – is one who gains satisfaction from giving pleasure to others (this is consistent with Hume's theory of sympathetic pleasure), whereas Kant held that the most 'moral' actions are those performed from a sense of duty and responsibility, even if this went against rather than with the grain of our emotional inclinations. As we have seen, Klein recognised the necessary role of the superego in development and in the recognition of moral norms, but observed that in its most punitive form it caused suffering not only to the self but also to its objects. One can think of Kantian moral theory as giving an unfortunately philosophical legitimacy to the power of the punitive superego.

There are other traditions of moral philosophy which seem able to absorb Kleinian insights into the origins and nature of the moral sense more readily than the different moral individualisms of utilitarian and Kantian philosophy. Aristotle's more 'social' or, as modern Aristotelians have put it, more 'communitarian' conception of how a good life is to be understood approximates more closely to the Kleinian idea of the self living within a matrix of relationships than individualist models of selfhood. His idea of the 'virtues' as the primary terms of the moral life corresponds in psychoanalytic terms to the idea of the internal objects or 'ego ideals' around which lives are oriented. Aristotle thought that nurture, education and the formation of good habits were fundamental to moral development, but he had a more 'external' and pedagogic idea of this than is adequate to a psychoanalytic understanding of the development of the self. But the idea that relationships with others are at the centre of the moral life, and that moral life is lived in the context of many specific interactions between the self and its objects, does establish a philosophical context in which a psychoanalytic understanding can find a central place.

Arguments within British moral philosophy in the 1960s and 1970s against the prevailing assumptions of individualism opened up space to which the Kleinian understandings of moral psychology are relevant. Philosophers such as Philippa Foot (1958, 2001), Alasdair MacIntyre (1966) and Iris Murdoch (1961) challenged the twin orthodoxies of utilitarianism and Kantianism, arguing that each of them denuded ethical discussion of any substantive idea of value. The idea that the spheres of facts and values are logically entirely separate, and that moral judgements did not logically depend on any facts of human nature, was argued by Foot to fail to recognise how much of everyday discourse is composed of descriptions of behaviour which refer both to dimensions of fact *and* value. When a person is described as envious, or jealous, or kind, or aggressive, this is both an assertion of a fact about that person, but also implies an assessment of its moral relevance. Klein's descriptions of states of mind, intentions and behaviours are both descriptive and evaluative in this way. Theoretically and clinically, one aim of psychoanalysis is to establish how such relations to persons or objects (envious or reparative ones, for example) come about, and how they cohere in distinct forms of personality organisation. On this argument, moral philosophy necessarily depends on assumptions and beliefs about the facts of human nature, and psychoanalytic investigation has provided valuable new understandings of this.

A belief that Klein shared with Freud, and which characterises all of psychoanalysis, is that there is a significant unconscious dimension to the human psyche, and that the freedom and well-being of individuals can be enhanced through its understanding, whether this is brought about through the relationships of everyday life, through literature and other forms of art or through the psychoanalytic process. This essential psychoanalytic idea was of course resisted by many philosophers, even to the extent of sustained antagonism towards it. But some philosophers, in the context of this controversy, sought to clarify ways in which key psychoanalytic ideas could be justified and defended. These writers included Stuart Hampshire, whose influential text *Thought and Action* (1959) had as its central commitment the idea that a condition of being able to act freely was the understanding of the causal influences on human thought and action, which in Hampshire's view plausibly included unconscious beliefs and desires. Hampshire's work was part of a larger current of ideas which characterised human action as being distinct in virtue of its being subject to the rational will of individuals. An anti-materialist current in post-war Anglo-Saxon philosophy was committed to clarifying what was distinctive about rational and self-governed action.[11]

A later important contribution to this debate was Donald Davidson's paper, 'Paradoxes of irrationality' (1982). Davidson's argument began with a definition of rational human actions as characterised by their bringing together a subject's beliefs and desires. A belief, for example, that unkind words cause pain to those who hear them, and a desire not to cause pain, may in combination lead to decisions to avoid unkindness of expression. Davidson proposed that the phenomenon of compulsive behaviours which might seem irrational, in that they may lead to consequences which are undesired by subjects, can be explained by positing the existence of a divided mind, one part of which entertains beliefs and desires unrecognised by the other. Unconscious beliefs and desires may thus be rational in their own terms (if a person is perceived as a dangerous enemy, it may make sense to hate and wish to harm that person), but if the belief does not correspond to reality it is in that sense irrational. It can be suggested that many of the behaviours and states of mind which are investigated by psychoanalysts are of this kind. Part of the work of analysis is to bring false beliefs and irrational desires into a closer relation to reality, as a way of lessening the extreme anxieties to which these can give rise. The model of different parts of the mind, relatively cut off from one another, postulated by Davidson is analogous to the idea of 'parts of the self' which has a large place in Kleinian analytic thinking.

There have also been contributions from philosophers more closely engaged with the work of Melanie Klein. Richard Wollheim, and a circle of philosophers associated with him, is the foremost of these. In many papers, and especially in his book *The Thread of Life* (1984), Wollheim set out a description of how a good and ethical life might be understood, which drew substantially on Klein's ideas. Wollheim writes of 'the evolution of morality as the transition from the dominion of the superego to the cultivation of the ego-ideal', taking up the important insight into the nature of morality and the good which is developed in Klein's theory of the paranoid-schizoid and depressive positions.

Jim Hopkins's work on the convergences between psychoanalytic, and especially Kleinian thinking, and developments in the neighbouring fields of attachment theory, evolutionary psychology and neuroscience, has already been referred to.

A third philosopher who has contributed in important ways to this debate is Sebastian Gardner (1992, 1993). He argues that the understanding of irrationality demands a more radical acknowledgement of the role of emotion and phantasy in mental life than Davidson's rationalistic model of 'parallel minds', of conscious and unconscious beliefs and desires, had

11 The classical philosopher whose ideas about the contribution of understanding to freedom, and indeed to the integration and harmony of the self, have a close affinity with psychoanalytic perspective, is Spinoza, as Hampshire (1951; pp. 141–144) has pointed out.

acknowledged.[12] The understanding of the place of emotions in the psyche is greatly enriched by Klein's theory of unconscious phantasy. Gardner acknowledges that we do think of emotions as appropriate or inappropriate to their objects and circumstances, and evaluate their rationality accordingly – for example, we decide when it is reasonable or unreasonable to feel anger with someone or something. But emotions are more than mere concomitants of our beliefs. The traditional conception of emotions as potentially disruptive and ungovernable, in good and bad ways, is correct. But they are not merely disordered states, but are rather in Gardner's view shaped by structures of phantasy, which function as schemata through which we perceive the world in affective terms. These underlying schemata function much as conceptual schemata do in organising our perceptions of the natural world. Gardner suggests that Klein's model of the paranoid-schizoid and depressive positions is an example of the schemata or templates which organise our experience of the world, and that characteristic patterns of emotion are their effects. One highly significant aspect of these schemata is the way in which they encode deep-seated expectations of how human beings will normally behave towards one another. Klein's account of these innate expectations is of course a complex one, which allows for many different developmental possibilities. But her theory of the depressive position establishes an expectation that human beings are capable of recognition of and care for one another as basic to the structures of their minds.

Since such mental schemata are essentially unconscious, this argument is consistent with the psychoanalytic view that emotions (e.g. seemingly irrational hatred or enthusiasm) cannot always be modified merely by pointing out their inconsistency or poor fit with relevant facts. It is the role of structures of unconscious phantasy in causing disturbances of feeling or belief that need to be addressed if changes in these are to occur. There has been a substantial psychoanalytic literature, following James Strachey's seminal 1934 paper devoted to the problems of technique involved in accessing and addressing these levels of unconscious phantasy.

Conclusion

Our argument is that Klein's psychoanalytic writing provides a ground-breaking account of the origins and nature of the moral sense, significantly modifying Freud's earlier view in the direction of a less individually centred and more relational view of human nature. We have briefly indicated how Klein's moral psychology can be understood in the context of the broader context of moral philosophical debate, and given some examples of how her ideas have been taken up within philosophy. Her theory of the paranoid-schizoid and depressive positions asserts that the capacity for taking responsibility for the self's destructive emotions and actions, and the desire to make reparation for harms done, are essential concomitants of the integration of the personality. In her account, the integration and internal harmony of the self, the capacity for symbolic functioning, and for recognition and concern for others are linked together in a view of human development which is in many ways hopeful, even though fully realist in its recognition of the power of more negative human propensities.

12 Gardner's argument was an element in a larger shift of attention from the 1980s onwards on to the field of the emotions, which gave rise to new areas of study in sociology (Hochschild, 1983) and history (Reddy, 2001) as well as in psychology (Panksepp, 1998) and philosophy (Wollheim, 1999).

Chapter 11

Kleinian aesthetics

One of the fascinations of psychoanalysis has always been its 'aesthetic' dimension. By this we mean the sense which Freud first conveyed in 'The interpretation of dreams' (1900) of the unconscious as an extraordinary unknown world, a space in which the mind seemed able to think in ways which were free of the everyday constraints of reason, but which nevertheless contained and conveyed deep kinds of meaning. The psychoanalytic process itself often brings its practitioners in contact with experiences of beauty, through the images which emerge in their patients' dreams or flow of associations, and through moments of unexpected recognition and illumination of emotional truth. In the psychoanalysis of children too, such an aesthetic dimension is added to by the directness and freshness with which children express themselves, and this was vividly present in much of Klein's presentation of her child cases.

Psychoanalysis has influenced and been of interest to many writers and artists in the last century or so – it has indeed become an unavoidable part of the cultural environment – though most often these connections have been implicit, rather than matters for conceptual appropriation. But many attempts at connection have been in the opposite direction, as psychoanalysts have sought to relate their forms of understanding to the imaginative artifacts of art and literature. Many psychoanalysts from Freud onwards have sought to develop these links and literary critics and philosophers, for example, Lionel Trilling, Harold Bloom, William Empson and Richard Wollheim, have also made important links between these fields of understanding, as mediators of each to the other.

Klein's psychoanalytic ideas have made a significant contribution to reflection on aesthetics – the study of the nature and meaning of beauty – and on the arts – even though her writings focused mainly on the clinical practice of psychoanalysis and on its theories and techniques. She herself wrote three papers which demonstrated how one could investigate literary texts from a psychoanalytic perspective. In the volume *New Directions in Psycho-Analysis: The Significance of Infant Conflict in the Pattern of Adult Behaviour* which Klein co-edited, there are papers by Klein and by Joan Riviere and Hanna Segal, which begin the distinctive contribution of Kleinian psychoanalysis to literature. The parallel development of Kleinian aesthetics in the field of the visual arts is represented in that volume in papers by the art historian and critic, Adrian Stokes.[1]

This Kleinian development in the field of aesthetics has continued up to the present, with the important additional influence of Bion's and subsequently Meltzer's writing. This later work has given a greater emphasis to the aesthetic dimensions of the mind and of

1 Marion Milner also contributed a paper to this volume, although her work evolved in a different direction.

psychoanalysis itself than was the case for Klein, whose concerns were ultimately more ethical than aesthetic. However, in this volume we are principally concerned with Klein's own work and direct influence, and not with this subsequent development, which Glover (2009) valuably reviews.[2]

Before we discuss Klein and her colleagues' own writing on literature and the arts, we are going to set out the principal psychoanalytic concepts in her clinical and theoretical writing which we believe were foundational for the development of a Kleinian aesthetics. In fact, the links between Klein and her colleagues' understanding of works of literature and their work in the clinical consulting room was a close one. Psychoanalytic ideas which had proved powerful in the understanding of clinical cases were also found to bring new understanding to characters and their interactions in novels, plays or poems. But just as new theoretical ideas were sometimes developed through the struggle to understand an individual patient in psychoanalysis, so it seems that encounters with works of literatures were also stimulating – even formative – for analysts in thinking through the implications of their theoretical ideas. In papers such as Klein's 'On identification' (1955), Riviere's 'The inner world in Ibsen's *Master-Builder*' (1952a) and Hanna Segal's 'A psycho-analytical approach to aesthetics' (1952), key psychoanalytic ideas are enriched and elaborated, just as in this tradition they have always been through these exemplifications. A similar deepening of psychoanalytic thinking through a writer's engagement with literary works can be seen in some of the best subsequent papers written in this tradition, such as those by Ronald Britton (1998b) on the poets Wordsworth, Coleridge, Rilke, Milton and Blake. Particularly important has been the recognition that poets' representations of the mind and its development have often anticipated more theoretical understandings, and have been an inspiration to psychoanalytic thinking.

Key themes in Klein's psychoanalytic writing

We will now outline areas of Klein's work which have been key to the development of Kleinian aesthetics. These include her writings about the functions of play in psychotherapy; her theory of the 'epistemophilic instinct' (later developed in important ways by Bion and by Meltzer); her theory of the depressive position and its significance for the development of the capacity for symbol formation and symbolic thinking; her understanding of the significance of mourning for psychological development; and her theory of projective identification.

Klein's technique of 'play therapy'

Here first is a description by Klein of her 'play technique' for the conduct of psychoanalysis with children, which she first described in early papers written in the 1920s, as discussed in Chapter 4. The significance of this is its understanding that the symbolic play of children in the therapy room was a means of gaining access to the internal world of child patients, and thus to the possibility of analysing them through interpretation. This was in her view a necessary means, since Freud's classical methods of psychoanalytic consultation with adults, with dreams as their 'royal road to the unconscious', were plainly unfeasible in the analysis of children, especially very young children. The 'stories' which children created and narrated

2 Among the contributors to psychoanalytic aesthetics of significance from the post-Kleinian tradition are Ronald Britton, John Steiner, Ignêz Sodré, Donald Meltzer, Thomas Ogden, Meg Harris Williams and Margot Waddell.

in their play, involving humans and animals who 'stood for' significant figures in their lives, were interpreted by Klein as representations of the inner world of her patients.

The simple toys Klein provided for her patients in the consulting room were chosen to facilitate their use for the expression to unconscious feelings and phantasies about their primary objects (usually objects within the family constellation), and about their transference relationship to the analyst. Play may therefore take the form of the elaboration of narratives and scenarios, in which toys and other objects in the consulting room figure as imagined representatives of the patient and those of greatest emotional significance to him or her.[3]

The idea that fictional narratives convey significant information about the inner world is highly significant for subsequent psychoanalytical approaches to literature, although the application of this idea to works of fiction was far from straightforward. In the context of 'play therapy', plainly the analyst's interest is in the inner world of her patient, which it is hoped the patient may come in time to share. But works of art are not therapy, and the audience's or critic's roles are not those of therapists. Is the 'inner world' which a psychoanalyst might convincingly see represented in a work of literature that of the writer himself, or is it rather that of the characters he portrays in his fiction? It is surely the understanding of the inner world of 'as if real' characters, who represent kinds of people relevant to readers' own lives and experiences, which is of most interest to fiction readers, not the reader's understanding of the author himself, who may indeed seem scarcely to be present in his fiction at all. But even if most imaginative writing is clearly not autobiographical in its form or manifest purpose, might there nevertheless be *some* relationship which a psychoanalytic reader might discern between an 'objectified' inner world of fictional characters, and inner preoccupations of the artist himself? Such questions have remained significant for psychoanalytic cultural criticism since its beginnings.

The epistemophilic instinct

In the paper from which the following passages are taken, Klein makes clear the essential role of symbolism and symbolic capacity in the process of analysis, as much with a child as with an adult. She explains the inhibition of symbolic capacity in this patient as a consequence of his extreme anxiety, which leads him to withdraw from reality, the objects of his environment being without affective or symbolic meaning for him. Klein describes her essential task as to mobilise her patient's interest in the world – his epistemophilic instinct or desire to know – believing that in so far as his capacity to symbolise develops, his anxieties will be reduced. This idea that anxieties are reduced and modified by understanding, and that the desire to know and understand is a primary human disposition, is a fundamental one. It enables us to understand both the therapeutic value of psychoanalysis, but also the central significance for development of symbolisation, and thus of cultural forms generally. This is a key link, summarised in the idea of sublimation which Klein takes up from Freud, between psychoanalysis and aesthetic experience.

> After a feeble beginning, symbol-formation in this child had come to a standstill. The early attempts had left their mark in one interest, which, isolated and unrelated to reality, could not form the basis for further sublimations. The child was indifferent to most of

3 Lynne Reid Banks' novel for children, *The Indian in the Cupboard*, is a vivid imagining of the way a toy can have such intense inner meaning to a child (Banks, 1980; Rustin and Rustin, 1987).

> the objects and playthings around him, and did not even grasp their purpose or meaning. But he was interested in trains and stations and also in door-handles, doors and the opening and shutting of them . . .
>
> . . . The unusual difficulty I had to contend with in the analysis was not his defective capacity for speech. In the play-technique, which follows the child's symbolic representations and gives access to his anxiety and sense of guilt, we can, to a great extent, dispense with verbal associations. But this technique is not restricted to an analysis of the child's play. Our material can be derived (as it has to be in the case of children inhibited in play) from the symbolism revealed in details of his general behaviour. But in Dick symbolism had not developed. This was partly because of the lack of any affective relation to the things around him, to which he was almost entirely indifferent. He had practically no special relations with particular objects, such as we usually find in even severely inhibited children. Since no affective or symbolic relation to them existed in his mind, any chance actions of his in relation to them were not coloured by phantasy, and it was thus impossible to regard them as having the character of symbolic representations. His lack of interest in his environment and the difficulty of making contact with his mind were, as I could perceive from certain points in which his behaviour differed from that of other children, only the effect of his lack of a symbolic relation to things. The analysis, then, had to begin with this, the *fundamental* obstacle to establishing contact with him.
>
> ('The importance of symbol-formation in the development of the ego', 1930; pp. 224–225)

Klein recognised that the desire to know and understand (the epistemophilic instinct) is one of the primary dispositions of human nature. She first set out this understanding in her texts ('Early stages of the Oedipus conflict', 1928; 'The importance of symbol-formation in the development of the ego', 1930; 'A contribution to the theory of intellectual inhibition', 1931) without giving it a full theoretical formulation. This idea became fully developed later, in Bion's work, when he established the equivalence between the instincts to know (K) to love (L) and to hate (H), in what has become the most significant revision of Freud's metapsychology since Klein's discovery of the paranoid-schizoid and depressive positions.[4]

Also of great significance for a psychoanalytic perspective on culture is not only the existence of an epistemophilic drive, but its distinctive object. Klein believed that this desire to know was focused initially, in the minds of infants, on the primary 'facts of life' (as Money-Kyrle later called them) of gender, generation and mortality. Klein followed Freud in this respect, in holding that it was sexual preoccupations, concerning the relationships between parents and children, that were the initial drivers of the child's desire to know and understand.

These ideas later become foundational for the Kleinian understanding of culture, in so far as they lead to an understanding of the importance of symbolic capacity in human life, and to those dimensions of symbolic meaning which relate to these primary 'facts of life'. This had been Freud's focus too, although Klein's later discovery of the paranoid-schizoid and depressive positions, and the revision which this brought about

4 O'Shaughnessy (1981b) gives a lucid account of the significance of Bion's discovery.

to Freud's metapsychology, pointed to different structures of unconscious meaning than those which had figured in Freud's own cultural investigations. The idea of an autonomous drive towards meaning and understanding, and the idea that its primary objects are the unconscious preoccupations of infancy, are guiding principles of the Kleinian approach to works of culture.

The paranoid-schizoid and depressive positions

In two previous chapters, we have presented these central ideas of Klein in some depth, and here we provide only a short extract which sets out the essence of Klein's view. Crucial to Kleinian cultural theory is the link between the mental integration achieved in the depressive position, and symbol formation and symbolic capacity. It was in Hanna Segal's writing that this fundamental implication of Klein's idea became recognised and elaborated.

> I have so far described some aspects of mental life during the first three or four months. (It must be kept in mind, though, that only a rough estimate can be given of the duration of stages of development, as there are great individual variations.) In the picture of this stage, as I presented it, certain features stand out as characteristic. The paranoid-schizoid position is dominant. The interaction between the processes of introjection and projection – re-introjection and re-projection – determines ego-development. The relation to the loved and hated – good and bad – breast is the infant's first object-relation. Destructive impulses and persecutory anxiety are at their height. The desire for unlimited gratification, as well as persecutory anxiety, contribute to the infant's feeling that both an ideal breast and a dangerous devouring breast exist, which are largely kept apart from each other in the infant's mind.
>
> ('Some theoretical conclusions regarding the emotional life of the infant', 1952; p. 70)

> [F]urther development on the line of integration and synthesis is initiated when the depressive position comes to the fore. The various aspects – loved and hated, good and bad – of the objects come closer together, and these objects are now whole persons. The processes of synthesis operate over the whole field of external and internal object-relations . . . All these processes of integration and synthesis cause the conflict between love and hatred to come out in full force. The ensuing depressive anxiety and feeling of guilt alter not only in quantity but also in quality. Ambivalence is now experienced predominantly towards a complete object. Love and hatred have come much closer together and the 'good' and 'bad' breast, 'good' and 'bad' mother, cannot be kept as widely separated as in the earlier stage. Although the power of destructive impulses diminishes, these impulses are felt to be a great danger to the loved object, now perceived as a person.
>
> (pp. 72–73)

> There are grounds to assume that as soon as the infant turns his interest towards objects other than the mother's breast – such as parts of her body, other objects around him, parts of his own body, etc. – a process starts which is fundamental for the growth of sublimations and object-relations. Love, desires (both aggressive and libidinal) and anxieties are transferred from the first and unique object, the mother, to other objects; and new interests develop which become substitutes for the relation to the primary object. This primary object is, however, not only the external but also the internalized good breast; and this deflection of the emotions and creative feelings, which become related to the external world, is bound up with projection. In all these processes, the function of symbol-formation and phantasy activity is of great significance. When depressive anxiety arises, and particularly with the onset of the depressive position, the ego feels driven to project, deflect and distribute desires and emotions, as well as guilt and the urge to make reparation, on to new objects and interests. These processes, in my view, are a mainspring for sublimations throughout life. It is, however, a precondition for a successful development of sublimations (as well as of object-relations and of the libidinal organization), that love for the first objects can be maintained while desires and anxieties are deflected and distributed. For, if grievance and hatred towards the first objects predominate, they tend to endanger sublimations and the relation to substitute objects.
>
> (p. 83)

Significant here is Klein's recognition that it is with the onset of the depressive position (that is to say, the integration within the infant's mind of its feelings of love and hate, and the perception of the mother no longer as discrete loved and hated part-objects ('the good and the bad breast') but as a whole person, sometimes loved and sometimes hated) that the capacity for symbolisation emerges. While the extreme splitting of the paranoid-schizoid position is necessary for the infant's security, it is with the lessening of splitting (Bion's idea of fragmentation is its more extreme form) that a mind capable of understanding is able to develop.

The second crucial point in this passage concerns the shift of the infant's attention away from the breast towards other objects and interests, with the onset of the depressive position. Klein describes the growth of the capacity for phantasy and symbol formation once a loving internal object becomes established.

It is in papers by Hanna Segal, however, that the links between the development of symbolic capacity and the onset of the depressive position are fully set out, in an essential development of Klein's own work.

Klein's theory of mourning

Klein believed, following Freud, that the experience of mourning was central to development, with its beginnings in the loss of the breast at the time of weaning, but recurring throughout life as other losses are inevitably sustained. Mourning involves the reinstatement or restoration in the mind of lost 'real objects'. This process involves renewed internal conflict between loving and hating impulses towards internal objects, the balance between these forces shaping the difference between the successful working through of mourning, and its failure in melancholia. The drive towards symbolisation is in part driven by the need to cope with this primary experience of loss, to find a way of creating symbolic representations of lost objects. Kleinian aesthetic theory focuses on the symbolic work of reparation involved in the making of cultural artifacts. Their idea is that works of art represent the struggle between loving and destructive desires towards primary objects – their quality and depth depending on the extent to which the reality of internal conflict is able to be faced by the artist. The work of art is the expression and record of these internal struggles, in the minds of artists and writers, made for the satisfaction and enrichment of their audiences.

Here is Klein on mourning:

> In my paper on 'Mourning and its relation to manic-depressive states', I expressed the following view: 'My experience leads me to conclude that, while it is true that the characteristic feature of normal mourning is the individual's setting up the lost loved object inside himself, he is not doing so for the first time but, through the work of mourning, is reinstating that object as well as all his loved *internal* objects which he feels he has lost.' Whenever grief arises, it undermines the feeling of secure possession of the loved internal objects, for it revives the early anxieties about injured and destroyed objects – about a shattered inner world. Feelings of guilt and persecutory anxieties – the infantile depressive position – are reactivated in full strength. A successful reinstating of the *external* love object which is being mourned, and whose introjection is intensified through the process of mourning, implies that the loved *internal* objects are restored and regained. Therefore the testing of reality characteristic of the process of mourning is not only the means of renewing the links to the external world but of *re-establishing the disrupted inner world.*
>
> ('Some theoretical conclusions regarding the emotional life of the infant', 1952; p. 77)

The understanding of works of art as the working through of loss was a theme of some of the most valuable Kleinian writings on works of art. Proust's own elaboration of this idea had a considerable influence on Segal's thinking, and is an example of a fruitful interaction between the understandings of imaginative writers and of psychoanalysts. Ronald Britton's idea (1998b) that the best of Wordsworth's poetry, including *The Prelude* in its original form, involves the presence and experience of loss is another example of the significance of mourning to Kleinian aesthetics.

Projective identification

The processes of projective and introjective identification discovered by Klein, and subsequently developed by many subsequent analysts, is fundamental to Kleinian and post-Kleinian aesthetics. Ideas of this kind are present in Freud's own writing on aesthetic questions; for example, in his idea that Leonardo da Vinci expresses his own maternal identification in his paintings of the Mona Lisa and St Anne. Artists and writers project aspects of themselves into their symbolic creations, which then are given a life that becomes independent of their creators. They also internalise aspects of others (including their artistic forerunners) in their own creative work.

> Projective identification is based on the splitting of the ego and the projection of parts of the self, into other people; first of all the mother or her breast. This projection derives from the oral–anal–urethral impulses, the parts of the self being omnipotently expelled in the bodily substances into the mother in order to control and take possession of her. She is not then felt to be a separate individual but an aspect of the self. If these excrements are expelled in hatred the mother is felt to be dangerous and hostile. But it is not only bad parts of the self that are split off and projected, but also good parts. Ordinarily, as I have discussed, as the ego develops, splitting and projection lessen and the ego becomes more integrated. If, however, the ego is very weak, which I consider to be an innate feature, and if there have been difficulties at birth and the beginning of life, the capacity to integrate – to bring together the split-off parts of the ego – is also weak, and there is in addition a greater tendency to split in order to avoid anxiety aroused by the destructive impulses directed against the self and external world. This incapacity to bear anxiety is thus of far-reaching importance. It not only increases the need to split the ego and object excessively, which can lead to a state of fragmentation, but also makes it impossible to work through the early anxieties.
>
> ('On the sense of loneliness', 1963; p. 303)

Klein's own paper 'On identification' (1955) in the *New Directions* volume is an exploration of the phenomena of projective and introjective identification conducted through the means of an analysis of a novel (*If I Were You*, by Julian Green, 1950). This paper has the form of a case study, in which the 'case' is the fictional hero, not a clinical patient, and its title makes clear that its principal aim is to explore a specific psychological process, rather than just to throw light on a work of literature. The paper describes the depletion of self involved in the extreme projective identifications of its central character, who is allowed within the fictional convention of the novel to take over other people's identities and then live out the unforeseen consequences of losing his own self and taking on the attributes of others. (A better-known story with a similar theme is Wilde's *The Picture of Dorian Gray*, 1891.)

Joan Riviere's two papers in the *New Directions* volume also concern projective and introjective identification. The first of these, 'The unconscious phantasy of an inner world reflected in examples from literature' (1952b), shows how different poets have represented in their work the experience of having incorporated an object – sometimes a beloved person – into themselves, following Klein's understanding of the introjection into the self of aspects of the mother. The second, 'The inner world in Ibsen's *Master-Builder*' (1952a), is an analysis of the disturbed object relations of its central character, Solness. Hilda, the young woman who comes into Solness's life as he struggles with the fear of ageing, failure and supercession by the young, and guilt about his deeply depressed wife and her dead twin babies, awakens in Solness the feelings of manic omnipotence which underpinned his emotional seduction of her as a child, when he had kissed her, telling her she was his princess. Under the sway of these projections, he now tries to re-enact his earlier triumph, when he had climbed to the top of the church tower of which he had been the architect, in his phantasy defying God. This time he falls to his death. Hilda's projection was in part one of hatred and envy for the failed father figure embodied in Solness, her childhood hero. Riviere's paper shows that several psychoanalytical ideas, besides those of identification, are of value in understanding this play. As is usually the case with the best work of this kind, a creative writer's understanding in his own terms of what psychoanalysts much later were able to express in theoretical terms is one of the principal discoveries of the paper.

The idea of the countertransference, which we have shown to be closely linked with that of projective identification, is also important in Kleinian aesthetic theory, although Klein herself expressed scepticism about its place in therapeutic technique. But it came to be argued that it is through something akin to a countertransference experience that audiences and readers give emotional meaning to actions as these unfold in a fictional narrative or on stage or screen. In regard to responses to paintings and other visual arts, and to architecture, Adrian Stokes and Richard Wollheim give great emphasis to reflection on the emotional experience of the viewer to the perceived work, as a crucial means of ascertaining the intentions of the artist, and the force and meaning of the work. These concepts have been important in moving the focus of Kleinian aesthetics from a primary concern with the inner struggles of the artist, as these are represented in works of art, to attention to their meaning for their audiences, and to the transactions of meaning and feeling between artists and audiences. These conceptions have brought the dimension of the 'here and now' from the consulting room to the experience of works of art.

But before we turn to Klein's papers on literature, there is the aesthetic dimension of psychoanalysis itself. In literary terms this has been present from Freud onwards, who was after all awarded the Goethe Prize in 1930. In Klein, what we become very much aware of are the beauties of the psychoanalytic method. We are going to quote two passages which illustrate this in different ways.

The first comes from an early session with Richard, the child whose analysis is recounted in full in *Narrative of a Child Analysis* (1961). The session follows a weekend during which Richard's older brother Paul, who is serving in the war, has been back on leave. For the first time Richard brought his fleet of toy warships which were to become a large feature of his play and of the wonderful drawings he did to explain their activities to Mrs Klein. These drawings are reproduced in volume 3 of Klein's complete works.

> Richard brought some toys of his own, a small fleet of warships, and began to play with them. He put some destroyers on one side and said they were German. On the other side battleships, cruisers, destroyers, and submarines represented the British fleet. (Richard was excited and elated.) The two battleships were attacking the destroyers; one blew up, the others were scuttled and sunk. While Richard moved the ships, he made sounds that were supposed to come from the ships and were most expressive and varied, something between the noise of engines running and human voices, clearly indicating whether the ships felt happy, friendly, angry, etc. When two or three ships were together this sounded like a conversation, although no words were used. (Richard was even more conscious than usual of noises outside and of children passing the house. He repeatedly jumped up to look out.)
>
> Mrs K. interpreted that the German destroyers stood for Mummy's babies, whom he felt he had attacked because he was jealous and hated them, and therefore he expected them to be hostile to him. While he was playing with the destroyers, he was afraid and suspicious of children passing by; he had been listening to noises, being 'on guard'. All children in the world had come to stand for Mummy's babies and therefore he would expect to find enemies wherever he met children.

Richard opened the door and asked Mrs K. to look at the lovely view. He pointed out that there were many butterflies. They looked nice but were destructive, eating cabbages and other vegetables; last year he had destroyed sixty of them in one day. He came back into the playroom.

Mrs K. interpreted that the butterflies were to him the same as the starfishes – that is, greedy babies, just as he felt that he himself was greedy; they should all be destroyed in order to save Mummy. Mrs K., too, should be saved from him when he became jealous of her other patients and wanted to get as much as possible from her: attention, time, ultimately her exclusive love. [Starfishes: this refers back to the material from the previous week which features dangerous starfishes.] But while one reason for attacking the children was to preserve Mummy, there was also his fear of them, and of what they would do to him – the children on the road, the hostile destroyers. This fear drove him to attack them.

Richard now put the whole fleet on one side and said that they were all British; they were one happy family. He pointed out to Mrs K. that the two battleships were the parents, the cruisers were the cook, maid, and Paul, and the destroyers were babies which were still inside Mummy. Richard now began to play with the other toys. He arranged a town with people beside a railway line and said that nothing would move, not even the trains (which were standing one behind the other). He told a little girl figure not to go on to the railway line because it was dangerous. He made various groups, including the three animals in two trucks, but put aside the pink woman and a few other figures which he had frequently used in earlier play. The dog was supposed to be wagging its tail but otherwise to be motionless. Then Richard said that the whole family was now happy. Suddenly, however, he moved both trains, made them collide, and everything was knocked over. Richard said that the trains had begun to quarrel; one said to the other that he was the more important, and the other answered that *he* was, and then they began to fight and made a mess of everything.

Mrs K. interpreted his longing for the whole family to be happily united and his wish to have only friendly feelings towards them, but his jealousy of Paul – in the play the collision of the two trains – produced disaster. At the weekend and on the preceding days, when Paul had been at home and Richard in 'X', he had felt extremely jealous of Paul. Paul, having come home on leave, received much attention and Richard felt that Paul was admired and considered to be so much more important than himself. The fighting trains also represented the parents in sexual intercourse. In the previous hour he had felt they were inside him. Therefore only by keeping them all, including himself, motionless and under control could he hope to remain friendly and the family happy, for controlling them also implied keeping his feelings in check.

(*Narrative of a Child Analysis,* 1961; session 19; pp. 85–87)

This is only about one-third of the total session material (!) but it does represent the vibrant interchange of child and analyst, the child's imagination responded to by the analyst's making emotional meaning out of the sequence of his activities, in relation to his mood in the session. The unconscious Oedipal phantasies Klein recognises in Richard's play are put into words to help him to understand himself. It is this process of giving meaning and creating understanding in the patient which is so deeply satisfying, and the reader can feel the anxiety, hope, excitement and achievement of the way that child and analyst are working together. Following this sequence Richard told Mrs Klein a secret (about his sexual activities) which makes it clear that his trust in her grew as she helped him to grasp his feelings through her interpretations. There is a sense of beauty in this process of development.

The second example is from the analysis of an adult who Klein described as neither unhappy nor ill, but quite successful in his life. What it exemplifies is her attunement to her patients' experience of the physical world and the meaning of his particular responsiveness to the beauties of nature. She understands this aspect of his character as an instance of the ways in which reparation and recovery can take place through the discovery of goodness and beauty in art or nature.

> He was aware that he had always felt lonely as a child and that this feeling of loneliness had never entirely gone. Love of nature had been a significant feature in this patient's sublimations. Even from earliest childhood he found comfort and satisfaction in being out of doors. In one session he described his enjoyment of a journey which led him through hilly country and then the revulsion he felt when he entered the town. I interpreted as I had done previously, that to him nature represented not only beauty, but also goodness, actually the good object that he had taken into himself. He replied after a pause that he felt that was true, but that nature was not only good because there is always much aggression in it. In the same way, he added, his own relation to the countryside was also not wholly good, instancing how as a boy, he used to rob nests, while at the same time he had always wanted to grow things. He said that in loving nature he had actually, as he put it, 'taken in an integrated object'.
>
> In order to understand how the patient had overcome his loneliness in relation to the countryside, while still experiencing it in connection with the town, we have to follow up some of his associations referring both to his childhood and to nature. He had told me that he was supposed to have been a happy baby, well fed by his mother; and much material – particularly in the transference situation – supported this assumption. He had soon become aware of his worries about his mother's health, and also his resentment about her rather disciplinarian attitude. In spite of this his relation to her was in many ways happy, and he remained fond of her; but he felt himself hemmed in at home and was aware of an urgent longing to be out of doors. He seemed to have developed a very early admiration for the beauties of nature; and as soon as he could get more freedom to be out of doors, this became his greatest pleasure. He described how he, together with other boys, used to spend his free time wandering in the woods and fields. He confessed to some aggression in connection with nature, such as robbing nests and damaging hedges. At the same time he was convinced that such damage would not be lasting because nature always repaired itself. Nature he regarded as rich and invulnerable, in striking contrast to his attitude towards his mother. The relation to nature seemed to be relatively free from guilt, whereas in his relation to his mother for whose frailty he felt responsible for unconscious reasons, there was a great deal of guilt . . .

> . . . In connection with home and mother he felt very lonely, and it was this sense of loneliness which was at the root of his revulsion against town. The freedom and enjoyment which nature gave him were not only a source of pleasure, derived from a strong sense of beauty and linked with appreciation of art, but also a means of counteracting the fundamental loneliness which had never entirely gone.
>
> ('On the sense of loneliness', 1963; pp. 307–308)

This material is in Klein's last paper, unpublished at her death. While this patient was not overly ill, what she describes in him is the loneliness she also saw as inherent in states of mental illness when the individual is cut off from good relationships to other people, internal and external. By contrast this patient had a developed capacity for symbolic representation and for sublimation.

Klein's psychoanalytic essays on literature

Klein wrote three papers which reflected on fictional works from a psychoanalytical point of view. Her main purpose in writing these papers was not to develop a psychoanalytic theory or method of literary analysis, but rather to develop her and readers' understanding of certain key psychoanalytic ideas, with these texts serving rather as working through the meaning as a clinical case might do. She does not refer at all to the problems of method which must arise in a consideration of works of art, and we may infer that she had decided to leave these specialist matters to her colleagues.[5]

Nevertheless, her literary papers are not without interest, and do throw new light on the imaginative works she discusses. We have already made reference above to 'On identification', and will confine our attention in this section to her 1929 paper 'Infantile anxiety situations reflected in a work of art and in the creative impulse', which discusses Ravel's opera, *L'Enfant et les Sortilèges,* and a biographical account of a painter, and her paper 'Some reflections on *The Oresteia*' (1963).

The 1929 paper gives primacy in its title to its psychoanalytical topic, just as 'On identification' (1955) did later. The main literary work she discusses is the libretto by Colette to Ravel's opera *L'Enfant et les Sortilèges.*[6] Through her analysis of the story Klein sets out her view of the violent destructiveness which can be provoked in infants by their encounter with the Oedipal situation. The text shows the sadism of the infant as he trashes its household and then becomes terrified by the consequences of his actions, as the inanimate damaged objects and the creatures in the park attack him in response. But the child's display

5 Robert Hinshelwood (2006) has pointed out that Klein appears to have completely disengaged from the philosophical issues which are involved in the changing metapsychology of psychoanalysis, following Freud's move away from his earlier 'scientific' and biological approach, to a more interpretive one. He suggests that Klein was ill equipped through her lack of medical training, or even university degree, to take part in such debates, or even recognise their significance. Perhaps similar considerations apply to her distance from analogous methodological discussions in the field of literature and the humanities.

6 Not only is the paper about the libretto rather than the opera, but it is even further removed from the artwork since Klein writes that her knowledge of its content 'is taken almost word for word from a review'.

of love and concern for an injured squirrel restores the situation. An identification with a good internal mother takes place, and the child is able to conquer his sadism by means of pity and sympathy.

> A squirrel which has been bitten falls to the ground, screaming beside him. He instinctively takes off his scarf and binds up the little creature's paw. There is great amazement amongst the animals, who gather together hesitatingly in the background. The child has whispered: 'Mama!' He is restored to the human world of helping, 'being good'. 'That's a good child, a very well-behaved child,' sing the animals very seriously in a soft march – the finale of the piece – as they leave the stage. Some of them cannot refrain from themselves calling out 'Mama'.
>
> ('Infantile anxiety situations reflected in a work of art and in the creative impulse', 1929; p. 211)

Klein's discussion both of *L'Enfant et les Sortilèges* and of the biographical account of the painter Ruth Kjär which follows it focuses on the resolution of infantile anxiety through acts of reparation. Although there are links between the anxiety states she discusses in relation to the two texts, and a theoretical paper 'Early stages of the Oedipus conflict' (1928) published in the previous year, the literary discussions are more than illustrations of a theoretical argument. Their conceptual focus is more specific than in the theoretical paper, and abstract ideas are rendered emotionally powerful in their embodiment in these narratives in the way that they are in Klein's clinical descriptions.

Her discussion of Aeschylus's trilogy, 'Some reflections on *The Oresteia*' (1963), is the most impressive of her three literary papers, and also of course has a great classical work as its named subject. Whilst one imagines that rather few readers have been led by Klein's analysis of Green's *If I Were You* to read the novel, her *Oresteia* paper prompts its readers to revisit these plays in the light of her interpretation of them. She states that she relied on Gilbert Murray's translation of this play to make her analysis.

The *Oresteia* is the tragedy of the house of Atreus, and consists of three plays, *Agamemnon*, the *Libation Bearers* and *The Eumenides*. Prior to their action, Agamemnon has sacrificed his daughter Iphigenia, to aid the Greek cause in the war on Troy, and has been away leading the siege and destruction of Troy for ten years. In the first play, Agamemnon returns home to be murdered by his wife Clytemnestra; in the second Orestes kills his mother in revenge for her murder of his father; and in the third Orestes is brought to judgement before the gods for his crime. Klein is interested in the states of mind of these characters, their mental conflicts and the presence or otherwise in them of remorseful and reparative feelings. Is the drama merely one of revenge – the enactment of a talion principle in the successive killings – or are the tragedies inviting reflection and assessment of the morality of each these actions? Klein describes a conflict between conflicting principles of *hubris* (overweening pride), to which all the principal characters are liable to succumb, and *dike* (justice). The eventual judgement and exoneration of Orestes, and the debate which precedes it, make clear that reflecting on what is just and reasonable, and what is not, is what Aeschylus invited his audience to do. It seems that the struggle of the ancient Greek tragedians was to bring into question the norms of a warrior society committed to honour and revenge justice, by demonstrating their catastrophic consequences for families and societies. Klein may see parallels between the Greek tragedies' exploration of the catastrophic consequences of irrational impulses when they are enacted and the investigations of psychoanalysis.

She notes the complicated Oedipal dimensions of this drama, and the displacements of objects that take place in it. She interprets Orestes' killing of his mother's lover, Aegisthus, as a displacement of his hatred of his father (analogous to Hamlet's relationship with his uncle, Claudius). While characters act out from their own sense of honour and for their own gratification (for example, Agamemnon expresses no regret for his destruction of Troy), the plays give us glimpses of its characters' more positive emotions too. Orestes, Klein says, loves his sister Electra, and experiences guilt for the revenge killing of his mother. Clytemnestra, although she entraps and kills Agamemnon, and calls her spearmen to attack Orestes when she fears he will attack her, also responds to the evidence of Agamemnon's remorse, and has loved her son. Klein's interest is in the emergence of some depressive states of mind in this situation. The tempering of the persecuting rage of the Eumenides (the Furies) in their pursuit of Orestes, so that they become merely permanent reminders of his misdeeds (a milder superego) demonstrates the shift of the trilogy towards its end into a more depressive register. The paper is a powerful demonstration of the particular insight Klein can bring to a text, through her understanding of the complexities of the Oedipal situation and of paranoid-schizoid and depressive states of mind.

The development of Klein's ideas in aesthetics

Hanna Segal

Hanna Segal's aim was to develop the implications of Klein's ideas for aesthetics, as Klein herself had scarcely attempted to do. Her classic 1952 paper 'A psycho-analytical approach to aesthetics' sets out the aims of this project, almost as a manifesto.

She begins by discussing the contribution of Freud and other psychoanalytic writers to aesthetic issues, but also their limitations, since they did not address:

> [T]he central problem of æsthetics, which is: what constitutes good art, in what essential respect is it different from other human works, more particularly from bad art? . . .
>
> . . . Maybe it is possible now, [she asks] in the light of new analytical discoveries, to ask new questions. Can we isolate in the psychology of the artist the specific factors which enable him to produce a satisfactory work of art? And if we can, will that further our understanding of the æsthetic value of the work of art, and of the æsthetic experience of the audience?
>
> It seems to me that Melanie Klein's concept of the depressive position makes it possible at least to attempt an answer to these questions.
>
> (Klein *et al.*, 1955; pp. 385–386)

She then succinctly sets out Klein's theory of the depressive position, which provides the basis for her approach to aesthetics. The artist's struggle, she believes, is essentially with depressive anxiety, and good art comes from an artist's courage and realism in facing up to depressive pain. This is the psychological task which audiences find represented for them in literature and in art, and it is this which explains its great importance for human societies.

She describes the essentially reparative task of the artist: 'the creation of a world of his own'. To understand what this means, she draws on the writing of an artist:

> Of all artists the one who gives us the fullest description of the creative process is Marcel Proust: a description based on years of self-observation and the fruit of an amazing insight. According to Proust, an artist is compelled to create by his need to recover his lost past. But a purely intellectual memory of the past, even when it is available, is emotionally valueless and dead. A real remembrance sometimes comes about unexpectedly by chance association. The flavour of a cake brings back to his mind a fragment of his childhood with full emotional vividness. Stumbling over a stone revives a recollection of a holiday in Venice which before he had vainly tried to recapture. For years he tries in vain to remember and re-create in his mind a living picture of his beloved grandmother. But only a chance association revives her picture and at last enables him to remember her, and to experience his loss and mourn her. He calls these fleeting associations: "intermittences du coeur", but he says that such memories come and then disappear again, so that the past remains elusive. To capture them, to give them permanent life, to integrate them with the rest of his life, he must create a work of art . . .
>
> . . . Through the many volumes of his work the past is being recaptured; all his lost, destroyed and loved objects are being brought back to life: his parents, his grandmother, his beloved Albertine . . . A book is a vast graveyard where on most of the tombstones one can read no more the faded names . . .
>
> . . . What Proust describes corresponds to a situation of mourning: he sees that his loved objects are dying or dead. Writing a book is for him like the work of mourning in that gradually the external objects are given up, they are reinstated in the ego, and re-created in the book.
>
> (pp. 388–390)

The paper goes on to describe clinical work by its author with four patients all of whom had been artists, and all of whom had suffered from inhibitions in their creativity, through their difficulties with depressive anxiety. She ends her discussion of her fourth patient with the following conclusion:

> One of Freud's greatest contributions to psychology was the discovery that sublimation is the outcome of a successful renunciation of an instinctual aim; I would like to suggest here that such a successful renunciation can only happen through a process of mourning. The giving up of an instinctual aim, or object, is a repetition and at the same time a re-living of the giving up of the breast. It can be successful, like this first situation, if the object to be given up can be assimilated in the ego, by the process of loss and internal restoration. I suggest that such an assimilated object becomes a symbol within the ego. Every aspect of the object, every situation that has to be given up in the process of growing, gives rise to symbol formation.
>
> (pp. 396–397)

She addresses two further questions, the first being the difference between the successful and unsuccessful artist. Quoting Freud (1911), she describes the artist's acute sense of reality, in regard for example to his 'assessment of the nature, needs, possibilities and limitations of his material, be it words, sounds, paints or clay'.

This is how Segal answers her question:

> The æsthetic pleasure proper, that is, the pleasure derived from a work of art and unique in that it can only be obtained through a work of art, is due to an identification of ourselves with the work of art as a whole and with the whole internal world of the artist as represented by his work. In my view all æsthetic pleasure includes an unconscious re-living of the artist's experience of creation. In his paper on 'The Moses of Michelangelo', Freud says 'What the artist aims at is to awaken in us the same mental constellation as that which in him produced the impetus to create.'
>
> (Klein *et al.*, 1955; p. 399)

She gives the example of classical tragedy:

> In creating a tragedy I suggest the success of the artist depends on his being able fully to acknowledge and express his depressive phantasies and anxieties. In expressing them he does work similar to the work of mourning in that he internally re-creates a harmonious world which is projected into his work of art.
>
> The reader identifies with the author through the medium of his work of art. In that way he re-experiences his own early depressive anxieties, and through identifying with the artist he experiences a successful mourning, re-establishes his own internal objects and his own internal world, and feels, therefore, re-integrated and enriched.
>
> (p. 400)

She extends this argument from tragedy to aesthetic experiences in general. Referring to work by John Rickman and Ella Freeman Sharpe, she rejects the common equation of the aesthetic with the beautiful. She writes:

> Ugliness is what expresses the state of the internal world in depression. It includes tension, hatred and its results – the destruction of good and whole objects and their change into persecutory fragments . . .
>
> . . . my contention is that 'ugly' is a most important and necessary component of a satisfying æsthetic experience.
>
> (p. 401)

While she agrees that beauty is an expression of order and harmony, she argues that it is only when this has involved assimilating and working through experiences of depression and mourning that this leads to deep aesthetic satisfaction, quoting Rilke:

> Beauty is nothing but the beginning of terror that we are still just able to bear.

She links her aesthetic argument to the concept of the death instinct and concludes:

> Re-stated in terms of instincts, ugliness – destruction – is the expression of the death instinct; beauty – the desire to unite into rhythms and wholes – is that of the life instinct. The achievement of the artist is in giving the fullest expression to the conflict and the union between those two . . .
>
> . . . All artists aim at immortality; their objects must not only be brought back to life, but also the life has to be eternal. And of all human activities art comes nearest to achieving immortality; a great work of art is likely to escape destruction and oblivion.
>
> It is tempting to suggest that this is so because in a great work of art the degree of denial of the death instinct is less than in any other human activity, that the death instinct is acknowledged, as fully as can be borne. It is expressed and curbed to the needs of the life instinct and creation.
>
> (pp. 404–405)

Segal provided an essential addition to the argument of 'A psycho-analytical approach to aesthetics' in her later paper, 'Notes on symbol formation' (1957). In this paper she showed the connection between the onset of the depressive position and the development of symbolic capacity. This was a link, further developed by Bion, which was crucial for psychoanalytic theory as well as for its cultural extensions.

She sets out a distinction between a symbolic equivalent (a function of 'concrete', sometimes psychotic) thinking, and an actual symbol. Symbolic activity in general is undertaken in an attempt to alleviate unconscious anxieties. In the paranoid-schizoid position, this meets with great difficulties, and the symbol may be experienced as identical to the object it stands for – thus Segal's famous case example of a patient who could not play the violin before an audience because it would be like masturbating in public. But in the depressive position, it becomes possible to recognise a difference between the object and the symbol which represents it, and then to work through anxieties through their symbolic representations. Of course regression can always occur, if paranoid-schizoid states of mind come to the fore, when symbolic capacity will be inhibited. Some works of art may forcefully confront their audiences with the experience of 'symbolic equations' or 'concrete thinking'.

Here is how Segal puts this:

> Symbol formation is an activity of the ego attempting to deal with the anxieties stirred by its relation to the object. That is primarily the fear of bad objects and the fear of the loss or inaccessibility of good objects. Disturbances in the ego's relation to objects are reflected in disturbances of symbol formation. In particular, disturbances in differentiation between ego and object lead to disturbances in differentiation between the symbol and the object symbolized and therefore to concrete thinking characteristic of psychoses.

> Symbol formation starts very early, probably as early as object relations, but changes its character and functions with the changes in the character of the ego and object relations. Not only the actual content of the symbol, but the very way in which symbols are formed and used seem to me to reflect very precisely the ego's state of development and its way of dealing with its objects . . .
>
> . . . The early symbols, however, are not felt by the ego to be symbols or substitutes, but to be the original object itself. They are so different from symbols formed later that I think they deserve a name of their own. In my paper of 1950 I suggested the term 'equation'. This word, however, differentiates them too much from the word 'symbol' and I would like to alter it here to 'symbolic equation' . . .
>
> . . . In favourable circumstances of normal development, after repeated experiences of loss, recovery, and re-creation, a good object is securely established in the ego . . . Earlier on, the aim was to possess the object totally if felt as good, or to annihilate it totally if felt as bad. With the recognition that the good and the bad objects are one, both these instinctual aims are gradually modified. The ego is increasingly concerned with saving the object from its aggression and possessiveness. And this implies a certain degree of inhibition of the direct instinctual aims, both aggressive and libidinal.
>
> This situation is a powerful stimulus for the creation of symbols, and symbols acquire new functions which change their character. The symbol is needed to displace aggression from the original object, and in that way to lessen the guilt and the fear of loss. The symbol is here not an equivalent of the original object, since the aim of the displacement is to save the object, and the guilt experienced in relation to it is far less than that due to an attack on the original object. The symbols are also created in the *internal* world as a means of restoring, re-creating, recapturing and owning again the original object. But in keeping with the increased reality sense, they are now felt as created by the ego and therefore never completely equated with the original object.
>
> (Segal, 1957; pp. 393–394)

Segal's work on reparative impulses in art has been the basis for the continuing vitality of much of the discourse between psychoanalysis and literature.

Adrian Stokes

The most significant writer on painting and the visual arts who was influenced by Klein was Adrian Stokes, who was already a well-known art historian and art critic when he entered psychoanalysis with her, and whose writing remains of contemporary interest.[7] He develops the idea that art is an expression of both destructive and reparative impulses in relation to internal objects, which find representation and aesthetic resolution in paintings, sculptures and architecture. Like Segal, he believes that those who respond to such works of art find their own internal conflicts symbolised and worked through in their experience of them. Stokes's paper in *New Directions in Psycho-Analysis*, 'Form in art', is a reflection of his engagement with psychoanalysis.

7 See, for example, *Art and Analysis: An Adrian Stokes Reader*, edited by Meg Harris Williams (2014) and *Art, Psychoanalysis, and Adrian Stokes: A Biography* by Janet Sayers (2015).

Stokes wrote in a tradition of art criticism in which aesthetic and emotional response to the art object was crucial to its understanding, in contrast to more 'external' iconographic or art-historical kinds of interpretation.[8] His own extensive writings about painting and architecture have a strongly 'subjective' dimension. Generally it is more difficult to establish the psychoanalytic meaning of works in the visual arts and in music than it is in literature, where the shared medium of language provides a bridge between the two fields. Thus a lot depends on the reader being guided to see in particular works of art the significant forms that the critic finds there. Also influenced by Klein's ideas, and by Stokes's writing on art, was the philosopher Richard Wollheim, whose *Painting As an Art* (1987) provides extensive interpretations of works of art influenced by this perspective. Wollheim believes that we learn to 'see in' a work of art the meaning which the artist has intentionally given to it. Both authors believe that unconscious intentions are embodied in art works, and that through processes of identification these are communicated to spectators and are responded to by them, both consciously and unconsciously. One aspect of this identification is the artist's own experience as a constant spectator of his own work of art as he creates it.

> The psychological account of meaning which I favour . . . roots meaning in some mental condition of the artist which, when it finds outlet in the activity of painting, will induce in the mind of the spectator an appropriately related, mental condition.
>
> (Wollheim, 1987; p. 357)

Just as Segal argued is the case with works of literature, we experience through a work of art an author's struggle to resolve the conflicts of his inner world. Stokes's and Wollheim's idea that the experience of the viewer of a work of art is essential to understanding the work itself has an affinity with the contemporary view that the transference–countertransference relationship is central to psychoanalytic practice. Wollheim describes in his book different ways in which painters seek to draw viewers of a painting into the space it evokes. One example is his discussion of certain paintings by Manet, which invite their viewer to recognise that human subjects of the painting themselves appear to be engaged in thought, and to identify with them in that mental space.

It is in the essays Stokes wrote between 1955 and 1967, and published in the third and final volume of his collected *Critical Writings* (Gowing, 1978), that his psychoanalytic approach to the arts and architecture was most fully developed. He wrote, however, that many of the concepts which had been central to his earlier writing – such as the idea of the enveloping and incantatory effects of works of art, and the distinction between 'carving' and 'modelling' in their creation – already had a close affinity with Kleinian ideas. He held that these then made possible a deeper explanation of their psychological meaning.[9]

8 Wollheim (1973) has describes Stokes's approach, which is similar to and also influenced his own, as having been influenced by Walter Pater's writing, and by the idea of an aesthetic sensibility.

9 Stokes found that the carving and modelling distinction which he had developed in his early work corresponded respectively to the 'depressive' or 'whole-object' and the paranoid-schizoid or part-object kinds of relating described by Klein. He wrote:

> My greater interest has been for works conceived primarily from the carving side, since I value the meaning conveyed by the accentuated otherness, by the self-subsistence, as it were, of forms, rather than by those juxta-positions through which we are made vividly conscious of tensions of the mind. I have more concern with restoration, reparation, than with the versatile interior giants that seem to infect the artist's material with shadowy or stark power.
>
> (Stokes, 1951; p. 242)

Like Segal, Stokes held that works of art did crucial work for the members of the societies who saw them, in giving symbolic expression to their own conflicting impulses, and in creating forms through which their anxieties could be contained.

Stokes argued that architecture is, or at least until modern times was, central among the arts as the external, public expression of primary object relations.

> We will agree that the work of art is a construction. Inasmuch as man both physically and psychologically is a structure carefully amassed, a coalescence and a pattern, a balance imposed upon opposite drives, building is likely to be not only the most common but the most general symbol of our living and breathing: the house, besides, is the home and the symbol of the Mother . . .
>
> (Stokes, 1959; p. 149)

> No-one will deny many references to the body in architectural art. Proportion, symmetry, derive from ourselves; the alternations of architectural features suggest to many the rhythm of breathing. Buildings are giants of ourselves, as well as symbols of the mother and of the womb.
>
> (Stokes, 1958; p. 109)

> To put the matter the other way round: how Gothic is the female genital. Think of the pointed arches, fold within fold, of a cathedral door, of turret slits and narrow apertures . . . Gothic iconography juxtaposes the sublime and the very bad: angel and gargoyle attend entry into the mother's body . . . Temples and sculptures of classical India architecture display with corresponding richness a more phallic architecture. Our responses to architecture, mother of the arts, show best that the whole-object constructions of art are based on part-object symbolic representations, or, more generally, part-object relationships; perhaps only architecture is so tied to part-object representations.
>
> (Stokes, 1965; pp. 284–285)

Stokes believed that forms of artistic expression and the states of mind they represent evolve socially and historically. Here is his psychoanalytic reflection on the inception of scientific thinking in ancient Greece:

> There seem to me only two psycho-analytic concepts that fill the bill. They are both Kleinian: first the concept of the integrated ego of which I have already spoken, the bringing together of the good and the bad, the fitting together of various strains in the psyche that are neither split-off continuously nor denied; and second, the Kleinian conception of creativeness or recreativeness of a whole object following upon the sense of loss. The two concepts are close to each other since the recognition of an independent
>
> *(continued)*

(continued)

longer unrelated; depressive anxiety takes precedence of paranoid anxiety; there is far more responsibility for the attacks upon what is good, and a corresponding growth in the sense of loss. Applied to what a society considers to be the norm, this means smaller emphasis upon the transcendental values of regression, a greater value attached to the individual, at the expense of social rigidity to some degree, inasmuch as society, and Nature if it be assimilated with society, are the largest targets for projective identification. And again, it means a far stronger relish for seizing the precise nature of objects in themselves, a relish that at times adds force to the spur of the reality principle.

(Stokes, 1958; pp. 131–132)

Stokes saw modern societies as deficient in aesthetic harmony and order, of which he believed the decline of architecture as an expressive and containing form was a major aspect – he held that this had freed the graphic arts, as with Cubism, to take up the task of investigating and giving form to the new state of perceptual and emotional confusion.

Here then, in the work of Adrian Stokes and Richard Wollheim, are substantial applications of Klein's ideas to the fields of architecture and the visual arts, comparable to the work which Hanna Segal and her successors have undertaken in the field of literature.

Chapter 12

Klein and society

As we have said previously, there was little reflection in Klein's own work on the wider implications of her ideas for society or politics. It is only in her reflections on the nature and meaning of criminality and delinquency that she addresses a potentially contentious social question. But despite her own disinclination to extend her thinking beyond its primary clinical context, Klein's ideas have been found valuable by many psychoanalysts and social scientists in reflecting on wider social issues. In this chapter we will show how this development has come about.

The central ideas from which Kleinian reflections on society have come arise from the centrality she gives to the place of anxiety in human development. Particularly influential in the subsequent assimilation of ideas in the broader social sphere have been her models of the paranoid-schizoid and depressive positions, and the different anxieties against which these are a defence. Her thoughts about criminality have these ideas as their source, since the primitive and punitive superego associated with the paranoid-schizoid position explains the unconscious compulsions which in her view underlie much criminal behaviour.

In this chapter we will first present Klein's ideas on the meaning of criminal and anti-social behaviour, before going on to writings by Elliott Jaques, Isobel Menzies Lyth and Wilfred Bion, who first, with Roger Money-Kyrle, extended her ideas to a wider field of social application. Our starting point, as with our two earlier chapters in Part 2, will be essays published in *New Directions in Psycho-Analysis* (1955), which we can assume were recognised by Klein herself to be significant developments of her own psychoanalytic project. Although Menzies Lyth's (then Menzies) 1960 paper was not published in that volume, it was written soon afterwards, and is often regarded, with the work of Elliott Jaques, as having initiated and inspired the social application of Klein's theory of paranoid-schizoid and depressive anxieties and the mechanisms of defence associated with them.

Klein and anti-social behaviour

The social issue which Klein addressed most directly in her own writings was the understanding of anti-social and criminal behaviours and their unconscious motivations. She wrote two papers specifically on this topic, both based on her analytic work with children. In these she related criminal dispositions to the functions of the punitive superego. Her ideas implicitly challenge conventional beliefs about criminal and delinquent motivations, as indeed did those of Freud and Winnicott.

She describes how in what she calls play analysis she observed how her patient's aggressive activities, attacking toys and objects which represent mother's body and breasts, and its parents and siblings more generally, alternate with severe anxiety:

> But when in analysis anxiety gradually gets resolved and thus sadism diminishes, feelings of guilt and constructive tendencies come to the fore . . . The more the tendency and capacity to restitute increases and the more the belief and trust in those around him grows, the milder does the super-ego become, and vice versa. But in those cases in which, as a result of a strong sadism and an overwhelming anxiety . . . the vicious circle between hatred, anxiety and destructive tendencies cannot be broken, the individual remains under the stress of the early anxiety situations and retains the defensive mechanisms belonging to that early stage. If then fear of the super-ego, either for external or intrapsychic reasons, oversteps certain bounds, the individual may be compelled to destroy people and this compulsion may form the basis for the development either of a criminal type of behaviour or of a psychosis.
>
> ('On criminality', 1934; pp. 259–260)

She explains how these developments may take place:

> Thus we see that the same psychological roots may develop into paranoia, or into criminality. Certain factors will in the latter case lead to a greater tendency in the criminal to suppress unconscious phantasies and to act them out in reality. Phantasies of persecution are common to both conditions; it is because the criminal feels persecuted that he goes about destroying others. Naturally, in cases where children, not only in phantasy, but also in reality, experience some degree of persecution through unkind parents and miserable surroundings, the phantasies will be greatly reinforced. There is a common tendency to over-estimate the importance of unsatisfactory surroundings, in the sense that the internal psychological difficulties, which partly result from the surroundings, are not sufficiently appreciated. It depends, therefore, on the degree of the intrapsychical anxiety, whether or not it will avail much merely to improve the child's environment.
>
> (p. 260)

She believes that the roots of this anti-social behaviour lie in the presence of violent and sadistic feelings in the infant, in its response to normal bodily frustrations, deprivations and anxieties, and from the jealousies and anxieties provoked by the Oedipal situation. Klein thought that infants responded to threats to their sole possession of a parent (from the other parent, and from siblings, existing or potential) with unconscious phantasies in which violent oral, urethral and anal attacks are launched on its objects. But such attacks bring fear of punishment and retribution, and fear for the survival of the infant's internal objects. In unfavourable circumstances, for example, where such destructive phantasies are amplified by a depriving or abusive care environment, rather than contained and mitigated by it, the outcome can be the child's identification with 'bad' internal objects, an overwhelming burden of guilt because of the destructive phantasies which he harbours, and the dominance of a persecutory superego which is felt to administer deserved punishments to the self. A sado-masochistic vicious circle can develop, in which the self has to be punished for its phantasied crimes, but then falls into resentment and hatred of the imagined authority which inflicts pain on it. Klein is essentially imagining juvenile and adult delinquent behaviour as following patterns set up during a destructive process of socialisation in early life. She sees the endless cycle of offending, reoffending and further punishment, which is one of the self-reinforcing patterns of the criminal justice system, as sometimes the re-enactment of a damaged form of early relationship. It is a matter of fact that there is a considerable correlation between those who find themselves in cycles of chronic reoffending and punishment, and traumatic or catastrophic early experiences suffered by such individuals.

Klein's argument, in her two papers on this topic ('Criminal tendencies in normal children' (1927) and 'On criminality' (1934)), challenges the conventional view which sees the superego as the guarantor and enforcer of morality. She argues on the contrary that the superego, if it develops in a severe and punitive form, can function to provoke delinquent or criminal behaviour, rather than to restrain it. This has important implications if one wishes human beings to behave responsibly and with care for one another. Personality formations dominated by internal persecution are unlikely to be changed for the better by repeated experiences of punishment and retribution. These may even induce a compulsive cycle of behaviour which invites punishments which are unconsciously believed to be deserved, but which then further weaken the self's inner trust and hopefulness.

Her thinking on this topic developed from the brief suggestion made by Freud in his paper 'Criminals from a sense of guilt' (1916). Like Freud, she draws upon Nietzsche's idea of the 'pale criminal'. Winnicott (1956) set out a related view of delinquent behaviour in children, and how it may signify a need for a deep-seated sense of guilt to be addressed.

These ideas have proved fertile in reflections on the nature of the criminal justice system, though their implications are far from having been fully recognised. Richard Wollheim (1993a) suggested that the implication of these insights was that severe punishments – he particularly had in mind capital punishment, a practice then still extant in Britain – might constitute a 'lure' or an attraction to certain criminals, preoccupied with their own sense of extreme wickedness. He held that they might imagine this ritualised and spectacular punishment with a kind of perverse masochistic pleasure, as a potential public expiation of their sense of guilt. We can add that some offenders may be attracted compulsively to the prospect of incarceration as providing a means of containment of their criminal impulses.

Arthur Hyatt Williams (1998) was able to work with individuals, including murderers who had been given life sentences. Hyatt Williams undertook psychoanalytic therapy with some of these offenders, and had responsibility to advise on their eventual suitability for release from confinement. He identified the existence of psychotic dispositions in these individuals, often cut off from and disavowed by the non-psychotic parts of their minds. It was the existence of these psychotic 'pockets' which made it so difficult to have confidence that violent reoffending would not occur. This is related to the fact that many violent crimes are perpetrated on family members or other persons with whom offenders have had a close relationship. Hyatt Williams observed that for much of the time these offender/patients were perfectly sane and rational, but that unintegrated psychotic parts of their minds were still latent in them, and liable to be provoked by incidents which could not be predicted. His experience as an analyst made him very cautious about the possibility of bringing about the deep changes in character which were needed if the risk associated with such patients' freedom were to be sufficiently reduced. It is the concept of unconscious paranoid-schizoid and depressive anxiety which links Hyatt Williams's work to Klein's thinking.

Donald Meltzer (1968) and Herbert Rosenfeld (1971) later developed Klein's idea that the self could be captured by the persecutory superego in their concept of the 'internal gang', in which the self becomes the victim of an internal tyrant. This fierce internal persecutor disavows and splits off vulnerability in the self, by cruel attacks on any perceived weakness, whether in the self (that is, on any feelings of love or trust which might render it vulnerable in phantasy to betrayal) or in others in whom weakness can be discerned. The idea of the sometimes seductive internal gang (and gangster) captures the essential cynicism of this mental state, in which a self which is identified with the persecutory superego gains pleasure in finding any moral weaknesses in its victims. This then provides a spurious moral justification for inflicting cruel punishments on them, as displacements of the superego's cruel attacks on the self and its internal objects. This understanding, developing Klein's original insight, illuminates the way in which those being punished, in external reality and internally, for their own crimes may find relief in locating and punishing those whom they can define as even worse criminals than themselves (for example, assaults which take place in prisons on those who have committed offences against children).

Klein believed that the balance established between feelings of love and hate in early life is crucial in determining whether the superego-dominated paranoid-schizoid position can be overcome, and more 'depressive' or reparative states of mind come to the fore. The later developments by Bick, Bion and others of the concept of the container–contained relation, through which infantile anxieties are allayed and destructive impulses lessened, extended Klein's early insights.

It has often been suggested, in criticism of Klein, that she was so focused on the internal world of infants and children that she was largely uninterested in the actual environment in which they were nurtured. Her writing does not support this view. A paper in which she summarised her understanding of child development, 'Our adult world and its roots in infancy' (1959), describes the range of developmental patterns that can take place, generally in consequence of the relation established between the innate dispositions of the individual child, and the care provided by parents.

While she saw infants as liable to be subject to considerable anxieties and feeling of persecution, she was also intensely aware of the essential life-giving importance of mothers' response to their babies. Thus:

> I have put forward the hypothesis that the newborn baby experiences, both in the process of birth and in the adjustment to the post-natal situation, anxiety of a persecutory nature. This can be explained by the fact that the young infant, without being able to grasp it intellectually, feels unconsciously every discomfort as though it were inflicted on him by hostile forces. If comfort is given to him soon – in particular warmth, the loving way he is held, and the gratification of being fed – this gives rise to happier emotions. Such comfort is felt to come from good forces and, I believe, makes possible the infant's first loving relation to a person, or, as the psycho-analyst would put it, to an object. My hypothesis is that the infant has an innate unconscious awareness of the existence of the mother. We know that young animals at once turn to the mother and find their food from her. The human animal is not different in that respect, and this instinctual knowledge is the basis for the infant's primal relation to his mother. We can also observe that at an age of only a few weeks the baby already looks up to his mother's face, recognizes her footsteps, the touch of her hands, the smell and feel of her breast or of the bottle that she gives him, all of which suggest that some relation, however primitive, to the mother has been established.
>
> ('Our adult world and its roots in infancy', 1959; p. 248)

It is true, however, that Klein gave particular emphasis to internal forces, to the potential for aggressiveness that she believed was innate in all human beings, believing that this aspect of human development was neglected when she was writing.[1]

> Innate aggressiveness is bound to be increased by unfavourable external circumstances and, conversely; is mitigated by the love and understanding that the young child receives; and these factors continue to operate throughout development. But although the importance of external circumstances is by now increasingly recognized, the importance of internal factors is still underrated. Destructive impulses, varying from individual to individual, are in integral part of mental life, even in favourable circumstances, and therefore we have to consider the development of the child and the attitudes of the adults as resulting from the interaction between internal and external influences.
>
> (p. 249)

She goes on to discuss how such interactions continue to have formative effects throughout childhood:

> My work with young children has shown me that even from babyhood onwards the mother, and soon other people in the child's surroundings, are taken into the self, and this is the basis of a variety of identifications, favourable and unfavourable . . .
>
> . . . If we look at our adult world from the viewpoint of its roots in infancy, we gain an insight into the way our mind, our habits, and our views have been built up from the earliest infantile phantasies and emotions to the most complex and sophisticated adult manifestations. There is one more conclusion to be drawn, which is that nothing that ever existed in the unconscious completely loses its influence on the personality.
>
> (pp. 260–262)

Although Klein herself scarcely wrote about social practices such as those of education, the wider implications of her understanding of development have been widely understood and taken up. The essential conclusion to be drawn from her insights is the central importance of the quality of emotional care that should be provided by children, and the need for this to be supported in every possible way. The idea that it is the balance between loving and hating impulses in the human character that determines well-being, and the damage that is caused by excesses of persecutory anxiety, also has implications beyond childhood. There is thus what one might term a preventive application of Klein's ideas, in the maintenance of social structures and relationships which support the development of responsible and reparative orientations towards others. These perspectives are among those which have contributed to the development of community mental health services in Britain which support families in these ways.

More intractable are the problems involved in the reparative or 'curative' applications of Klein's ideas to established anti-social or criminal states of mind. She herself

1 There are some passages, however, in which Klein overstates this aspect of the infant's experience. 'In my view, omnipotent destructive impulses, persecutory anxiety, and splitting are predominant in the first three to four months of life' (p. 253). As most of this paper suggests, the reality is more differentiated than this.

acknowledged that it was easier to bring about changes in young children through psychoanalytic interventions than in adults whose characters are fully developed before psychotherapies are attempted.

This psychoanalytic understanding of unconscious motivations raises ethical and juridical issues too, since it does not fit well with everyday expectations concerning individuals' own responsibilities for their actions. The common belief is that individuals should be held responsible for what they do as free and rational beings, and that where they cause injury or harm in contravention of the law they are justly liable to receive punishment. There are two overlapping philosophical justifications of this view. The first proposes that the law should reinforce individuals' natural desire to seek pleasure and avoid pain, by ensuring that criminal deeds may be punished with 'a just measure of pain', the prospect of which serves as a rational disincentive to transgression. The second idea appeals to a moral faculty held to be innate in human beings, such that punishment is understood to be a merited consequence of having committed an offence. These framings do indeed function to encourage conformity to laws, and to justify appropriate sanctions being applied to offenders.

The idea of unconscious motivation is very difficult to incorporate within such common-sense assumptions. Only at the extreme point of psychotic states – the judicial defence of 'unsound mind' – does a psychiatric or psychoanalytic understanding of criminality have a formal place in the criminal justice system, although more complex assessments of motivation and its reasons do enter into the particular assessments which law enforcement authorities make of specific criminal acts, for example, in deciding upon appropriate sentences. It is indeed difficult to see how the acknowledgement of unconscious motives can be allowed access to the formal judicial decision-making process without undermining the common convention that individuals should be expected to take responsibility for their own freely chosen actions. (It is what actions are freely chosen and what are not that is called into question by psychoanalytic understanding.)

There is a larger potential impact for psychoanalytic insights when the form and nature of punishment are considered. If one follows Klein in holding that criminality is a form of character disorder, arising from the predominance of hate over love in the personality, and/or of an excessively punitive superego, then the question for a social system is: how are such character disorders most likely to be repaired, or their harmful aspects mitigated? Mere repeated experiences of punishment seem unlikely in themselves to give rise to favourable character development. Indeed, it is known that the prison system is largely ineffective in this respect, since rates of reoffence following custodial sentences are high. 'Prison works' sometimes seems to mean little more than that, whilst criminals are incarcerated, they are unfree to commit crimes outside prison.

One of the problems in sustaining practices in the criminal justice system which might be more effective in modifying criminal and anti-social dispositions is the resentment and hostility which is felt towards offenders by members of wider society. Reparative measures directed towards convicted offenders, or leniency towards them, are liable to be seen by the law-abiding as unjust 'rewards' for their offences. If rehabilitative forms of punishment were really effective, (for example, through remedial therapeutic or educational provision), it may be that some former offenders would indeed find their lives and opportunities improved as a consequence. This can feel unjust to those who feel they have restrained their anti-social impulses, at cost to themselves, and who feel they have received little reward for their law-abiding lives. Elements of the dominant culture prefer to see offenders suffer, bearing the projected burden of the anti-social impulses of the larger society, than to acknowledge a human bond of recognition and identification with them.

Klein's reflections on criminal dispositions provide an example of the way in which psychoanalytic understanding can unsettle conventional assumptions about individual and social behaviour.

Elliott Jaques and the theory of unconscious defences against anxiety

Elliott Jaques' 1955 essay on social defences against anxiety was the first exposition of a theory which has been perhaps the most influential application of Klein's ideas for the understanding of social institutions. Jaques argued that states of both persecutory and depressive anxiety pervade social institutions, and that defences against these states of anxiety are often prominent features of their organisational structure and of the division of roles and functions within them. Here is how he put this:

> The specific hypothesis I shall consider is that *one* of the primary cohesive elements binding individuals into institutionalized human association is that of defence against psychotic anxiety. In this sense individuals may be thought of as externalizing those impulses and internal objects that would otherwise give rise to psychotic anxiety, and pooling them in the life of the social institutions in which they associate. This is not to say that the institutions so used thereby become "psychotic". But it does imply that we would expect to find in group relationships manifestations of unreality, splitting, hostility, suspicion, and other forms of maladaptive behaviour. These would be the social counterpart of – though not identical with – what would appear as psychotic symptoms in individuals who have not developed the ability to use the mechanism of association in social groups to avoid psychotic anxiety.
>
> (Jaques, 1955; p. 479)

> One example of social mechanisms of defence against paranoid anxieties is that of putting bad internal objects and impulses into particular members of an institution who, whatever their explicit function in a society, are unconsciously selected, or themselves choose to introject these projected objects and impulses and either to *absorb* them or *deflect* them. By absorption is meant the process of introjecting the objects and impulses and containing them; whereas by deflection they are again projected but not into the same members from whom they were introjected.
>
> The phantasy social structuring of the process of absorption may be seen, for example, in the case of the first officer in a ship, who, in addition to his normal duty, is held responsible for many things that go wrong, but for which he is not actually responsible. Everyone's bad objects and impulses may unconsciously be put into the first officer, who is consciously regarded by common consent as the source of the trouble. By this mechanism the members of the crew can unconsciously find relief from their own internal persecutors. And the ship's captain can thereby be more readily idealized and identified with as a good protective figure.
>
> (pp. 482–483)

Jaques describes two kinds of defences against depressive anxiety. In the case of the scapegoating of a minority group, which seems like an instance of the deflection of projection of persecutory anxiety from the self into a bad object, he suggests there may be a dimension of unconscious depressive anxiety located in the minority group, which may explain how they have been chosen for persecution.

> [W]e must consider the possibility that the one of the operative factors in this selection is the consensus in the minority group, at the phantasy level, to seek contempt and suffering in order to alleviate unconscious guilt. That is to say, there is an unconscious co-operation (or collusion) at the phantasy level between persecutor and persecuted. For the members of the minority group, such a collusion reinforces their own defences against depressive anxiety – by such mechanisms as social justification for feelings of contempt and hatred for an external persecutor, with consequent alleviation of guilt and reinforcement of denial in the protection of internal good objects.
>
> (pp. 485–486)

This idea has relevance to what Klein had to say about criminal behaviour and the unconscious guilt which may motivate it and punishment which may follow from it.

A second form of defence is this:

> Another way in which depressive anxiety may be alleviated by social mechanisms is through manic denial of destructive impulses, and destroyed good objects, and the reinforcement of good impulses and good objects, by participation in group idealization. These social mechanisms are the reflection in the group of mechanisms of denial and idealization shown by Melanie Klein to be important mechanisms of defence against depressive anxiety.
>
> (p. 486)

Jaques illustrated his argument with an organisational case study which was based on his work as a consultant with the Tavistock Institute of Human Relations. He sought to understand the relations which prevailed between the management and the workforce, in a period (the 1950s) in which organised conflict between employers and workers was endemic in Britain. Jaques proposed that there was an unconscious dimension to this relationship, operating beneath the surface, as well as the more manifest dimension of conflicts over material rewards and local power. He argued that each of the two principal kinds of anxiety which had been theorised by Klein had an active presence in this system, and that these were managed through mechanisms of splitting and projection.

The case study was of a department of the Glacier Metal Company, with about 60 employees, which was engaged in a renegotiation of its payment system with its workforce. Jaques reported that defences against both persecutory and depressive anxieties had an active presence in the relationship between management and employees. The workers projected into their elected representatives (which included two shop stewards) states of persecutory anxiety, which led them to be suspicious and intransigent in their dealings with management. Sometimes these persecutory feelings were directed towards the representatives themselves, who were thought of as too subservient to the management. But while suspicion and hostility were projected into their representatives and their negotiations, much better relations with supervisors prevailed on the shop floor, where work proceeded in a co-operative, life-as-usual way.

Jaques reported that on the management side depressive anxiety was the predominant mode of defence against the unconscious guilt which management experienced for its exercise of power over the workforce, and as a defence against the anger directed towards them by the workers' representatives. Management was reported to idealise the workforce, and did not wish to call into question its good intentions, despite the antagonism it was facing. Jaques suggested that management's persisting belief in its workers' good faith occasioned depressive anxiety in workers, in so far as they felt that they were taking advantage of management's good will. This depressive anxiety was then defended against through an intensification of persecutory anxiety.

In his account, Jaques was describing two parallel and complementary forms of unconscious splitting in the relationship between management and employees. Management dealt with its more aggressive feelings by disavowal, and by holding on to a more depressive orientation towards its workforce. The workforce dealt with the persecuted states of mind evoked by the discipline of the work and management's power over them by projecting these hostile feelings into their representatives. One has no reason to doubt Jaques' account of this particular situation, although one knows that managements can engage in a form of splitting parallel to that of their workforce. Its phantasy may be that, while the elected shop stewards are malicious, the workforce itself is not, and would not be in conflict with management if it were not for their influence on them as trouble makers or 'agitators'. In such a context, it can become a function of management–union negotiations to regulate the elements of hostility inherent in the employer–employee relationship, taking some of the burden of anxiety and persecution away from the workplace itself. As Jaques himself suggests, Bion's distinction between work group and basic assumption group has relevance to this division of functions.

The crucial discovery announced in Jaques's paper was that unconscious mechanisms of defence, including splitting, play an important part in organisational behaviour. And indeed, that the institutionalisation of industrial conflict in the relationships between union and management representatives could serve as a means of containing conflict, leaving both sides less encumbered by anxiety in the daily conduct of their work. This added a psychoanalytic dimension to what is widely recognised in the field of industrial relations, namely that trade unions often have a regulating role in industrial organisations, and not a disruptive one. It is the recognition of these dimensions of unconscious anxiety, and organisational defences against them such as splitting and projection, that was the first important contribution by Jaques to the social application of Klein's ideas.[2]

Isobel Menzies Lyth: defences against anxiety in a nursing service

The important paper which followed Jaques in developing these connections was Isobel Menzies's Lyth's 'A case-study in the functioning of social systems as a defence against

2 Jaques later repudiated his commitment to psychoanalytic ways of thinking about employment relations, instead adopting a model of organisation in which a rational calculus of the just relation between levels of reward and responsibilities was recommended as the most effective model of organisational design.

anxiety: a report on a study of the nursing service of a general hospital' which she first published in 1960. Menzies Lyth had been invited as a consultant to investigate problems being encountered in the training of nurses. Her report provided an extremely rich description of the experiences of the student nurses, and of the organisation of the nursing system. Among the presenting problems were that an excessive proportion of student nurses were failing to complete their training or were soon afterwards lost to the profession. Sickness rates among trainees were high. She reported an atmosphere of demoralisation and dissatisfaction, with many of the nurse trainees saying that the work they were expected to do did not satisfy the main aspiration which had brought them into nursing, which was to provide care. Patients' experience of their nursing was understandably not as it should have been, though this was not the main focus of the study. Senior members of the nursing staff had invited Menzies Lyth to investigate why this system was working so poorly.

She developed an explanation of the situation she found based on what she understood to be the powerful unconscious anxieties, evoked by the sufferings of the patients, and by exposure to damaged bodies and their functions, to feelings of disgust, and to situations of intimacy where sexual feelings had to be coped with. She developed what is still one of the foremost analyses ever written of a social organisation seen as dominated by a system of social defences against anxiety. The theory of unconscious social defences against anxiety still rests significantly on the foundation which Menzies Lyth laid down for it.

Her analysis was based on a fine-grained description of the experiences of the student nurses, and the form of organisation which framed and constrained their work. She observed that nurses were required to work in a depersonalised environment and were discouraged from forming relationships with individual patients. Feelings towards patients were denied and deemed unprofessional. The work of nursing was defined as sequences of discrete and somewhat mechanical tasks, making it difficult for nurses to recognise their purpose and meaning. Menzies Lyth referred to them as 'ritual task performances', which were unconsciously designed to obscure responsibility for decisions. Anxiety was further managed by routines of checks and counterchecks, and by lack of clarity about who held responsibility for what. There was little team work, or supervision of student nurses, either as individuals or in groups. In effect they were left to survive as individuals, as best they could. Nursing was held up as an ideal, but the nurses' actual capacity for development was underestimated. The idea seemed to be that a good nurse was born and not made. Individuals among the senior staff seemed to be aware of some of these problems, and were not without sympathy for their students, but the system itself remained rigid and resistant to change. There were indications that it was the most capable student nurses who withdrew from their training, and that the senior staff were those who had learned to survive this system, which, though unconscious in its origin, had become an external reality for its members.

Menzies Lyth understood this hospital system as an unconscious defence against the anxieties evoked by the nursing tasks, and drew directly on Melanie Klein's theory of the emotional development of the infant in formulating her ideas. Here is how she relates the anxieties evoked by nursing experience to the primitive anxieties of infancy:

> A hospital accepts and cares for ill people who cannot be cared for in their own homes. This is the task the hospital is created to perform, its 'primary task'. The major responsibility for the performance of that primary task lies with the nursing service, which must provide continuous care for patients, day and night, all the year round.

The nursing service, therefore, bears the full, immediate, and concentrated impact of stresses arising from patient-care.

The situations likely to evoke stress in nurses are familiar. Nurses are in constant contact with people who are physically ill and injured, often seriously. The recovery of patients is not certain and will not always be complete. Nursing patients who have incurable diseases is one of the nurse's most distressing tasks. Nurses are confronted with the threat and the reality of suffering and death as few lay people are. Their work involves carrying out tasks which, by ordinary standards, are distasteful, disgusting and frightening. Intimate physical contact with patients arouses strong libidinal and erotic wishes and impulses that may be difficult to control. The work situation arouses very strong and mixed feelings in the nurse: pity, compassion, and love; guilt and anxiety; hatred and resentment of the patients who arouse these strong feelings; envy of the care given to the patient.

The objective situation confronting the nurse bears a striking resemblance to the phantasy situations that exist in every individual in the deepest and most primitive levels of the mind. The intensity and complexity of the nurse's anxieties are to be attributed primarily to the peculiar capacity of the objective features of her work situation to stimulate afresh these early situations and their accompanying emotions. I will comment briefly on the main relevant features of these phantasy situations.

The elements of these phantasies may be traced back to earliest infancy. The infant experiences two opposing sets of feelings and impulses, libidinal and aggressive. These stem from instinctual sources and are described by the constructs of the life-instinct and the death-instinct. The infant feels omnipotent and attributes dynamic reality to these feelings and impulses. He believes that the libidinal impulses are literally life-giving and the aggressive impulses death-dealing. The infant attributes similar feelings, impulses and powers to other people and to important parts of people. The objects and the instruments of the libidinal and aggressive impulses are felt to be the infant's own and other people's bodies and bodily products. Physical and psychic experiences are very intimately interwoven at this time. The infant's psychic experience of objective reality is greatly influenced by his own feelings and phantasies, moods and wishes.

Through his psychic experience the infant builds up an inner world peopled by himself and the objects of his feelings and impulses. In the inner world, they exist in a form and condition largely determined by his phantasies. Because of the operation of aggressive forces, the inner world contains many damaged, injured, or dead objects. The atmosphere is charged with death and destruction. This gives rise to great anxiety. The infant fears for the effect of aggressive forces on the people he loves and on himself. He grieves and mourns over their suffering and experiences depression and despair about his inadequate ability to put right their wrongs. He fears the demands that will be made on him for reparation and the punishment and revenge that may fall on him. He fears that his libidinal impulses and those of other people cannot control the aggressive impulses sufficiently to prevent utter chaos and destruction. The poignancy

(continued)

(continued)

of the situation is increased because love and longing themselves are felt to be so close to aggression. Greed, frustration, and envy so easily replace a loving relationship. This phantasy world is characterized by a violence and intensity of feeling quite foreign to the emotional life of the normal adult . . .

. . . Unconsciously, the nurse associates the patients' and relatives' distress with that experienced by the people in her phantasy-world, which increases her own anxiety and difficulty in handling it.

(Menzies, 1960; pp. 97–99)

After describing the organisation of the nursing system, Menzies Lyth summarised the situation thus:

The characteristic feature of the social defence system, as we have described it, is its orientation to helping the individual avoid the experience of anxiety, guilt, doubt, and uncertainty . . . this is done by eliminating situations, events, tasks, activities, and relationships that cause anxiety or, more correctly, evoke anxieties connected with primitive psychological remnants in the personality. Little attempt is made positively to help the individual confront the anxiety-evoking experiences and, by so doing, to develop her capacity to tolerate and deal more effectively with the anxiety. Basically, the potential anxieties in the nursing situation are felt to be too deep and dangerous for full confrontation, and to threaten personal disruption and social chaos.

(p. 109)

Menzies Lyth acknowledges the significance for her work of Jaques's and Bion's insights into the role of social defences against anxiety in groups and institutions, as well as of Klein's concepts of primitive anxieties and defences.

One can infer from her rich descriptions that both depressive and paranoid-schizoid anxieties were pervasive for the nurse trainees. Depressive anxiety was aroused by the sufferings of patients, and persecutory anxiety by the ever-present fear of making errors and failing them. The system was imbued with a broader persecutory anxiety, displaced from the primary nursing task, in so far as nurses were expected at all times to maintain a high degree of compliance to rules, and feared being shamed or punished if they failed to comply. The effect of pervasive paranoid-schizoid anxiety was to inhibit symbolic capacity (in Kleinian theory, a function of the depressive position) and thus the ability of both the nursing system and the individual nurses to learn from experience. Although both paranoid-schizoid and depressive kinds of anxiety are strongly present in Menzies Lyth's descriptions of the hospital system, in her paper she is less conceptually specific than Jaques, explicitly referring only to paranoid-schizoid anxiety.

In a valuable recent paper, William Halton (2015)[3] has proposed a reformulation of Menzies Lyth's analysis of her findings. He suggests that repressed in this system of defences

3 Halton's paper is published in a volume (Armstrong and Rustin, 2015) which reviews the development of these ideas in the 60 years since their initial formulation, and shows their continuing fertility.

is an unacknowledged hatred of patients, for the pain their sufferings cause to their nurses and others, and that what is being described by Menzies Lyth is an obsessional form of defence, in which attention is removed from the physical and emotional reality of the patients as whole persons, and is instead displaced on to particular details and routines. There are many situations in medical care, of course, in which attention to details (for example, which symptoms are present, which drugs need to be given, when) is essential. But patients have needs which go beyond their physical care, that is, for recognition, understanding and care, and it is these needs which Menzies Lyth's study described as having been disavowed and neglected by the nursing system.

Following broadly psychoanalytic principles, Menzies Lyth recommended that if the anxieties she had identified could be openly acknowledged in the nursing situation, and settings provided in which they could be shared and reflected on by nurse trainees and their supervisors, their harmful impact could be lessened. But the implications of her study go beyond this, since they imply that a changed model of authority, task organisation and training would produce better outcomes for patients and nursing staff alike. She suggested, following Jaques and Bion, that resistance to social change is likely to be greatest in institutions dominated by paranoid-schizoid defences, whose nature is to inhibit understanding.

Like Elliott Jaques' Glacier Metal research, Menzies Lyth's study of nursing was path breaking. Each of these studies contributed to the development of a genre of organisational research and consultancy in which psychoanalytic principles of investigation and intervention could be applied in institutional settings. Klein's belief in the primary therapeutic value of the understanding of unconscious states of mind which could be achieved in interpretative work with patients was transposed by Jaques, Menzies Lyth and contemporaries and successors in this field to work within organisations of many kinds. Her concept of unconscious anxieties and the defences which are mobilised against them has thus proved to be powerful resources in the understanding of organisational and social dynamics. Menzies Lyth developed the insights she had first elaborated in her nursing study into other settings, such as day care for young children, where they proved equally powerful in identifying dysfunctional modes of organisation. In the case of day care, it was the anxieties evoked by the sufferings of small children having to cope with long hours of separation from their parents which were the primary source of stress for care staff. Menzies Lyth identified methods of defence similar to those of the nursing system ('multiple indiscriminate care' was her formulation for this) employed by care staff as a defence against these anxieties (Menzies Lyth *et al.*, 1971; Menzies Lyth, 1989).

The later development of the Kleinian concepts of paranoid-schizoid and depressive anxiety has also proved to have relevance to broader institutional and social phenomena. The post-Kleinian theory of 'borderline states' and of libidinal and destructive narcissism has provided further diagnostic and conceptual resources not only for the understanding of individual patients, but also of organisational behaviour. The idea that organisations and networks may resort to an unconscious defence of 'not knowing' ('turning a blind eye', in John Steiner's (1985) phrase) to intolerable anxieties has turned out to illuminate several kinds of failure and dysfunction. For example, in the numerous instances of sexual and other forms of abuse within families and institutions which have been revealed in recent years, there are of course the responsibilities of the actual perpetrators to consider, the theoretical understanding of whose behaviour often seems to lie in the realm of psychological perversion. But there have also been gross failures of institutional authorities, staff members and regulators, to take note of danger signs which should have alerted them to the existence of serious risks, and to take urgent preventive action (Rustin, 2005). The mechanisms of splitting and denial, and the substitution of empty routines and rule following for an active cognitive and emotional engagement with a whole situation, are illuminated by these Kleinian and post-Kleinian models of unconscious anxieties and defences.

Bion's theory of groups

A second highly significant text which was included in the *New Directions* anthology was Wilfred Bion's 1955 paper 'Group dynamics – a re-view'. Here Bion outlined his model for the understanding of group behaviour, which was based on work he conducted with small groups convened for the purpose of investigating unconscious group phenomena. The principal connection with Klein's ideas lies in the importance of unconscious anxiety in shaping the response of the group to the situation in which it is placed. Bion described three kinds of 'valency' or unconscious disposition in the group. These were respectively 'fight–flight', 'dependency' and 'pairing'. In the first of these, the group's shared phantasy was of a threatening enemy, which needed to be either confronted or fled from. (It seems likely that this understanding drew on Bion's experiences in front-line military combat.) In the second, the group assumed a wholly passive orientation, with the phantasy that the group leader, or someone or something else, would take care of all its problems. In the third, 'pairing', all hope is invested in a phantasy of a creative act, perhaps undertaken by a couple, perhaps a single person, which would give rise to a magical 'object', Messiah or idea which would answer all unconscious needs. There is a fourth kind of orientation, fundamental to Bion's model, which is that of the 'work group', the state of mind in which the group is able to functional rationally and address itself to the completion of whatever tasks it has taken responsibility for. The three 'basic assumptions' each describe means of avoiding or turning away from an orientation towards reason and work.

Here is Bion's own description of his experience with these groups:

> Participation in basic assumption activity requires no training, experience, or mental development. It is instantaneous, inevitable, and instinctive: I have not felt the need to postulate the existence of a herd instinct to account for such phenomena as I have witnessed in the group. In contrast with work group function basic assumption activity makes no demands on the individual for a capacity to co-operate but depends on the individual's possession of what I call valency – a term I borrow from the physicists to express a capacity for instantaneous involuntary combination of one individual with another for sharing and acting on a basic assumption. Work group function is always in evidence with one, and only one, basic assumption. Though the work group function may remain unaltered the contemporary basic assumption that pervades its activities can be changing frequently; there may be two or three changes in an hour or the same basic assumption may be dominant for months on end.
>
> (Bion, 1955; p. 449)

> To recapitulate: any group of individuals met together for work shows work group activity, that is mental functioning designed to further the task in hand. Investigation shows that these aims are sometimes hindered, occasionally furthered, by emotional

> drives of obscure origin. A certain cohesion is given to these anomalous mental activities if it is assumed that emotionally the group acts as if it had certain basic assumptions about its aims. These basic assumptions, which appear to be fairly adequately adumbrated by three formulations, dependence, pairing, and fighting or flight, are, on further investigation, seen to displace each other, as if in response to some unexplained impulse. They appear, furthermore, to have some common link, or, perhaps, even to be different aspects of each other. Further investigation shows that each basic assumption contains features that correspond so closely with extremely primitive part objects that sooner or later psychotic anxiety, appertaining to these primitive relationships, is released. These anxieties, and the mechanisms peculiar to them, have been already displayed in psycho-analysis by Melanie Klein, and her descriptions tally well with the emotional states which find an outlet in mass action of the group in behaviour that seems to have coherence if it is considered to be the outcome of a basic assumption. Approached from the angle of sophisticated work group activity the basic assumptions appear to be the source of emotional drives to aims far different either from the overt task of the group or even from the tasks that would appear to be appropriate to Freud's view of the group as based on the family group. But approached from the angle of psychotic anxiety associated with phantasies of primitive part object relationships, described by Melanie Klein and her co-workers, the basic assumption phenomena appear far more to have the characteristics of defensive reactions to psychotic anxiety, and to be not so much at variance with Freud's views as supplementary to them. In my view, it is necessary to work through both the stresses that appertain to family patterns and the still more primitive anxieties of part object relationships. In fact I consider the latter to contain the ultimate sources of all group behaviour.
>
> (p. 476)

The framing of these study groups[4] was like that of an experiment, or quasi-laboratory for the study of group processes. Bion as conductor of these groups confined himself rigorously to an analytic function, that is, to offer insights into the groups' states of mind whenever it seemed illuminating to do so. Because group members had to learn from their experience what the work of the group was to be there was no externally defined task to be completed or problem to be solved – it was not easy for them to maintain the mode of functioning of a 'work group'. The setting of the group thus had the effect of inducing the unconscious anxieties which it was the work of the group to investigate. Just as the consulting room can be described as comparable to a laboratory (Rustin, 2001), evoking and making visible in the transference relationship to the analyst the states of mind which are to be explored, so Bion's setting functions as a laboratory for the study of the unconscious state of mind of the group.

Bion holds that the anxieties which groups struggle to defend themselves against are of a psychotic kind. This signifies that they are analogous to the anxieties experienced in early infancy, in which the question of the infant's survival and the role of mother or primary carer are central. The role of the mother in early life, according to Bion, is emotionally and mentally to process the anxieties of her infant, and thus contain them. It is through introjection of the mother's mental function that the infant develops a mental apparatus, a

4 *Experiences in Groups* is the title of the book (Bion, 1961) in which he described this work at greater length. These 'study groups' are a practice distinct from psychoanalytic group therapy, whose development was greatly influenced by Bion's work. On this development, see Garland (2010).

capacity for thought, we might say a functioning ego, of its own. The effect of the group experience is to threaten group members with a situation in which there appears to be no available containment. Following Freud, Bion holds that states of mind are liable to become unconsciously transmitted in fluid and volatile ways within groups. Thus the states of mind observed in a group can often not be correctly attributed to individual members and the specific anxieties which they bring to the group, but may, through the mechanisms of projective and introjective identification, become located in any members at particular moments. Freud (e.g. 1921, 1930) had argued that a group can have the effect of weakening the egos of its individual members, leading them to become identified with an object of fantasy (e.g. leader, nation, god): Bion develops this view. The occurrence of a sudden state of panic and flight in a crowd, or of the mob's turning on a victim chosen in phantasy and without reason (Shakespeare's *Julius Caesar* dramatises the role of such a mob[5]) is a familiar example of the operation in the world of one of Bion's basic assumptions, 'fight–flight'.

Bion nowhere tries to integrate fully his model of basic assumptions, as defences against anxiety, with Klein's theory of paranoid-schizoid and depressive anxieties, although 'fight–flight' does seem to correspond closely with the paranoid-schizoid position, and the 'work group' orientation has a strongly 'depressive' character in so far as it can apprehend the real qualities of its 'object' and is capable of symbolic functioning. One reason why this theoretical integration is incomplete may be because the psychotic states of mind in which Bion is most interested (and which are a central theme of his later writing) occur in an early phase of development which precedes formation of the paranoid-schizoid position, and the definite forms of splitting which accompany this. That is to say, a phase of development which Klein did not fully explore in her own work, but which is explored more fully in Bion's writing. One knows of child patients suffering from psychotic states in whom the capacity for splitting, and thus the capacity to push hated and feared objects outside the self, was seen as a crucial step at their stage of development, and the prerequisite for a further process of integration.[6] Psychoanalytic writers on autistic states, such as Frances Tustin and Thomas Ogden, have written about such undifferentiated formations of the mind, in which no separation between self and its object is felt to be tolerable. Perhaps the basic assumption of 'dependency' can understood as a phantasied state of reliance on an omnipotent mother figure, leaving the group and its members feeling freed from responsibility or the need for thought or action of any kind.

Klein had understood, contrary to Freud, that Oedipal anxieties arose in the first months of life, and were linked with unconscious fears and hatreds of potential 'new babies', whose existence could threaten the well-being and survival of the infant. The basic assumption of

5 3 Pleb.: Your name, sir, truly.
Cinna: Truly, my name is Cinna.
1 Pleb.: Tear him to pieces; he's a conspirator!
Cinna: I am Cinna the poet, I am Cinna the poet.
4 Pleb.: Tear him for his bad verses, tear him for his bad verses!
Cinna: I am not Cinna the conspirator.
4 Pleb.: It is no matter, his name's Cinna; pluck but his name out of his heart, and turn him going.
3 Pleb.: Tear him, tear him!

(*Julius Caesar*, III, 3)

6 Klein wrote 'that it is essential for normal development that a division between the good and bad object, between love and hate, should take place in earliest infancy. When such a division is not too severe, and yet sufficient to differentiate between good and bad, it forms in my view one of the basic elements for stability and mental health' ('On the development of mental functioning', 1958; p. 242).

'pairing' is an idealised phantasy of procreation of a magical child or product whose arrival will solve all problems, but this may be thought of primarily as an unconscious denial of its fear and envy of potential rivals. 'Our baby must be so beautiful or marvellous that it will save us from the fate of being cast out', may be the primitive Oedipal fantasy. It is to be noted that the Kleinian model of early Oedipal anxiety has as much to do with the fear of being displaced by new babies through the sexual activities of the parents than with its libidinal desire for them. Bion stresses that the basic assumptions are unconscious phantasies, and that there is no possibility that these can in reality be fulfilled, and the basic assumption of pairing seems to be exactly of this kind. These are in any case conjectures, since the conceptual frames constituted by Bion's basic assumptions and Klein's paranoid-schizoid and depressive positions do not precisely map on to each other.

Bion's early work with groups has proved immensely fertile and influential, giving rise to a large development in group therapy, and group relations training, the latter becoming a significant element in the practice of psychoanalytic organisational consultancy. These are two of the many wider contexts of practice in which Klein's ideas have proved seminal.

Chapter 13

Afterword

It has been a remarkable and moving experience for the authors of this book to re-read all of the published writings of Melanie Klein. The four volumes record an immensely productive psychoanalytic life, both conveying a rich sense of what took place in her consulting room and demonstrating how much it mattered to Klein to communicate with her colleagues, students and those interested in psychoanalytic ideas what she had discovered and what she believed it revealed about the human mind and the potential of psychoanalytic therapy.

The purpose of this book has primarily been to introduce readers to Klein's own published writing, and to demonstrate its evolution over her long professional career. There was not the space, nor was it our intention, to write much about the influence of her work on subsequent generations of psychoanalysts, child psychotherapists and other professionals concerned with mental health. This is, however, a significant omission, although we have indicated some lines of later development in some of our chapters. However, much of her influence is left unexplored, despite the fact that Klein was herself from early in her career one of a group of psychoanalysts who were able to work creatively together,[1] and in the years since her death her writings have had a continuing major influence on the later development of psychoanalytic theory and technique. Her writings and her personal influence on a generation of future analysts have had a great influence on the later development of psychoanalysis. Whilst the development of a 'Kleinian school' of psychoanalysis has been accompanied by factional disputes and tensions within the psychoanalytic movement, and indeed to some degree within Klein's original circle, its more significant feature has surely been the generative potential of so many of the ideas which she developed together with her colleagues.

We will briefly summarise some of the key developments for which Klein had, or shared, responsibility, and suggest the influence which these have had.

First, her impact on the lives of young children and their families. Here, there is her development of the technique of psychoanalytic play therapy, which has had a formative influence on the development of child analysis and subsequently of psychoanalytic child psychotherapy. Then there is her conviction that an intense emotional relationship between a baby and its mother or primary carer exists from the moment of birth. This picture of the early bond between baby and mother gave impetus to the development of very early psychoanalytically informed interventions when such relationships are troubled, and to the practice of psychoanalytic infant observation, now a part of many psychoanalytic trainings world-wide.

Second, her theoretical contributions to our understanding of mental life. Klein's theory of paranoid-schizoid and depressive anxiety has proved to be extremely influential as a

1 One notes, for example, the defence of Klein's ideas in the 'Controversial Discussions' of 1941–1945 (King and Steiner, 1991) by Paula Heimann, Susan Isaacs and Joan Riviere, as well as Klein herself.

conceptualisation of the vicissitudes of personality development, both normal and abnormal. This gave rise to further discoveries and elaborations, as additional kinds of personality organisation (for example, borderline, narcissistic and autistic aspects of personality) were encountered in the consulting room, and given their own theoretical formulations by successors of Klein, such as Herbert Rosenfeld, Frances Tustin, John Steiner and Ronald Britton. Klein's recognition that projective identification can serve the function of unconscious communication was taken up by Paula Heimann, in her recognition of the potential clinical significance of the countertransference, and further developed by Wilfred Bion in his understanding of the relation of 'container and contained', which he saw as the central dynamic of the relationship between infant and mother. Bion's understanding of projective identification, and its functions both as the evacuation of intolerable parts of the mind, and as a communication seeking understanding, made possible a deeper understanding of 'primitive' (i.e. infantile) and psychotic states of mind, and broadened the field of mental disorders with which psychoanalytic therapists are able to work. Her continuing commitment to the relevance of Freud's theory of the life and death instincts set her apart from some subsequent revisions of psychoanalytic theory, but it is notable that the idea of the death instinct and its link to the repetition compulsion remain of contemporary clinical interest to many analysts, including, for example, Michael Feldman and John Steiner. Finally, the importance of Klein's detailed picture of the internal world and her emphasis on the necessity for a central focus on psychic reality in psychoanalysis remains undimmed. Donald Meltzer's writings bring this out with especial clarity.

With respect to technique, the phenomenon of the transference relationship, which was always at the centre of Klein's own therapeutic technique, became the subject of intense further study, taking into account its countertransferential dimensions, giving rise to Betty Joseph's elaboration of the 'total transference relationship', which has now become an important point of reference for post-Kleinian psychoanalysts.

In the final chapters of this book, we have outlined the influence of Klein's ideas, through the work of Hanna Segal and others, on the psychoanalytic understanding of symbolism and culture. We have described the influence of her concepts of paranoid-schizoid and depressive anxiety on the application of psychoanalytic ideas to the understanding of organisations and society, through the work of Elliot Jaques and Isobel Menzies Lyth. More broadly, we have argued that Klein's theory of the 'innate object-relatedness' of human beings contributed to a reorientation of psychoanalysis from its more individualistic formulation in Freud's own work, towards a more 'social' and morally complex perspective. In this respect, although not in all others, Kleinian ideas have become part of the broader 'object relations' tendency in psychoanalysis.

These and many other later developments of Klein's ideas have been set out in excellent scholarly expositions by psychoanalyst writers such as Elizabeth Spillius and Robert Hinshelwood. It is because Klein's work provided such remarkable resources for further thinking that her influence has been so considerable, and has given rise to the development of a distinctive tradition of psychoanalytic thought. We believe that this was a remarkable achievement, and that Klein was surely one of the foremost female scientists of the twentieth century.

Suggestions for further reading

The Melanie Klein Trust website has a wealth of material, both historical and contemporary, including both text and video: http://www.melanie-klein-trust.org.uk.

Bronstein, C. (ed.) (2001) *Kleinian Theory: A Contemporary Perspective*. London: Whurr. This book provides a modern overview of Klein's thought.

Frank, C. (2009) *Melanie Klein in Berlin: Her First Psychoanalyses of Children*. London: Routledge. This is a scholarly presentation of Klein's work with children in Berlin, drawing on the Klein Archive.

Grosskurth, P. (1986) *Melanie Klein: Her World and Her Work*. Cambridge, MA: Harvard University Press, 1987. This is the only substantial biography of Melanie Klein. It is however seen as contentious by many sympathetic to Klein.

Hinshelwood, R. (1989) *A Dictionary of Kleinian Thought*. London: Free Association Books. This invaluable work provides concise expositions of Klein's main concepts and theories and their subsequent evolution.

Hinshelwood, R. (1994) *Clinical Klein*. London: Free Association Books. This book is a companion to Hinshelwood's *Dictionary of Kleinian Thought* and outlines Klein's theoretical contributions and their subsequent development, giving many contemporary clinical examples.

Kristeva, J. (2001) *Melanie Klein* [trans. Ross Guberman]. New York: Columbia University Press. This is a sympathetic account of Klein's work by a leading French psychoanalyst and feminist.

Likierman, M. (2001) *Melanie Klein: Her Work in Context*. London: Continuum. This book is a fine study of Klein's work, and is particularly interesting in tracing Ferenczi's importance to her development.

Meltzer, D. (1978) *The Kleinian Development*. Perthshire: Clunie Press. [Reprinted London: Karnac, 1998.] The second part of this volume, which in three parts outlines a view of psychoanalytic development from Freud to Bion, consists of a detailed study of Klein's *Narrative of a Child Analysis*.

Segal, H. (1964) *Introduction to the Work of Melanie Klein*. London: Heinemann. [Reprinted London: Karnac, 1988.] This book remains a classic study.

Sherwin-White, S. (in press) *Melanie Klein Revisited: Pioneer and Revolutionary in the Psychoanalysis of Young Children*. London: Karnac.

Spillius, E.B. (ed.) (1988) *Melanie Klein Today: Developments in Theory and Practice, Vol. 1: Mainly Theory; Vol. 2: Mainly Practice*. London: Routledge. These two volumes include an impressive range of the work of psychoanalysts in the Klein tradition, with authoritative introductions by Elizabeth Spillius.

Spillius, E.B. (2007) *Encounters with Melanie Klein: Selected Papers of Elizabeth Spillius*. London: Routledge. These papers outline important features of Kleinian thought, and investigate Melanie Klein's unpublished archive.

Spillius, E.B., Milton, J., Garvey, P, Couve, C. and Steiner, D. (eds.) (2011) *The New Dictionary of Kleinian Thought*. London: Routledge. This volume is a revised and updated edition of R.D. Hinshelwood's 1989 *Dictionary of Kleinian Thought*, adding significant new material.

Publications by Melanie Klein

Love, Guilt and Reparation and Other Works 1921–1945 (1975) *(The Writings of Melanie Klein, Vol. I)* London: Hogarth Press. [Reprinted London: Vintage, 1988.]

Contents

The development of a child (1921)

Inhibitions and difficulties at puberty (1922)

The role of the school in the libidinal development of the child (1923)

Early analysis (1923)

A contribution to the psychogenesis of tics (1925)

The psychological principles of early analysis (1926)

Symposium on child-analysis (1927)

Criminal tendencies in normal children (1927)

Early stages of the Oedipus conflict (1928)

Personification in the play of children (1929)

Infantile anxiety situations reflected in a work of art and in the creative impulse (1929)

The importance of symbol-formation in the development of the ego (1930)

The psychotherapy of the psychoses (1930)

A contribution to the theory of intellectual inhibition (1931)

The early development of conscience in the child (1933)

On criminality (1934)

A contribution to the psychogenesis of manic-depressive states (1935)

Weaning (1936)

Love, guilt and reparation (1937)

Mourning and its relation to manic-depressive states (1940)

The Oedipus complex in the light of early anxieties (1945)

The Psycho-Analysis of Children (1932) (*The Writings of Melanie Klein, Vol.* 2) London: Hogarth Press, revised edition, 1975. [Reprinted London: Vintage, 1997.]

Contents

Part I

The technique of child analysis

The psychological foundations of child analysis

The technique of early analysis

An obsessional neurosis in a six-year-old girl

The technique of analysis in the latency period

The technique of analysis in puberty

Neurosis in children

The sexual activities of children

Part II

Early anxiety-situations and their effect on the development of the child

Early stages of the Oedipus conflict and of super-ego formation

The relations between obsessional neurosis and the early stages of the super-ego

The significance of early anxiety-situations in the development of the ego

The effects of early anxiety-situations on the sexual development of the girl

The effects of early anxiety-situations on the sexual development of the boy

Appendix

The scope and limits of child analysis

Envy and Gratitude and Other Works 1946–1963 (1975) (*The Writings of Melanie Klein, Vol.* 3). London: Hogarth. [Reprinted London: Vintage, 1997.]

Contents

Notes on some schizoid mechanisms (1946)

On the theory of anxiety and guilt (1948)

On the criteria for the termination of a psycho-analysis (1950)

The origins of transference (1952)

The mutual influences in the development of ego and id (1952)

Some theoretical conclusions regarding the emotional life of the infant (1952)

On observing the behaviour of young infants (1952)

The psycho-analytic play technique: its history and significance (1955)

On identification (1955)

Envy and gratitude (1957)

On the development of mental functioning (1958)

Our adult world and its roots in infancy (1959)

A note on depression in the schizophrenic (1960)

On mental health (1960)

Some reflections on *The Oresteia* (1963)

On the sense of loneliness (1963)

Short contributions

The importance of words in early analysis (1927)

Note on 'A Dream of Forensic Interest' (1928)

Theoretical deductions from an analysis of dementia praecox in early infancy (1929)

Review of *Woman's Periodicity* by Mary Chadwick (1933)

Some psychological considerations: a comment (1942)

Narrative of a Child Analysis: The Conduct of the Psycho-Analysis of Children as Seen in the Treatment of a Ten-Year-Old Boy (1961) (*The Writings of Melanie Klein, Vol. 4*). London: Hogarth. [Reprinted London: Vintage, 1998.]

Other works

Klein, M. (2013) *Autobiography*. Annotated and transcribed by Janet Sayers. http://melanie-klein-trust.org.uk/domains/melanie-klein-trust.org.uk/local/media/downloads/2013_Klein_autobiography___Janet_Sayers_transcription.pdf (accessed 3 August, 2016). The full autobiography was transcribed and edited by Robert Hinshelwood (2016) http://melanie-klein-trust.org.uk.surface3.vm.bytemark.co.uk/domains/melanie-klein-trust.org.uk/local/media/downloads/_MK_full_autobiography.pdf

Klein, M., Heimann, P., Isaacs, S. and Riviere, J. (1952) *Developments in Psychoanalysis*. [Reprinted London: Karnac, 1989.]

Klein, M., Heimann, P. and Money-Kyrle, R.E. (eds.) (1955) *New Directions in Psycho-Analysis: The Significance of Infant Conflict in the Pattern of Adult Behaviour*. [Reprinted London: Karnac, 1993.]

Klein, M. and Riviere, J. (1937) *Love, Hate, and Reparation*. (Psycho-Analytical Epitomes No. 2.) [Reprinted in 1953.] [Reprinted London: Norton, 1964.]

Bibliography

Abraham, K (1973) 'A short study on the development of the libido, viewed in the light of mental disorders'. In *Selected Papers of Karl Abraham*. London: Hogarth and the Institute of Psychoanalysis.

Alvarez, A. (1992) *Live Company: Psychoanalytic Psychotherapy with Autistic, Borderline, Deprived and Abused Children*. London: Routledge.

Alvarez, A. and Reid, S. (eds.) (1999) *Autism and Personality: Findings from the Tavistock Autism Workshop*. London: Routledge.

Armstrong, D. and Rustin, M.J. (2015) *Social Defences Against Anxiety: Explorations in a Paradigm*. London: Karnac.

Banks, L.R. (1980) *The Indian in the Cupboard*. New York: Doubleday.

Bick, E. (1964) 'Notes on infant observation in psycho-analytic training'. *International Journal of Psycho-Analysis*, 45: 558–566. [Reprinted in: Harris, M. and Bick, E. (1987) *Collected Papers of Martha Harris and Esther Bick*. Strath Tay, Perthshire: Clunie Press.]

Bick, E. (1968) 'The experience of the skin in early object-relations'. *International Journal of Psycho-Analysis*, 49: 484–486. [Reprinted in: Harris, M. and Bick, E. (1987) *Collected Papers of Martha Harris and Esther Bick*. Strath Tay, Perthshire: Clunie Press.]

Bion, W.R. (1955) 'Group dynamics: a re-view'. In Klein, M., Money-Kyrle, R. and Heimann, P. (eds.) *New Directions in Psycho-Analysis: The Significance of Infant Conflict in the Pattern of Adult Behaviour*. London: Tavistock. [Reprinted London: Karnac, 1977.]

Bion, W.R. (1961) 'Experiences in groups'. In *Experiences in Groups and Other Papers*. London: Tavistock. [Reprinted London: Routledge.]

Bion, W.R. (1962a) 'A theory of thinking'. *International Journal of Psycho-Analysis*, 43: 306–310. [Reprinted in: Bion, W.R. (1967) *Second Thoughts*. London: Heinemann.]

Bion, W.R. (1962b) *Learning from Experience*. London: Heinemann.

Bion, W.R. (1970) *Attention and Interpretation*. London: Tavistock. [Reprinted London: Karnac, 2016.]

Boston, M. and Szur, R. (eds.) (1983) *Psychotherapy with Severely Deprived Children*. London: Routledge and Kegan Paul.

Bowlby, J. (1969) *Attachment and Loss, Vol. 1: Attachment*. London: Hogarth Press.

Bowlby, J. (1973) *Attachment and Loss, Vol. 2: Separation: Anxiety and Anger*. London: Hogarth Press.

Bowlby, J. (1980) *Attachment and Loss, Vol. 3: Loss: Sadness and Depression*. London: Hogarth Press.

Britton, R.S. (1989) 'The missing link: parental sexuality in the Oedipus complex'. In Steiner, J. (ed.) *The Oedipus Complex Today: Clinical Implications*. London: Karnac.

Britton, R.S. (1998a) 'Before and after the depressive position: $Ps(n) \rightarrow D(n) - Ps(n + 1)$'. In *Belief and Imagination: Explorations in Psychoanalysis*. London: Routledge.

Britton, R.S. (1998b) *Belief and Imagination: Explorations in Psychoanalysis*. London: Routledge.

Britton, R.S. (1998c) 'Wordsworth: the loss of presence and the presence of loss'. In *Belief and Imagination: Explorations in Psychoanalysis*. London: Routledge.

Caper, R. (1999) *A Mind of One's Own: A Kleinian View of Self and Object*. London: Routledge.

Chaucer, G. (1951) *The Canterbury Tales* (translated into modern English by Nevill Coghill). London: Penguin.
Davidson, D. (1982) 'Paradoxes of irrationality'. In Wollheim, R. and Hopkins, J. (eds.) *Philosophical Essays on Freud*. Cambridge: Cambridge University Press. [Reprinted in: Davidson, D. (2004) *Problems of Rationality*. Oxford: Oxford University Press.]
Donne, J. (1624) 'Meditation XVII'. *Devotions Upon Emergent Occasions*. In Hayward, J. (ed.) (1967) *John Donne: Complete Poetry and Selected Prose*. London: Nonesuch Press.
Empson, W. (1935) 'Alice in Wonderland: the child as swain'. In *Some Versions of Pastoral*. London: Chatto and Windus.
Feldman, M. (1989) 'The Oedipus complex: manifestations in the inner world and the therapeutic situation'. In Steiner, J. (ed.) *The Oedipus Complex Today: Clinical Implications*. London: Karnac.
Fonagy, P. (2001) *Attachment Theory and Psychoanalysis*. New York: Other Press.
Fonagy, P. and Target, M. (2003) *Psychoanalytic Theories: Perspectives from Developmental Psychopathology*. London: Whurr.
Foot, P. (1958) 'Moral beliefs'. *Proceedings of the Aristotelian Society*, 59: 83–104. [Reprinted in: Foot, P. (1978) *Virtues and Vices and Other Essays in Moral Philosophy*. Oxford: Blackwell.]
Foot, P. (2001) *Natural Goodness*. Oxford: Oxford University Press.
Frank, C. (2009) *Melanie Klein in Berlin: Her First Psychoanalyses of Children*. Leighton, S. and Young, S. (trans.); Bott Spillius, E. (ed.). London: Routledge.
Freud, S. (1900) 'The interpretation of dreams'. *Standard Edition of the Complete Psychological Works of Sigmund Freud (S.E.)*. London: Hogarth Press [1950–1974], 4–5.
Freud, S. (1905) 'Three essays on the theory of sexuality'. *S.E.* 7: 125–243.
Freud, S. (1909) 'Analysis of a phobia in a five-year-old boy'. *S.E.* 10: 5–149.
Freud, S. (1910) *Leonardo da Vinci and a Memory of his Childhood. S.E.* 11: 63–137.
Freud, S. (1911) 'Formulations on the two principles of mental functioning'. *S.E.* 12: 213–226.
Freud, S. (1916) 'Criminals from a sense of guilt' ('Some character-types met with in psycho-analytic work, part III'). *S.E.* 14: 332–333.
Freud, S. (1917) 'Mourning and melancholia'. *S.E.* 14: 243–260.
Freud, S. (1918) 'From the history of an infantile neurosis'. *S.E.* 17: 7–121.
Freud, S. (1920) 'Beyond the pleasure principle'. *S.E.* 18: 7–64.
Freud, S. (1921) 'Group psychology and the analysis of the ego'. *S.E.* 18: 69–143.
Freud, S. (1930) 'Civilization and its discontents'. *S.E.* 21: 64–145.
Freud, S. (1937) 'Constructions in analysis'. *S.E.* 23: 255–269.
Gardner, S. (1992) 'The nature and source of emotion'. In Hopkins, J. (ed.) *Psychoanalysis, Mind and Art: Perspectives on Richard Wollheim*. Oxford: Blackwell.
Gardner, S. (1993) *Irrationality and the Philosophy of Psychoanalysis*. Cambridge: Cambridge University Press.
Garland, C. (2010) *The Groups Book: Psychoanalytic Group Therapy: Principles and Practice*. London: Karnac.
Glover, N. (2009) *Psychoanalytic Aesthetics: An Introduction to the British School*. London: Karnac.
Goodyer, I.M., Tsancheva, S., Byford, S., Dubicka, B., Hill, J., Kelvin, R., Reynolds, S., Roberts, C., Senior, R., Suckling, J., Wilkinson, P., Target, M. and Fonagy, P. (2011) 'Improving Mood with Psychoanalytic and Cognitive Therapies (IMPACT): a pragmatic effectiveness superiority trial to investigate whether specialised psychological treatment reduces the risk of relapse in adolescents with moderate to severe unipolar depression: study protocol for a randomised controlled trial'. *Trials*, 12 (175). doi: 10.1186/1745-6215-12-175.
Gowing, L. (ed.) (1978) *The Critical Writings of Adrian Stokes, Vol. 2: 1937–1958*. London: Thames and Hudson.
Green, H., McGinnity, A., Meltzer, H., Ford, T. and Goodman, R. (2005). *Mental Health of Children and Young People in Great Britain 2004*. Basingstoke: Palgrave Macmillan.
Green, J. (1950) *If I Were You* [trans. McEwan, J.H.F]. London: Eyre and Spottiswoode.

Hagell, A. (ed.) (2012) *Changing Adolescence: Social Trends and Mental Health*. Bristol: Policy Press.

Halton, W. (2015) 'Obsessional-punitive defences in care systems: Menzies Lyth revisited'. In Armstrong, D. and Rustin, M. (eds.) *Social Defences Against Anxiety: Explorations in a Paradigm*. London: Karnac.

Hampshire, S. (1951) *Spinoza*. Harmondsworth: Penguin [revised ed. 1962].

Hampshire, S. (1959) *Thought and Action*. London: Chatto and Windus.

Hampshire, S. (1962) 'Disposition and memory'. *International Journal of Psycho-Analysis*, 43: 59–68. [Reprinted in: Hampshire, S. (1971) *Freedom of Mind and Other Essays*. Princeton, NJ: Princeton University Press.]

Harris, M. (1987) 'Consultation project in a comprehensive school'. In Harris Williams, M. (ed.) *Collected Papers of Martha Harris and Esther Bick*. Strath Tay, Perthshire: Clunie Press.

Heimann, P. (1950) 'On counter-transference'. *International Journal of Psycho-Analysis*, 31: 81–84.

Hinshelwood, R.D. (2006). 'Who wants to be a scientist?: the historical and psychoanalytic context at the start of Klein's career: circa 1918–1921'. In Mills, J. (ed.) *Other Banalities: Melanie Klein Revisited*. London: Routledge.

Hochschild, A.R. (1983) *The Managed Heart: The Commercialisation of Human Feeling*. Berkeley, CA: University of California Press.

Hopkins, J. (2003) 'Evolution, emotion, and conflict'. In Chung, M. and Feltham, C. (eds.) *Psychoanalytic Knowledge and the Nature of the Mind*. Basingstoke: Palgrave Macmillan.

Hopkins, J. (2014) 'The significance of consilience: psychoanalysis, attachment, neuroscience and evolution'. http://www.academia.edu/7719945/The_Significance_of_Consilience (accessed 3 August, 2016).

Hoxter, S. (1983) 'Some feelings aroused in working with severely deprived children'. In Boston, M. and Szur, R. (eds.) *Psychotherapy with Severely Deprived Children*. London: Routledge and Kegan Paul.

Hrdy, S.B. (1999) *Mother Nature: A History of Mothers, Infants, and Natural Selection*. New York: Pantheon.

Hug-Hellmuth, H. (1921) 'On the technique of child-analysis'. *International Journal of Psycho-Analysis*, 2: 287–305. [Reprinted in: Hinshelwood, R.D. (ed.) *Influential Papers from the 1920s*. London: Karnac, 2004.]

Jaques, E. (1955) 'Social systems as defence against persecutory and depressive anxiety: a contribution to the psycho-analytical study of social processes'. In Klein, M., Money-Kyrle, R. and Heimann, P. (eds.) *New Directions in Psycho-Analysis: The Significance of Infant Conflict in the Pattern of Adult Behaviour*. London: Tavistock. [Reprinted London: Karnac, 1977.]

Joseph, B. (1987) 'Projective identification: clinical aspects'. In Sandler, J. (ed.) *Projection, Identification, Projective Identification*. Madison, CT: International Universities Press. [Reprinted London: Karnac, 1988.]

Joseph, B. (1989) *Psychic Equilibrium and Psychic Change: Selected Papers of Betty Joseph*. Feldman, M. and Bott Spillius, E. (eds.) London: Tavistock/Routledge.

King, P. and Steiner, R. (eds.) (1991) *The Freud–Klein Controversies 1941–45*. London: Routledge.

Klein, M., Heimann, P. and Money-Kyrle, R.E. (eds.) (1955) *New Directions in Psycho-Analysis: The Significance of Infant Conflict in the Pattern of Adult Behaviour*. [Reprinted London: Karnac, 1993.]

Lear, J. (1990) *Love and Its Place in Nature: A Philosophical Interpretation of Freudian Psychoanalysis*. New York: Farrar, Straus and Giroux.

Likierman, M. (2001) *Melanie Klein: Her Work in Context*. London: Continuum.

Locke, J. (1947) 'An essay concerning human understanding'. In: *The Epistle to the Reader*. London: Everyman, p. xxiii.

MacIntyre, A. (1966) *A Short History of Ethics*. London: Macmillan.

Main, M. (1995) 'Recent studies in attachment: overview, with selected applications for clinical work'. In Goldberg, S., Muir, R. and Kerr, J. (eds.) *Attachment Theory: Social, Developmental and Clinical Perspectives*. Hillsdale, NJ: Analytic Press.

Mayes, L., Fonagy, P. and Target, M. (eds.) (2007) *Developmental Science and Psychoanalysis: Integration and Innovation*. London: Karnac.

Meltzer, D. (1967) *The Psycho-Analytical Process*. London: Heinemann. [Reprinted London: Karnac, 2008.]

Meltzer, D. (1968) 'Terror, persecution and dread: a dissection of paranoid anxieties'. *International Journal of Psycho-Analysis*, 49: 396–401.

Meltzer, D. (1973) *Sexual States of Mind*. Strath Tay, Perthshire: Clunie Press.

Meltzer, D. (ed.) (1978) *The Collected Papers of Roger Money-Kyrle*. Strath Tay, Perthshire: Clunie Press.

Menzies, I. (1960) 'A case-study in the functioning of social systems as a defence against anxiety: a report on a study of the nursing service of a general hospital'. *Human Relations*, 13 (2): 95–121. [Reprinted in: Menzies Lyth, I. (1988) *Containing Anxiety in Institutions: Selected Essays, Vol. 1*. London: Free Association Books.]

Menzies Lyth, I. (1989) 'Day care of children under five: an action research study'. In *The Dynamics of the Social: Selected Essays, Vol. 2*. London: Free Association Books.

Menzies Lyth, I., Robertson, J., Scott, S.M. and Gwynne, G. (1971) *An Action Research Study of the Day Care of Children Under Five*. Report to the Department of Health and Social Security. London: Tavistock Institute of Human Relations.

Milton, J. (1909) 'Paradise lost'. In: *The Complete English Poems*, revised edition. London: Everyman Library. [Reprinted: London: David Campbell Publishers, 1992.]

Money-Kyrle, R. (1951) *Psychoanalysis and Politics: A Contribution to the Psychology of Politics and Morals*. London: Duckworth.

Money-Kyrle, R. (1955) 'Psycho-analysis and ethics'. In Klein, M., Heimann, P. and Money-Kyrle, R.E. (eds.) *New Directions in Psycho-Analysis: The Significance of Infant Conflict in the Pattern of Adult Behaviour*. London: Tavistock. [Reprinted London: Karnac, 1977.]

Money-Kyrle, R. (1968) 'Cognitive development'. *International Journal of Psycho-Analysis*, 49 (4): 691–698. [Reprinted in: Meltzer, D. (ed.) *The Collected Papers of Roger Money-Kyrle*. Strath Tay, Perthshire: Clunie Press, 1978.]

Money-Kyrle, R. (1971) 'The aim of psychoanalysis'. *International Journal of Psycho-Analysis*, 52: 103–106. [Reprinted in: Meltzer, D. (ed.) *The Collected Papers of Roger Money-Kyrle*. Strath Tay, Perthshire: Clunie Press, 1978.]

Murdoch, I. (1961) 'Against dryness: a polemical sketch'. *Encounter*, January, 16–20.

O'Shaughnessy, E. (1981a) 'A clinical study of a defensive organization'. *International Journal of Psycho-Analysis*, 62: 359–428. [Reprinted in: Spillius, E. (ed.) *Melanie Klein Today: Developments in Theory and Practice, Vol. 2: Mainly Practice*. London: Routledge, 1988.]

O'Shaughnessy, E. (1981b) 'A commemorative essay on W.R. Bion's theory of thinking'. *Journal of Child Psychotherapy*, 7 (2): 181–192. [Reprinted in Rusbridger, R. (ed.) *Inquiries in Psychoanalysis, Collected Papers of Edna O'Shaughnessy*. London: Routledge, 2015.]

O'Shaughnessy, E. (1989) 'The invisible Oedipus complex'. In Steiner, J. (ed.) *The Oedipus Complex Today: Clinical Implications*. London: Karnac.

O'Shaughnessy, E. (1992) 'Enclaves and excursions'. *International Journal of Psycho-Analysis*, 73 (4): 603–614.

O'Shaughnessy, E. (1999) 'Relating to the superego'. *International Journal of Psycho-Analysis*, 80 (5): 861–870. [Reprinted in Rusbridger, R. (ed.) *Inquiries in Psychoanalysis: Collected Papers of Edna O'Shaughnessy*. London: Routledge, 2015.]

Panksepp, J. (1998) *Affective Neuroscience: The Foundations of Human and Animal Emotions*. Oxford: Oxford University Press.

Reddy, W.M. (2001) *The Navigation of Feeling: A Framework for the History of Emotions*. Cambridge: Cambridge University Press.

Rickman, J. (ed.) (1939) *On the Bringing-Up of Children*. London: Kegan Paul.

Riviere, J. (1952a) 'The inner world in Ibsen's *Master-Builder*'. *International Journal of Psycho-Analysis*, 33 (2): 173–180. [Reprinted in: Klein, M., Heimann, P. and Money-Kyrle, R.E. (eds.) *New Directions in Psycho-Analysis: The Significance of Infant Conflict in the Pattern of Adult Behaviour*. London: Tavistock.] [Reprinted London: Karnac, 1977.]

Riviere, J. (1952b) 'The unconscious phantasy of an inner world reflected in examples from literature'. *International Journal of Psycho-Analysis*, 33 (2): 160–172. [Reprinted in Klein, M., Heimann, P. and Money-Kyrle, R.E. (eds.) *New Directions in Psycho-Analysis: The Significance of Infant Conflict in the Pattern of Adult Behaviour*. London: Tavistock.] [Reprinted London: Karnac, 1977.]

Rosenfeld, H. (1964) 'On the psychopathology of narcissism: a clinical approach'. *International Journal of Psycho-Analysis*, 45: 332–337. [Reprinted in *Psychotic States*. London: Hogarth Press, 1965.]

Rosenfeld, H. (1971) 'A clinical approach to the psycho-analytical theory of the life and death instincts: an investigation into the aggressive aspects of narcissism'. *International Journal of Psycho-Analysis*. 52: 169–178. [Reprinted in Spillius, E. (ed.) *Melanie Klein Today: Developments in Theory and Practice, Vol. 1: Mainly Theory*. London: Routledge, 1988.]

Rosenfeld, H. (1987) *Impasse and Interpretation: Therapeutic and Anti-Therapeutic Factors in the Psychoanalytic Treatment of Psychotic, Borderline, and Neurotic Patients*. London: Tavistock.

Roth, P. and Lemma, A. (eds.) (2008) *Envy and Gratitude Revisited*. London: Karnac.

Rustin, M.E. (2005) A conceptual analysis of critical moments in the life of Victoria Climbié, *Child and Family Social Work*, 10 pp 10–19.

Rustin, M.E. (2012) 'Mattie as an educator'. In Harris Williams, M. (ed.) *Enabling and Inspiring: A Tribute to Martha Harris*. London: Karnac.

Rustin, M.E., Dubinsky, A., Dubinsky, H. and Rhode, M. (eds.) (1997) *Psychotic States in Children*. London: Duckworth. [Reprinted London: Karnac, 2002.]

Rustin, M.E. and Rustin, M.J. (1987) *Narratives of Love and Loss: Studies in Modern Children's Fiction*. London: Verso. [Reprinted London: Karnac, 2001.]

Rustin, M.J. (2001) 'Give me a consulting room: the generation of psychoanalytic knowledge'. In *Reason and Unreason: Psychoanalysis, Science and Politics*. London: Continuum.

Rustin, M.J. (2007) 'How do psychoanalysts know what they know?' In Braddock, L. and Lacewing, M. (eds.) *The Academic Face of Psychoanalysis: Papers in Philosophy, the Humanities and the British Clinical Tradition*. London: Routledge.

Salzberger-Wittenberg, I., Williams, G. and Osborne, E. (eds.) (1983) *The Emotional Experience of Learning and Teaching*. London: Routledge and Kegan Paul.

Sayers, J. (2015) *Art, Psychoanalysis, and Adrian Stokes: A Biography*. London: Karnac.

Segal, H. (1952) 'A psycho-analytical approach to aesthetics'. *International Journal of Psycho-Analysis*, 33 (2): 196–207. [Reprinted in Klein, M., Heimann, P. and Money-Kyrle, R.E. (eds.) (1955) *New Directions in Psycho-Analysis: The Significance of Infant Conflict in the Pattern of Adult Behaviour*. London: Tavistock. [Reprinted London: Karnac, 1977.] [Reprinted in: *The Work of Hanna Segal: A Kleinian Approach to Clinical Practice*. Northvale, NJ: Jason Aronson, 1981.]

Segal, H. (1957) 'Notes on symbol formation'. *International Journal of Psycho-Analysis*, 38: 391–397. [Reprinted in Bott Spillius, E. (ed.) (1988) *Melanie Klein Today: Developments in Theory and Practice, Vol. 1: Mainly Theory*. London: Routledge.]

Shakespeare, W. (1952) *Julius Caesar*. The Alexander Text of William Shakespeare: The Complete Works. London: Collins.

Sherwin-White, S. (2014) 'Melanie Klein's thoughts on brothers and sisters'. In D. Hindle and S. Sherwin-White (eds.) *Sibling matters: a psychoanalytic, developmental and systemic approach*. London: Karnac.

Sherwin-White, S. (2016) *Melanie Klein Revisited: Pioneer and Revolutionary in the Psychoanalysis of Young Children*. London: Karnac (in press).

Shuttleworth, A. (2002) 'Turning toward a bio-psycho-social way of thinking'. *European Journal of Psychotherapy and Counselling*, 5 (3): 205–223.

Sodré, I. (2008) 'Even now, now, very now: on envy and the hatred of love'. In Roth, P. and Lemma, A. (eds.) *Envy and Gratitude Revisited*. London: Karnac.

Spillius, E. and O'Shaughnessy, E. (eds.) (2012) *Projective Identification: The Fate of a Concept*. London: Routledge.

Steiner, J. (1985) 'Turning a blind eye: the cover up for Oedipus'. *International Review of Psycho-Analysis*, 12: 161–172. [Reprinted in Bell, D. (ed.) *Psychoanalysis and Culture: A Kleinian Perspective*. London: Duckworth, 1999.]

Steiner, J. (ed.) (1989) *The Oedipus Complex Today: Clinical Implications*. London: Karnac.

Steiner, J. (1993) *Psychic Retreats: Pathological Organizations in Psychotic, Neurotic and Borderline Patients*. London: Routledge.

Stokes, A. (1951) *Smooth and Rough*. London: Faber.

Stokes, A. (1955) 'Form in art'. In: Klein, M., Heimann, P. and Money-Kyrle, R.E. (eds.) *New Directions in Psycho-Analysis: The Significance of Infant Conflict in the Pattern of Adult Behaviour*. London: Tavistock.

Stokes, A. (1958) *Greek Culture and the Ego: A Psycho-Analytic Survey of an Aspect of Greek Civilization and of Art*. London: Tavistock. [Reprinted in Gowing, L. (ed.) *The Critical Writings of Adrian Stokes, Vol. 2: 1937–1958*. London: Thames and Hudson, 1978.]

Stokes, A. (1959) *Three Essays on the Painting of Our Time*. London: Tavistock. [Reprinted in Gowing, L. (ed.) *The Critical Writings of Adrian Stokes, Vol. 3: 1955–1967*. London: Thames and Hudson, 1978.]

Stokes, A. (1965) *The Invitation in Art*. London: Tavistock. [Reprinted in Gowing, L. (ed.) *The Critical Writings of Adrian Stokes, Vol. 3: 1955–1967*. London: Thames and Hudson, 1978.]

Strachey, J. (1930) 'Some unconscious factors in reading'. *International Journal of Psycho-Analysis*, 11: 322–331.

Strachey, J. (1934) 'The nature of the therapeutic action of psycho-analysis'. *International Journal of Psycho-Analysis*, 15: 127–159.

Trowell, J. (2007) 'Childhood depression: a place for psychotherapy. An outcome study comparing individual psychodynamic psychotherapy and family therapy'. *European Journal of Child and Adolescent Psychiatry*, 16 (3): 157–167.

Trowell, J. (2011) *Childhood Depression: A Place for Psychotherapy*. London: Karnac.

Tustin, F. (1972) *Autism and Childhood Psychosis*. London: Hogarth Press. [Reprinted London: Karnac, 1995.]

Wilde, O. (1891) *The Picture of Dorian Gray*. New York: Dover, 1993.

Williams, A.H. (1998) *Cruelty, Violence, and Murder: Understanding the Criminal Mind*. London: Karnac.

Williams, M.H. (ed.) (2014) *Art and Analysis: An Adrian Stokes Reader*. London: Karnac.

Winnicott, D.W. (1952) 'Anxiety associated with insecurity'. In *Collected Papers: Through Pediatrics to Psycho-Analysis*. London: Hogarth, 1958.

Winnicott, D.W. (1956) 'The anti-social tendency'. In *Collected Papers: Through Paediatrics to Psycho-Analysis*. London: Hogarth, 1958.

Winnicott, D.W. (1984) *Deprivation and Delinquency*. London: Routledge.

Wollheim, R. (1973) *On Art and the Mind*. London: Allen Lane.

Wollheim, R. (1984) *The Thread of Life*. Cambridge: Cambridge University Press.

Wollheim, R. (1987) *Painting as an Art*. London: Thames and Hudson.

Wollheim, R. (1993a) 'Crime, punishment and "pale criminality"'. In *The Mind and its Depths*. Cambridge, MA: Harvard University Press.

Wollheim, R. (1993b) 'The ends of life and the preliminaries of morality: John Stuart Mill and Isaiah Berlin'. In *The Mind and its Depths*. Cambridge, MA: Harvard University Press.

Wollheim, R. (1993c) 'The good and the bad self: the moral psychology of British Idealism and the English School of Psychoanalysis compared.' In *The Mind and its Depths*. Cambridge, MA: Harvard University Press.

Wollheim, R. (1999) *On the Emotions*. Newhaven, CT: Yale University Press.

Youell, B. (2006) *The Learning Relationship: Psychoanalytic Thinking in Education*. London: Karnac.

Index